Linguistic Knowledge and Language Use

One of the key challenges in linguistics is to account for the link between linguistic knowledge and our use of language in a way that is both descriptively accurate and cognitively plausible. This pioneering book addresses these challenges by combining insights from Construction Grammar and Relevance Theory, two influential approaches which until now have been considered incompatible. After a clear and detailed presentation of both theories, the author demonstrates that their integration is possible, and explains why this integration is necessary in order to understand exactly how meaning comes about. A new theoretical model is offered that provides groundbreaking insights into the semantics–pragmatics interface and addresses a variety of topics, including the nature of lexical and grammatical concepts, procedural meaning, coercion and idiom processing. This title is part of the Flip It Open Programme and may also be available Open Access. Check our website Cambridge Core for details.

BENOÎT LECLERCQ is an Associate Professor in English Linguistics at the University of Paris 8. His research focuses on the semantics–pragmatics interface, with a particular interest in the domain of modality. Recent publications include *Models of Modals* (co-authored, De Gruyter, 2023).

Linguistic Knowledge and Language Use

Bridging Construction Grammar and Relevance Theory

Benoît Leclercq

Université Paris 8

CAMBRIDGE
UNIVERSITY PRESS

CAMBRIDGE
UNIVERSITY PRESS

Shaftesbury Road, Cambridge CB2 8EA, United Kingdom

One Liberty Plaza, 20th Floor, New York, NY 10006, USA

477 Williamstown Road, Port Melbourne, VIC 3207, Australia

314–321, 3rd Floor, Plot 3, Splendor Forum, Jasola District Centre, New Delhi – 110025, India

103 Penang Road, #05–06/07, Visioncrest Commercial, Singapore 238467

Cambridge University Press is part of Cambridge University Press & Assessment, a department of the University of Cambridge.

We share the University's mission to contribute to society through the pursuit of education, learning and research at the highest international levels of excellence.

www.cambridge.org
Information on this title: www.cambridge.org/9781009273206

DOI: 10.1017/9781009273213

© Benoît Leclercq 2024

This publication is in copyright. Subject to statutory exception and to the provisions of relevant collective licensing agreements, no reproduction of any part may take place without the written permission of Cambridge University Press & Assessment.

First published 2024

A catalogue record for this publication is available from the British Library.

Library of Congress Cataloging-in-Publication Data
Names: Leclercq, Benoît, 1992– author.
Title: Linguistic knowledge and language use : bridging construction grammar and relevance theory / Benoît Leclercq.
Description: Cambridge, United Kingdom : Cambridge University Press, 2024. | Includes bibliographical references and index.
Identifiers: LCCN 2023024148 (print) | LCCN 2023024149 (ebook) | ISBN 9781009273206 (hardback) | ISBN 9781009273220 (paperback) | ISBN 9781009273213 (ebook)
Subjects: LCSH: Semantics. | Pragmatics. | Construction grammar. | Relevance.
Classification: LCC P325 .L335 2024 (print) | LCC P325 (ebook) | DDC 401/.43–dc23/eng/20230705
LC record available at https://lccn.loc.gov/2023024148
LC ebook record available at https://lccn.loc.gov/2023024149

ISBN 978-1-009-27320-6 Hardback

Cambridge University Press & Assessment has no responsibility for the persistence or accuracy of URLs for external or third-party internet websites referred to in this publication and does not guarantee that any content on such websites is, or will remain, accurate or appropriate.

Contents

Figures

Acknowledgments

This book contains the theoretical apparatus that I developed for my Ph.D. thesis, which I completed in 2019 at the University of Lille. I was and remain extremely grateful to my supervisor, Ilse Depraetere, to whom I am forever indebted. Thank you for your patient guidance and continuous support. In various ways, I have learned extensively from you. Challenging at times, your keenness and attention to detail and precision were truly stimulating. Your immense knowledge was a considerable source of inspiration. And your contagious joy and enthusiasm for research provided much-needed motivation during the tough times of the research process. Thank you for being a shining example of scientific rigor, open-mindedness and humility. You have made me a better linguist and a better person.

I also owe a great intellectual debt to Martin Hilpert and Billy Clark, who respectively introduced me to *Construction Grammar* and *Relevance Theory* during my MA studies in Lille. I thank them both for formative discussions and for instilling in me the passion that led to the work presented in this book. I am most grateful to Billy Clark for the countless discussions (on my research, Relevance Theory, and linguistics more generally) and for providing such a safe space for doubt and questioning.

I have learned a lot from my interactions with linguists from Lille, Paris and from around the world. It will be difficult to do justice to them all, but I need to mention Dany Amiot, Bert Cappelle, Agnès Celle, Guillaume Desagulier, Rita Finkbeiner, Dylan Glynn, Gunther Kaltenböck, Maarten Lemmens, Mégane Lesuisse, Cameron Morin, Cédric Patin, Christopher Piñón, Laurence Romain and Jasper Vangaever. They have been teachers, colleagues, co-authors, friends, and they have added considerably to my intellectual growth and my experience in academia. Special thanks go to Bert Cappelle, who has always been eager to share thoughts and whose feedback has greatly contributed to keeping a sharp critical mind.

Thanks are also extended to Helen Barton and Isabel Collins, from Cambridge University Press, for an enjoyable editorial process.

Last but not least, thank you, coffee. It is not just the taste of it, even though I have learned to appreciate a good double espresso. I generally think that people vastly underestimate the power of coffee. In particular, I have always been a fervent advocate of coffee breaks. Not that they make for good excuses, or anything. Coffee breaks directly contribute to the research process. Those shared with colleagues, after a seminar. Those at conferences, discussing each other's presentations. Those that are much needed before submitting an article. And most importantly, those with your family and friends, when you remember that their love is what matters most. For all of that, thank you, coffee.

1 Introduction

The aim of this book is to reassess the semantics–pragmatics interface by combining insights from Construction Grammar (Goldberg, 1995, 2006; Hoffmann and Trousdale, 2013a; Hilpert, 2019; Hoffmann, 2022) and Relevance Theory (Sperber and Wilson, 1995; Wilson and Sperber, 2012; Clark, 2013a).

The past seventy years have witnessed increasing attempts at describing linguistic knowledge and language use, from which various approaches gradually emerged. This growing interest can be traced back to Chomsky's (1965: 59) observation that appropriate descriptions of language use also necessarily require a good understanding of the underlying mechanisms, i.e. the cognitive abilities, that make communication possible. The extent to which performance and competence actually differ has caused a great deal of debate in the literature. Nevertheless, it is primarily this distinction that triggered a "*cognitive turn* in linguistics" (Schmid, 2012: 380). Of course, with this new approach to language came a host of new research questions, the different answers to which resulted in the emergence of various frameworks. Construction Grammar and Relevance Theory developed out of this quest to provide cognitively plausible accounts of language use and, in their respective domains of application, gained enough importance to become respected landmarks in the linguistic scene. These two theories are the starting point of this book.

In spite of their common interest in cognition, the two frameworks generally focus on different aspects of language use. In Construction Grammar, the main goal is to provide an accurate description of what constitutes linguistic knowledge and to explain how this knowledge is actually exploited in practice. In contrast, Relevance Theory grew out of a general concern to understand the cognitive underpinnings that enable us to make sense of our world and in particular, when applied to linguistic communication, to how they contribute to understanding the speaker's communicative and informative intentions. Although these two frameworks provide equally insightful understandings of verbal communication, there have been very few attempts to combine their perspectives. This is most probably due to the often-held assumption that grammar and pragmatics belong to different realms of cognition and deserve

1

separate attention since knowledge about one can hardly provide a better understanding of the other. The aim of the book is precisely to show, however, that this combination is not only useful, but is indeed necessary in order to provide a richer description of the underlying mechanisms of both grammar and pragmatics and of their respective contributions to the interpretation of an utterance.

Because they were developed independently on the basis of different underlying assumptions with an eye to answering different research questions, the two frameworks sometimes provide opposite analyses of the same phenomena. For instance, consider the discussion between Bilbo and Gandalf:

(1)   "Good morning!" said Bilbo, and he meant it. The sun was shining, and the grass was very green. But Gandalf looked at him from under long brushy eyebrows that stuck out further than the brim of his shady hat.
        "What do you mean?" he said. "Do you wish me a good morning, or mean that it is a good morning whether I want it or not; or that you feel good this morning; or that it is a morning to be good on?"
        "All of them at once," said Bilbo.   (from Tolkien, 1937)

Putting aside Gandalf's wit for a moment, one might wonder why he needs to ask Bilbo what exactly he intends to communicate when using the phrase *good morning*. As a linguist, the answer to this question will vary depending on the theoretical background in which it is couched. Exaggerating somewhat, a constructionist might answer that Gandalf's answer is indeed a bit odd given that *good morning* is a conventional construction of English which is a formula commonly used as a greeting when you meet a person for the first time early in the day. Given this convention, Gandalf should have known that Bilbo only meant to say *hello* and therefore answered *good morning* in return. In opposition, a relevance theorist might argue that Gandalf's answer is quite appropriate since, in spite of the linguistic conventions, the meaning of a lexical item remains usually underspecific and needs to be systematically enriched in context via pragmatic inferential processes. As a result, if the intended interpretation was not clear, then Gandalf is indeed entitled to ask what it was that Bilbo actually meant. This of course is a very simplistic demonstration, and theorists in the different frameworks probably have more moderate views than the ones they are associated with here. Nevertheless, this example is meant to capture a general observation that will become clear throughout the following chapters, namely that Construction Grammar and Relevance Theory respectively tend to over-emphasize the role played by linguistic conventions and pragmatic inferencing, and typically so at the cost of the other. It could of course be argued that this tendency is an inevitable side effect of the respective aims of the two theories. Unfortunately, this therefore means that for a broad range of linguistic phenomena, it is unclear which of the two frameworks actually achieves descriptive accuracy (a goal they both set out to achieve) since their respective predictions sometimes come into conflict. For the sake of cognitive accuracy, it is therefore necessary to compare the two frameworks in a systematic manner so as to pin down more specifically the respective contributions of grammar and pragmatics during the interpretation of an utterance. It is my aim to do so.

In order to appreciate the respective contributions of Construction Grammar and Relevance Theory to the understanding of verbal communication, it is essential to provide detailed overviews of the two frameworks first. In Chapter 2, each theory will be introduced in turn. Their strengths will be highlighted and the weaker points needing particular attention (especially those that concern the semantics–pragmatics interface) will be identified. On the basis of this review, focus on the main points of contention will lead me to articulate the discussion around two facets of lexical semantics–pragmatics. In Chapter 3, the aim will be to define exactly how the notions of semantics and pragmatics apply to a lexical item. It will be shown that although the two frameworks describe the meaning of a lexeme in conceptual terms, their opposite views on the nature of concepts affects the way these concepts are argued to contribute to the understanding of the lexemes with which they are associated. I will assess the exact nature of conceptual content and the way this content is exploited in context on the basis of various arguments. I will generally argue that understanding a lexeme depends on rich semantic knowledge together with strong pragmatic principles, and the notion of *lexically regulated saturation* will be used to capture the interpretation process of a lexical item. In the following chapter, Chapter 4, the aim is to discuss the ways in which the direct linguistic environment of a lexeme contributes to this particular interpretation process. First, I will critically assess the nature of a mechanism known as *coercion* and argue that, although clearly semantically constrained, coercion is itself also essentially pragmatic. I will then show that the pragmatic roots of coercion are linked to the *procedural* nature of the semantic content encoded by the grammatical constructions in which lexemes occur. In doing so, both the formal nature of these constructions and the notion of procedural encoding will be (re)defined. It will be shown that constructions that have a coercive force are necessarily (semi-)schematic constructions and that procedural meaning might best be described in meta-conceptual terms. Second, it will be shown that the interpretation of a lexeme is also largely determined by more lexically fixed (i.e. idiomatic) sequences. Upon recognition of these patterns, the process of *lexically regulated saturation* may thus be suspended. I will argue that interpreting these larger patterns is a context-sensitive process and that the *principle of relevance* introduced in Relevance Theory can explain the underlying mechanism.

The concluding section of this book will show that integrating the perspectives of Construction Grammar and Relevance Theory proves to be particularly beneficial in the search for descriptive accuracy. In addition to increasing the respective explanatory power of the two frameworks, conjoining these two approaches provides additional insights into the underlying cognitive mechanisms which make verbal communication successful.

2   Understanding Construction Grammar and Relevance Theory

Construction Grammar and Relevance Theory will now be presented in turn. In the case of Construction Grammar, it will be shown that its main strength resides in its capacity to provide a thorough understanding of linguistic knowledge. Its usage-based take on language provides profound insights into the forms and functions of the linguistic units that individuals can use. At the same time, the discussion will show that its focus on conventions makes for only a partial understanding of linguistic communication. Concerning Relevance Theory, the opposite observation will be made. I will show that while it provides a very elaborate analysis of the pragmatic processes that make verbal communication successful, the argumentation is sometimes weakened by theory-internal assumptions about linguistic knowledge.

2.1   Construction Grammar

Construction Grammar is a cognitively oriented theory of language whose central aim is to account for the entirety of linguistic knowledge. The term *construction grammar* was first used by Charles Fillmore and Paul Kay (Fillmore, 1985a, 1988, 1989; Fillmore, Kay and O'Connor, 1988; Fillmore and Kay, 1995), who were concerned about the lack of attention given in derivational generative grammars to allegedly more peripheral linguistic phenomena (e.g. idiomatic expressions, 'irregular' clausal structures). From a constructionist perspective, these phenomena are considered as much a part of an individual's linguistic knowledge as any general grammatical rules, and not merely by-products of some combinatorial or transformational operations (Hoffmann and Trousdale, 2013b: 3). That is, instead of a core–periphery view, constructionists adopt a more holistic approach to language. In this approach, knowing a language only (or mostly) consists in knowing *constructions*, hence the name of the theory. Like the Saussurean sign (de Saussure, 1916), constructions are defined as arbitrary form–function mappings (Goldberg, 1995: 4). However, whereas the Saussurean sign only applies to lexemes (and morphemes), the notion of construction extends to all aspects of grammar, including idioms as well as abstract phrasal patterns. To use

Goldberg's (2003: 223, 2006: 18) much-cited phrase, it is "constructions all the way down."

Adopting such a symbolic view of language is of course not distinctive of Construction Grammar. This idea is largely shared by functional/cognitive linguists (e.g. Lakoff, 1987; Langacker, 1987, 1991a, 2008; Talmy, 1988, 2000a, 2000b; Wierzbicka, 1988; Halliday, 1994; Givón, 1995, inter alia). Yet Construction Grammar stands out from other functional/cognitive-oriented frameworks in terms of how these symbols (i.e. *constructions*) are said to be acquired and mentally represented, as well as how they interact with one another. There are (naturally) different points of contention between constructionists themselves as well. The term 'Construction Grammar' in fact covers a range of different constructionist approaches (cf. Croft and Cruse, 2004: 257–290; Goldberg, 2006: 213–214, 2013; Hoffmann, 2022: 256–271; Ungerer and Hartmann, 2023). In this book, I will mostly work with the ideas developed within (Goldbergian) Cognitive Construction Grammar (Goldberg, 2006: 213; Boas, 2013: 233). The absence of formalism in this approach seems particularly well suited for its integration with Relevance Theory. Nevertheless, since I will not de facto ignore other constructionist approaches,[1] I will continue to use the umbrella term Construction Grammar and its conventional acronym CxG to refer to the theory.

2.1.1   Fundamental Principles

The use of the term *construction* in CxG can sometimes be unsettling when you are not familiar with the theory, for it does not only refer to complex combinations or grammatical structures such as is usually the case elsewhere in linguistics. Rather, all objects of linguistic knowledge are argued to be constructions: morphemes, lexemes, idioms as well as larger phrasal patterns (Goldberg, 2003: 219). In CxG, what defines a construction is not its internal complexity but its symbolic nature: constructions are conventional pairings of a specific form and a particular semantic or pragmatic function (Goldberg, 1995: 4, 2006: 5; Langacker, 2008: 5). In order to be conventional, i.e. in order to be part of the speaker's knowledge and obtain construction status, these pairings should exhibit at least one of two properties: (i) non-predictability, and/or (ii) sufficient frequency of occurrence. Goldberg (2006) puts it as follows:

Any linguistic pattern is recognized as a construction as long as some aspect of its form or function is not strictly predictable from its component parts or from other constructions recognized to exist. In addition, patterns are stored as constructions even if they are fully predictable as long as they occur with sufficient frequency. (Goldberg, 2006: 5)

---

[1] I also largely embrace Langacker's approach, Cognitive Grammar, which comes very close to Goldberg's Cognitive Construction Grammar (see Langacker, 2009).

Originally, Goldberg (1995: 4) defined non-predictability as the only defining criterion for construction status. From this perspective, constructions were all assumed to be either semantically or formally non-predictable, the paradigm case of which are idioms. The semantics of *piece of cake* and *kick the bucket*, for instance, are non-predictable because they are non-compositional, i.e. they cannot be understood solely on the basis of the individual lexemes that compose them. In the sentence in (2), the form of the construction *many a day* is non-predictable, given that *many* usually selects for a plural noun.

(2)   I have waited many a day for this to happen. (Hilpert, 2019: 10)

Linguistic expressions that show non-predictability are naturally good candidates for construction status, for they require language users to store them independently of the canonical patterns from which they cannot be derived (Hilpert, 2019: 12). This explains why morphemes and words are constructions, since their forms and functions are non-predictable and language users have to learn them individually (Goldberg, 2002a: 1). However, not all linguistic patterns are non-predictable. The phrases *Make a wish* and *I miss you*, for instance, are neither semantically nor formally deviant. The same is true of the multi-word patterns *legal action* and *in exchange* as well as the inflected forms *smaller* and *students*. What gives these patterns construction status is not non-predictability but frequency of occurrence. That is, these patterns are used frequently enough to be stored by the speaker as distinct constructions (cf. Langacker, 1988; Stemberger and MacWhinney, 1988; Arnon and Snider, 2010; Hanna and Pulvermüller, 2014, inter alia).[2]

In other words, in CxG, knowing a language consists in knowing patterns that combine a form and a meaning either non-predictively or that occur with sufficient frequency. According to this definition, all of the patterns in (3) to (9) are constructions.[3]

(3)   ADJ-*ish*
        a. Part of it is yellowish. (COCA, spoken)
        b. But, generally, I think of myself as a youngish person in an oldish body. (NOW)

(4)   *Roof*
        a. The roof is leaking in a lot of places. (COCA, spoken)
        b. Smoke rises through a hole in the roof. (COCA, spoken)

---

[2] See Ungerer and Hartmann (2023) for a recent discussion on the definition of constructions.

[3] Most of the examples used in this book were extracted from corpora available on Mark Davies' interface (english-corpora.org): BNC (British National Corpus), COCA (Corpus of Contemporary American English) and NOW (News on the Web) corpora (Davies, 2004, 2008-, 2016-).

(5)   *Private property*
       a. For example, there's no private property in the Soviet Union. (COCA, spoken)
       b. Trespassing upon private property is unlawful in all States. (COCA, written)

(6)   *Break the ice*
       a. What can I say to break the ice with a guy? (COCA, written)
       b. Did you try to do anything to break the ice with them? (COCA, spoken)

(7)   X *is the new* Y construction
       a. So that's why I say, you know, land is the new gold. (COCA, spoken)
       b. Strong is the new skinny according to the *New York Post*. (COCA, spoken)

(8)   WAY construction (form: [SUBJ V *one's way* OBL])
       a. Mickey Mouse tootled his way across the screen. (NOW)
       b. You can't buy your way into someone's heart and mind. (NOW)

(9)   CAUSED-MOTION construction (form: [SUBJ V OBJ OBL])
       a. Henry's friend moved the bookcases in Mr Emerson's study. (COCA, spoken)
       b. My constituents will vote me out of office. (COCA, spoken)

In the sentences in (3), the morphological schema ADJ-*ish* is used to indicate approximation or vagueness: vaguely yellow in (3a), and relatively young/old in (3b). The noun *roof* in (4) refers to the cover of a building. Regardless of their frequency of occurrence, these two constructions are neither semantically nor syntactically predictable from their component parts. This is not the case of the multi-lexeme construction *private property* in (5). This construction, used to indicate an individual's land or building, can be predicted both syntactically (as a particular instance of the [Adj N] pattern) and semantically (i.e. it is semantically transparent). Still, it certainly has construction status for most (native) English speakers due to its high frequency of occurrence. In (6), the idiomatic expression *break the ice* is syntactically predictable. It can be seen as an instantiation of the more general [V NP] and [Det N] constructions. However, it is not semantically predictable. Nothing in the individual meanings of *break*, *the* and *ice* can predict the interpretation of the idiom in terms of a particular social behavior between individuals who are meeting for the first time. In (7), the X *is the new* Y construction is neither entirely syntactically nor semantically predictable. This pattern is not syntactically predictable since Y can be realized by an adjective, as in (7b), although the string *the new* would normally select a nominal head (to instantiate the more regular [Det Adj N] pattern). Neither is it semantically predictable, because none of the elements that occur in this construction suggest that the X and Y items should be interpreted not literally but in a metonymic relationship to a bigger category

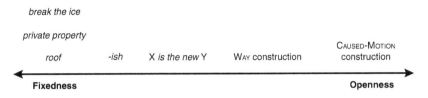

Figure 2.1 Lexicon–syntax continuum in CxG

that hearers need to infer in context, e.g. in (7b) *strong* and *skinny* have to be understood in relation to the category of what body type currently seems to be more attractive (cf. Dancygier and Sweetser, 2014: 154). The WAY construction in (8), used to convey manner (or means) of motion, is arguably syntactically predictable. It is not, however, semantically predictable. The meanings of the different items in (8b), for instance, and in particular that of the verb *buy*, do not themselves convey (metaphorical) manner of motion interpretations (cf. Jackendoff, 1990: 218; Israel, 1996: 218). Finally, a similar analysis can be given to the CAUSED-MOTION construction identified in (9). While the form of the construction can be derived from more canonical patterns, examples like (9b) show that the caused-motion meaning with which it is associated is not always predictable from its component parts (cf. Goldberg, 1995: 152–179).

CxG therefore establishes no principled distinction between elements of the lexicon and larger phrasal (or 'syntactic') patterns. Instead of a dichotomy between the two, it is assumed that there is a continuum of constructions from more lexical to more syntactic. This continuum is often referred to as the *lexicon–syntax continuum* (Langacker, 2005: 102; Croft and Cruse, 2004: 255; Goldberg, 2006: 220). One way of representing this continuum is to locate constructions on a gradient of lexical fixedness, i.e. from lexically fixed to lexically open (or schematic) constructions, as in Figure 2.1 (inspired by Kay and Michaelis, 2012: 4; Michaelis, 2017, 2019).

There are different reasons why no strict distinction is made between lexicon and syntax in CxG, all of which are closely related. The main reason has to do with the general aim of the theory. Although CxG directly takes its name from arguing that all levels of linguistic knowledge can be described in terms of constructions, it is primarily concerned with how linguistic knowledge relates to cognition in order to provide a "psychologically plausible account of language" (Boas, 2013: 233). A central assumption within CxG is that language does not require a specific cognitive mechanism but is the product of general cognitive abilities (Lakoff, 1987: 58, 1991: 62; Langacker, 1991b: 1; Tomasello, 2003: 3; Goldberg, 2006: 12, 2019: 52;

Bybee, 2010: 6–8, 2013: 49).[4] Like other models in functional/cognitive linguistics, CxG therefore rejects a modular view of language and in particular the autonomy of syntax (Croft and Cruse, 2004: 1; Fried and Östman, 2004: 24). That is, grammatical constructions are not separated from the rest of our linguistic knowledge and abilities. In addition, constructionists consider that the "primary function of language is to convey information" (Goldberg, 2013: 2).[5] From this perspective, all components of language are considered to be meaningful. Hence, like lexical items, grammatical constructions are assumed to have a specific meaning that contributes to the understanding of the sentences in which they occur. This is the case for the Way construction and the Caused-Motion construction in (8) and (9) discussed above. It is also true of the Ditransitive construction, different instantiations of which are found in (10).

(10)   a. The United Nations was giving them food. (COCA, spoken)
        b. Heloise passed me the wooden bowl. (COCA, written)
        c. He told his wife the same thing. (NOW)

Although the interpretations of these sentences differ, they are composed of similar constructions, one of which is called the Ditransitive construction (Goldberg, 1995: 141–151). In terms of semantics, it is this construction that conveys the notion of transfer, or more specifically X causes Y to receive Z (Goldberg, 1995: 141). And this meaning is said to be associated with the abstract phrasal form [Subj V Obj1 Obj2], which all sentences in (10) instantiate. Specifically, all the slots of this pattern are associated with a specific function:

(11)   Ditransitive: Syn: Subj   V   Obj1   Obj2
                            (   ) (   ) (   ) (   )
                      Sem: Agent   cause-receive   Recipient   Theme

As the representation in (11) indicates, each of the open slots of the construction is associated with a particular function which, in context, is inherited by the

---

[4] The psychological and neurological reality of this assumption is supported by empirical and experimental evidence (cf., for instance, overviews by Bates and Goodman, 1997, 1999; Tomasello and Slobin, 2005; Behrens, 2009, and references cited therein). See Cappelle (to appear) for a critical discussion, though.

[5] This quote is interesting as it could suggest that Construction Grammar falls prey to the "descriptive fallacy" (Austin, 1962: 3), namely the assumption that words and utterances are only used to convey (truth-evaluable) propositions while language is also used to perform a number of other functions (i.e. speech acts). Yet this is clearly not the view adopted in CxG. Not only does it reject truth-conditionality, but it also acknowledges the other types of (pragmatic) functions that language is used to perform (see next section). Nevertheless, as will be shown in Section 2.1.2.3, this quote is a good example of the symptomatic vagueness with which issues that relate to the semantics–pragmatics interface are treated.

lexical items that occur in that slot.[6] In (10a), for instance, *them* and *food* are respectively interpreted as 'recipient' and 'theme' because of their occurrence in the OBJ1 and OBJ2 slots of the DITRANSITIVE construction. Of course, it could also be argued that these interpretations of the lexemes are not due to their being used in a distinct DITRANSITIVE construction but to the subcategorization frame (i.e. valence)[7] of the main verb *give* of which they are the arguments. Although this might sometimes be the case, the perspective developed in CxG nonetheless seems to provide better insights into an individual's linguistic knowledge and about their use of the language. First of all, experimental data reveal that these constructions are psychologically real and that language users do store grammatical patterns in association with a specific function independently of the lexical items that occur inside them (cf. Hare and Goldberg, 1999; Bencini and Goldberg, 2000; Kaschak and Glenberg, 2000; Chang, Bock and Goldberg, 2003; Goldberg and Bencini, 2005; Ye, Zhan and Zhou, 2007; Bencini and Valian, 2008; Boyd, Gottschalk and Goldberg, 2009; Johnson and Goldberg, 2013; Shin and Kim, 2021; Li et al. 2022, inter alia).

More importantly for us, the observation that grammatical constructions, like lexical items, are meaningful necessarily shifts the semanticist's focus of attention. In (12), for instance, *kick* is interpreted in terms of transfer and the expressions *Bob* and *the football* respectively receive the roles of 'recipient' and 'theme' not because of the subcategorization frame of the verb *kick*, which usually only selects one object (e.g. *Pat kicked the ball*), but because of their occurrence in the DITRANSITIVE construction.

(12)   Pat kicked Bob the football. (Goldberg, 1995: 11)

(13)   Lyn crutched Tom her apple. (Kaschak and Glenberg, 2000: 512)

Similarly, the DITRANSITIVE construction is responsible for the transfer interpretation in (13) of the denominal verb *crutch*, whereby Lyn (SUBJ/agent) is understood to have used a crutch in order for Tom (OBJ1/recipient) to receive her apple (OBJ2/theme). In this case, not only are the respective roles of *Tom* and *her apple* inherited from the DITRANSITIVE construction, but also the CAUSE-RECEIVE interpretation of *crutch*. The particular interaction between a lexeme

---

[6] The representation in (11) is adapted from Goldberg (1995: 50, 2006: 138). Please note that although specific thematic roles and (Jackendovian) primitives (CAUSE and RECEIVE) have been used to describe the construction's semantics, they have no "theoretical significance" here (Goldberg, 1995: 49). That is, these labels are only used because they facilitate the semantic description of the argument-structure construction. However, the actual semantics of the DITRANSITIVE construction are more complex and require more than a list of rudimentary components (see Section 2.1.2.2).

[7] Subcategorization frames have been "an essential part of linguistic theorizing since Chomsky (1965)" (Goldberg, 2006: 65).

and a construction such as in (13) is often referred to as *coercion* and will be addressed more fully in Section 2.1.3.

Finally, CxG assumes no a priori distinction between the lexicon and syntax because of its usage-based approach to language. That is, no syntactic structures or linguistic items of any sort are considered to be innate. Rather, a central tenet within CxG consists in viewing all aspects of linguistic knowledge as resulting from language use (Langacker, 1991b: 264; Croft, 2001: 59; Goldberg, 2006: 44; Diessel, 2013: 347). From this perspective, one's linguistic knowledge consists in "the cognitive organization of one's experience with language" (Bybee, 2006: 711). In particular, regardless of their internal complexity, it appears that linguistic patterns emerge from a process of categorization (and generalization) over exemplars, i.e. concrete realizations (Kemmer and Barlow, 2000; Tomasello, 2003, 2006; Bybee, 2010). In CxG, these concrete realizations – which are found in utterances – are called *constructs*, while the generalizations that emerge from them are what form *constructions* (Fried, 2015: 980). Consider the sentences in (14) to (16).

(14)   a. It's about a cat who stole a dog's bed. (NOW)
        b. Why don't you have a cat? (COCA, spoken)
        c. The cat wanted a little air time. (COCA, spoken)

(15)   a. She was as calm as a pond on a windless day. (COCA, written)
        b. I felt as proud as a president. (COCA, written)
        c. Clare acted as serious as a nun. (COCA, written)

(16)   a. It was you who begged for those loans in the past. (NOW)
        b. In some cases, it is their wives who are the chief wage earners. (COCA, written)
        c. It is my son who made it. (COCA, written)

Constructionists believe that just like the form and meaning of the lexeme *cat* are acquired by generalizing over different usage events such as in (14), the *as* ADJ *as a* N construction is itself acquired by generalizing over examples like those in (15), and the *It*-CLEFT construction by generalizing over examples such as in (16). That is, all aspects of linguistic knowledge are acquired by a gradual process of categorization and generalization across usage events, and no grammatical pattern is therefore considered innate. As a result, linguistic knowledge is "viewed as emergent and constantly changing" (Bybee, 2013: 49). Indeed, new constructs have a systematic impact on the representation of a construction. The lexicon–syntax continuum represented in Figure 2.1 can therefore be seen as a consequence of this usage-based acquisition process, with different constructions being more or less abstract depending on the degree of generalization made possible by the input received by an individual. It also follows from this perspective that all constructions (lexical to grammatical) are not stored separately but are located in the same repository of linguistic knowledge. This repository is referred to in CxG as the *construct-i-con* (Jurafsky, 1992: 28; Goldberg, 2003: 219).

It is important to note that the construct-i-con does not contain only constructions, i.e. generalizations (cf. Section 2.1.2.2, footnote 14,), but these are stored alongside the individual constructs from which they emerge (Abbot-Smith and Tomasello, 2006; Bybee, 2010, 2013; Goldberg, 2006). According to Langacker (1987), arguing that linguistic knowledge is either composed of broad generalizations or specific instantiations amounts to committing to what he calls the "rule/list fallacy" (Langacker, 1987: 29), i.e. an either/or idealization that may not correspond to a speaker's cognitive reality. This assumption is in particular supported by the observation that frequency plays a major role in the mental representation of constructions (cf. Ellis, 2002; Diessel, 2007). The effects of frequency are often discussed in terms of a construction's degree of entrenchment (Langacker, 1987: 59, 2008: 16; Schmid, 2020: 205ff.). The more frequently a linguistic expression is used, the more cognitively entrenched it is. Among other characteristics, a high degree of entrenchment correlates with higher cognitive salience (i.e. accessibility) and faster processing (Harris, 1998; Schmid, 2007, 2017; Blumenthal-Dramé, 2012). How this particular view has an impact on the representation of meaning, which is the focus of this book, will be fully discussed in Section 2.1.2.2.

2.1.2 Constructions: What They Are

Constructions are considered the basic building blocks on the basis of which complex structures and sentences can be constructed. Given that constructions combine a form with a meaning, the interpretation of an utterance therefore depends on which constructions are being used in a given context and how they are being assembled. In order to understand the individual contribution of these constructions to the interpretation process, it is necessary to look more closely at how CxG defines the notions of *form* and especially that of *meaning*.

2.1.2.1 The Forms of Constructions The previous section already referred to the possible forms that constructions can have. It remains to be established exactly what constitutes the form of a construction. CxG considers that the formal pole of a construction includes phonological and morphosyntactic properties (cf. Boas, 2013: 234). To give one example, knowing the construction *admire* consists in knowing that it is pronounced /ədˈmaɪəʳ/ for instance,[8]

---

[8] I say 'for instance' since it follows logically from CxG's usage-based approach that not all English speakers have the pronunciation shown here (e.g. /ədˈmaɪr/ with a rhotic American accent).

and that it shares the morphosyntactic properties of verbs (e.g. subject–verb agreement, tense inflection, etc.). Not all constructions are phonologically specific, however. Because they are gradually acquired in context, it was shown earlier that constructions may be more or less schematic depending on the degree of abstraction involved (cf. the *lexicon–syntax continuum*, Figure 2.1). Like the verb *admire*, the lexeme *audience* and the idiom *by and large*, for instance, are lexically (and phonologically) fixed constructions. On the other hand, constructions like the *as* ADJ *as a* N construction identified in (15) are only partially specific. Some parts of this construction, the *as* and *as a* elements, are lexically (and phonologically) fixed. The two open slots ADJ and N, however, only specify the morphosyntactic properties that the (phonologically specific) items that fill them should have. Other constructions, such as the DITRANSITIVE construction, are, however, entirely schematic and only specify for morphosyntactic properties. As described in (11), for instance, the DITRANSITIVE construction takes the schematic form [SUBJ V OBJ1 OBJ2]. Only the items that fill the different slots of this construction are phonologically specific, e.g. *me*, *ball*, *threw*, *the* and *Jake* in (17).

(17)   Jake threw me the ball. (COCA, written)

The forms of constructions can therefore vary from fully lexically (and phonologically) specific to more schematic. This is not, however, the only way in which constructions have been approached and described in CxG. Constructions are also often discussed in terms of another continuum from atomic to complex constructions (see Croft and Cruse, 2004: 255; Langacker, 2005: 108). That is, as illustrated in Figure 2.2, in addition to being lexically specific or schematic, constructions can also vary in size. From this perspective, increased complexity does not correlate with increased schematicity. Rather, lexically specific constructions can also be very complex. In Figure 2.2, the idiom *break the ice* and the phrase *as soon as possible* are good examples of lexically specific and complex constructions. Partially specific constructions can also be relatively simple (e.g. the *How* ADJ! construction, as in *How adorable!* or *How confusing!*) as well as more complex (e.g. the X *is the new* Y construction, as in (7)). Finally, fully schematic constructions need not always be complex, such as the DITRANSITIVE construction, but can also be simpler (e.g. the AUX V construction as in *have slept* or *should write*).

Representations such as that in Figure 2.2 perfectly illustrate the position adopted in CxG that linguistic knowledge is not strictly divided between words on the one hand and syntactic rules on the other, but that it is composed of a network of more or less complex and schematic constructions. As such, it also nicely captures the perspective adopted in CxG that all of these forms gradually emerge from language use.

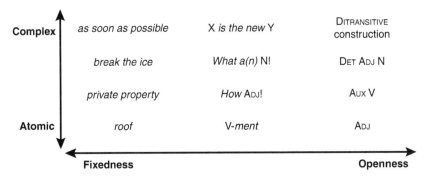

Figure 2.2 Fixity and complexity of constructions (adapted from Leclercq, 2023: 67)

There is, however, a central implication of the usage-based approach adopted in CxG that I have not yet discussed, and which directly concerns the form of constructions and in particular that of argument structure constructions (e.g. the DITRANSITIVE and CAUSED-MOTION constructions). The different surface forms in (18) to (19) illustrate what is commonly referred to as the "dative alternation" (cf. Pinker, 1989: 82; Rappaport Hovav and Levin, 2008: 129; Perek, 2015: 154).

(18)   [SUBJ V OBJ1 OBJ2]
    a. We'll give them a voucher. (COCA, spoken)
    b. They'll send you the tune beforehand. (COCA, spoken)

(19)   [SUBJ V OBJ2 *to* OBJ1]
    a. She gave the money to the suspect. (COCA, spoken)
    b. You can send a postcard to us. (COCA, spoken)

In a Chomskyan transformational account of grammar, it has been argued that these different surface forms are derived from a single (deep) underlying syntactic structure (cf. Akmajian and Heny, 1975: 185). In CxG, however, these forms are not treated as variants of the same structure but as two distinct constructions (cf. Perek, 2015: 148, and references cited therein). The pattern in (18), as mentioned before, is referred to as the DITRANSITIVE construction, and the pattern in (19) is referred to as the *To*-DATIVE construction. This distinction is argued to follow logically from the usage-based nature of linguistic knowledge, with generalizations emerging from surface structures (Goldberg, 2002b: 329).[9] In CxG, what is true for the dative

---

[9] Perek (2015: 149) argues that a speaker's knowledge most probably also includes knowledge of the commonalities between the two constructions, which he discusses, following Cappelle (2006), in terms of an *allostruction*. See Perek (2015: 151–166) for more details.

alternation is (of course) also true for other alternations, such as the causative alternation (cf. Romain, 2017, 2022) and the locative alternation (cf. Perek, 2015: 158). Here, each pattern in the alternation is considered a construction in its own right since each can be identified with its own set of idiosyncratic properties.

Note that the focus on form here is relevant to the semantics–pragmatics interface for a simple reason. Constructions are defined as form–meaning pairings. The DITRANSITIVE and the *To*-DATIVE constructions identified in (18) and (19) should therefore each be associated with a specific meaning. The main question has to do with what meaning is expressed exactly. The DITRANSITIVE construction was described in (11) in terms of a notion of transfer, whereby *X* CAUSES *Y* TO RECEIVE *Z*. At first sight, the *To*-DATIVE construction in (19) seems to convey a similar meaning. It is assumed in CxG, however, that differences in form should systematically correspond to differences in meaning. This has been discussed in terms of the *principle of no synonymy* (Goldberg, 1995: 67), recently reframed as the *principle of no equivalence* (Leclercq and Morin, 2023). According to this principle, the *To*-DATIVE construction should therefore serve a different function from the DITRANSITIVE construction. Thompson and Koide (1987: 400) argue that the iconic distance between the SUBJ and OBJ1 positions in fact reflects a conceptual distance, whereby the *To*-DATIVE construction conveys greater physical distance between the referents of SUBJ and OBJ1 than the DITRANSITIVE construction. Similarly, Goldberg (1995: 90) argues that the sentences in (18) are better interpreted as conveying *X* CAUSES *Y* TO MOVE TO *Z*.[10] That is, both analyses consider the *To*-DATIVE construction to convey greater motion than the DITRANSITIVE construction. As Diessel (2015) points out:

This explains why the verbs *bring* and *take* are particularly frequent in the *to*-dative construction, whereas verbs such as *give* and *tell* are proportionally more frequent in the ditransitive (cf. Gries and Stefanowitsch, 2004). (p. 313)

This observation is meant to show that even seemingly similar patterns can convey slightly different meanings.[11] Therefore, it is important for the semanticist, and in particular the pragmaticist, to pay careful attention to the forms of the constructions that speakers use, as they provide rich clues as to the intended interpretation. (In the next sections, it will be shown that this is not systematically the case in Relevance Theory.) It will have become clear that, like in the

---

[10] Note that Goldberg (1995: 89–97) considers the *To*-DATIVE alternative to be a metaphorical extension of the CAUSED-MOTION construction (SUBJ V OBJ OBL), which she calls the TRANSFER-CAUSED-MOTION construction and which explains her semantic description.

[11] That there is a semantic difference between the two constructions has received support from experiments in neuroscience (cf. Allen et al., 2012).

Chomskyan tradition, CxG also tries to account for the generativity of language, i.e. the ability to produce novel sentences (Fried and Östman, 2004: 24). Unlike in the Chomskyan tradition, however, this generativity is not attributed to transformational syntactic rules. Rather, generativity originates from the possibility for meaningful constructions to combine with (and be embedded in) other meaningful constructions. Therefore, as mentioned before, complex sentences are not only syntactically complex but also semantically complex, given that both their form and meaning have to combine. Some of the results behind this combination process will be discussed in Section 2.1.3.

2.1.2.2 Semantics in Construction Grammar The previous section illustrates the challenge that describing the form of a construction in isolation from its meaning can represent. The next step therefore naturally consists in spelling out more explicitly how meaning is defined in CxG. The reader will already have noticed that in spite of this section's title, I have just used the term *meaning* (twice) instead of the term *semantics*. This might appear as a confusing terminological laissez-faire to those working on the semantics–pragmatics interface. However, this is a deliberate choice that, as will become clear in this section and the next, actually reflects much of the CxG viewpoint with regard to the functional pole of constructions. For this reason, I will continue using the term *meaning* here and gradually elucidate the reasons why it is preferred – together with the term *function* – to the notion of *semantics*.

The perspective on meaning adopted in CxG can be attributed in particular to Charles Fillmore (1975, 1976, 1982, 1985b), George Lakoff (1987, 1988, 1989) and Ronald Langacker (1987, 1991a, 1991b), whose work has largely contributed to the development of CxG. It is important to understand, however, that CxG also generally embraces most of the ideas on meaning developed in the wider context of cognitive linguistics (see Geeraerts and Cuyckens (2007: 25–418), Geeraerts (2010: 182–272, 2017, 2021) and Lemmens (2016) for detailed overviews). To put it simply, the meaning of a construction is often discussed in terms of a concept, a conceptual structure or a conceptualization (cf. Langacker, 2008: 46). This view is prima facie similar to the one adopted in Relevance Theory, which, as we will see, also discusses meaning in terms of concepts (cf. Section 2.2.3.1). However, the two frameworks have a radically different understanding of the nature of concepts. In CxG, as in cognitive linguistics more generally, concepts are understood not in terms of atomic primitives but as more or less complex units of our conceptual system that are internally structured (cf. Lakoff, 1987). This approach was developed in direct opposition to atomic accounts of conceptual content such as the one developed by Jerry Fodor (cf. Fodor, Fodor and Garrett, 1975; Fodor et al., 1980; Fodor, 1998: 40–87, inter alia). That is, concepts are considered to be complex structures. The aim of this section therefore is to understand what type of information concepts make accessible and how this information is organized.

In order to discuss the nature of these conceptual structures, different theoretical constructs have been developed, such as *frames* (Fillmore, 1985b), *idealized cognitive models* (Lakoff, 1987) and *domains* (Langacker, 1987). Although these terms reflect slightly different standpoints, they "are often interchangeable" (Langacker, 2008: 46). For this reason, I will not delve into the particularities of each proposal but will discuss more generally the core assumptions that they all share.[12] A central assumption is that concepts are cognitive objects: "meanings are in our head" (Gärdenfors, 1999: 21). Meaning is therefore not understood in CxG as a bearer of truth-conditions in relation to the external (or some possible) world. Rather, meaning is understood in terms of the way speakers themselves construe and conceptualize the world and particular situations. This has been discussed in cognitive linguistics in terms of the notion of *construal* (Langacker, 1991b: 61, 2019). Consider the sentences in (20) to (21).

(20)   a. The rock is in front of the tree. (Langacker, 2008: 76)
        b. The tree is behind the rock. (Langacker, 2008: 76)

(21)   a. [This type of bird] spends its life on the ground. (Fillmore, 1982: 121)
        b. [This type of bird] spends its life on land. (Fillmore, 1982: 121)

In the sentences in (20), the same situation is being depicted (i.e. both sentences would have the same truth-conditions). They differ, however, in terms of their *vantage point* (cf. Langacker, 2008: 73), i.e. the perspective adopted by the speaker to describe the situation. Similarly, in the sentences in (21), the nouns *ground* and *land* can be used to refer to the same "dry surface of the earth" (Fillmore, 1982: 121). Choosing one or the other, however, depends on whether you construe this surface in relation to the air (22a), or in relation to the sea (22b).[13] That is, it is argued that their meanings consists of these particular construals, in which some content is understood in relation to a particular background.

---

[12] Note that there is a tendency among construction grammarians to discuss meaning in terms of *frames* (see Goldberg, 1995: 25; Boas, 2021). This is particularly true when describing the semantics of verbs and argument-structure constructions, for which *frames* offer a relatively more adapted perspective. As Goldberg (1995: 7) herself points out, however, all three approaches have been crucial to the development of CxG.

[13] Specific terminology has been used to describe the particular construal depicted here: *figure* and *ground* (Langacker, 2008: 58) or *profile* and *base* (p. 66). From this perspective, the nouns *ground* and *land* are used to denote a similar *figure/profile* but in relation to a different *ground/ base*.

(22)   a.   GROUND   b.   LAND

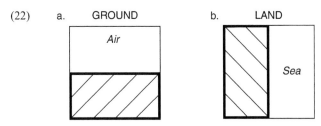

You will notice the particular schematic imagery that underlies the two representations in (22). This captures another central assumption in cognitive linguistics with respect to what meanings are actually composed of. It is assumed that much of a construction's meaning is made of a number of pre-conceptual *image schemas* (Johnson, 1987: xix; Langacker, 2008: 32; Hampe, 2005). Image schemas, as Evans and Green (2006: 184) point out, are not exactly the type of symbolic mental images such as the ones depicted in (22). Still, the notion of *image schema* is meant to capture the observation that much of our conceptual system is shaped by our perceptual and physical experiences, from which conceptual patterns can be abstracted. It was mentioned earlier that a central tenet of CxG is to view language as drawing on general cognitive mechanisms and emerging from language use. This does not only hold for linguistic forms but is also true at the level of meaning. Meaning also gradually emerges from renewed experiences and language use, and it is clear in cognitive linguistics that this experience is not purely mentalistic or intellectual but involves all of our perceptual and physical senses, as well as social and cultural practices:

"Experience," then, is to be understood in a very rich, broad sense as including basic perceptual, motor-program, emotional, historical, social, and linguistic dimensions. I am rejecting the classical empiricist notion of experience as reducible to passively received sense impressions, which are combined to form atomic experiences. By contrast, experience involves everything that makes us human – our bodily, social, linguistic, and intellectual being combined in complex interactions that make up our understanding of our world. (Johnson, 1987: xvi)

In other words, a central assumption within cognitive linguistics is that meaning is not a purely linguistic notion (and therefore not autonomous) but is encyclopedic in nature, i.e. concepts include knowledge about the world and how we experience it (Croft and Cruse, 2004: 30; Geeraerts and Cuyckens, 2007: 5; Langacker, 2008: 39; Lemmens, 2016: 92; Diessel, 2019: 93; Goldberg, 2019: 12). The meaning (i.e. semantics) of the noun *strawberry*, for instance, includes a whole set of knowledge ranging from its particular shape and color, that it is a (summer) fruit, as well as facts about how they grow and how they are usually sold (i.e. in a punnet), etc. Similarly, as Lemmens (2016: 92) points out, the meaning of the construction *school night* necessarily includes cultural knowledge of how weeks are divided and organized as well as social practices that are related to *school nights* with regard to the rest of this cultural/social organization (e.g. weekends). This analysis also applies to more phrasal patterns such as the DITRANSITIVE construction discussed earlier. Each of the open slots of this construction, [SUBJ V OBJ1 OBJ2], was described via conceptual primitives: *Agent* CAUSE-RECEIVE *Recipient Theme*. As mentioned in footnote 6, however, the exact meaning of this construction is actually more complex and cannot be reduced to these primitives (see Goldberg, 1995: 49). The meaning of the DITRANSITIVE construction more largely includes knowledge of how humans engage in acts of transfer (Goldberg, 1995: 39), i.e. knowledge of what a transfer actually involves, of the respective roles of agents, recipients and themes and the relation between them, as well as who/ what can usually perform these roles (Goldberg, 1995: 142–151).

Already, it should be clear why the more general terms *meaning* and *function* are therefore preferred to the term *semantics*. The perspective adopted here indeed rejects the traditional division between purely linguistic content on the one hand (usually referred to as *semantics*) and encyclopedic knowledge on the other (usually attributed to *pragmatics*). That is, what is often attributed to pragmatics – as is the case in Relevance Theory – is considered to directly contribute to a construction's *semantics*. There is therefore no strict division between the two (as in (23)), but rather a gradation from semantics to pragmatics (as in (24)), both adapted from Langacker (2008: 40, Fig. 2.4):

(23) | Semantics | | Pragmatics | Separate Components

(24)   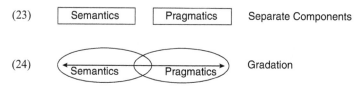   Gradation

What the representation in (24) is meant to capture is that it is not necessarily clear to what extent, during the interpretation of an utterance, some particular piece of encyclopedic knowledge is already part of a given conceptual structure or is pragmatically derived from the context. Rather, because of the constantly changing nature of conceptual structures, some pieces of knowledge are already well established in the speaker's conceptual structure (i.e. semantic) while others are only in the process of conventionalizing (i.e. partially semantic), and yet others are wholly contextual (i.e. pragmatic). This is not the only reason why the term *semantics* is not often used in cognitive frameworks. One of the reasons comes from another central assumption that meanings are not seen as (context-free) disposable packages that speakers and hearers simply access when using a particular construction. Rather, it is assumed that using a construction only provides a point of access to all of its associated knowledge, and that meaning is constructed in context (see Evans, Bergen and Zinken, 2007: 9; Radden et al., 2007: 1; Langacker, 2008: 41; Taylor, 2017: 261). That is, the actual meaning of a construction largely depends, in context, on "which portions of this encyclopedic knowledge are activated, and to what degree" (Langacker, 2008: 42). Some parts of this knowledge are so central to the understanding of a particular construction that they systematically get activated across usages, but other (more 'peripheral') aspects of knowledge will only get activated in some contexts and not others, i.e. will be more salient in some contexts and not others. For this reason, Langacker (2008: 30) prefers to talk about meaning in terms of *conceptualizations* rather than *concepts*, the former term conveying greater dynamicity than the latter notion, which conveys more stativity. It will become clear in the next chapter that some of these assumptions are also central to Relevance Theory, which I will present in Section 2.2.3.1.

Adopting an encyclopedic view of meaning (or semantics) necessarily requires some further explanation in terms of how this knowledge is organized and represented in the speaker's and hearer's minds. It is generally understood in cognitive linguistics that the conceptual structure associated with a particular construction does not simply represent an unstructured "grab bag" of encyclopedic knowledge (Lemmens, 2017: 107). Rather, this knowledge is well structured and organized. Conceptual structures are usually described in terms of categories. There are, however, various ways in which these categories can be described. In CxG, as in cognitive linguistics more generally, categories are often discussed in terms of either a *radial network* (Lakoff, 1987) or a *schematic network* (Langacker, 1987) of encyclopedic knowledge. In either case, it is assumed that our knowledge is organized in a number of interconnected bundles (or clusters) of knowledge, one of which is more central to a given category than others. This more central cluster of knowledge is usually referred to as the *prototype* (Rosch, 1975, 1978, 1983; Rosch and Mervis, 1975; Taylor, 1995).[14] Via an analogical process, the encyclopedic information associated with a given exemplar (i.e. construct) is located within the category in relation to the prototype, either as a more or less specific instance of that prototype or as an extension depending on its resemblance to previously encountered

---

[14] Note that two perspectives have developed concerning these networks: a prototype model and an exemplar-based model (see Bybee, 2006, 2010, 2013). The difference is whether the individual clusters are made up of all the individual traces (and uses) of encyclopedic knowledge (exemplar-based), or whether there is some form of abstraction involved (prototype). These two approaches are often seen as being in opposition. Like Barsalou (1990) and Hampton (2016), however, I think these are not necessarily opposite analyses but simply two sides of the same coin: while individuals do categorize on the basis of the individual usage events (i.e. exemplars), there is also most probably some abstraction of the knowledge involved (prototype). The possibility for abstractions to be derived does not preclude the possibility for individual exemplars to be stored, and vice versa. In this book, I will continue using the term *prototype*, but without the theoretical assumption that this necessarily precludes the storage by individuals of particular exemplars.

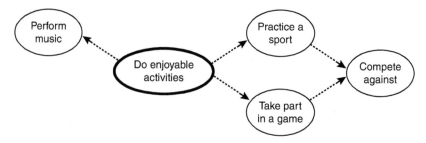

Figure 2.3 Radial network of *play*

exemplars. For instance, the verb *play* gives access to the radial category represented in Figure 2.3.[15]

This network represents the category of encyclopedic knowledge that the verb *play* gives access to, and which is organized in different clusters of various resemblance. These different dots (or clusters) constitute the different senses of the verb (which can then be understood as different but related concepts). In this network, one of the different clusters of encyclopedic knowledge (i.e. senses) – shown here in the bold circle – is more central than others and all other senses develop as extensions from this central sense. This representation captures the conventional polysemy of the verb *play*, each of the different clusters representing one of the senses of the verb.

Radial networks such as in Figure 2.3 nicely enable the identification and understanding of the various senses of a given construction by identifying the relation between the different clusters of encyclopedic information that a construction is associated with. Now, independently of whether any kind of abstraction or generalization occurs within the clusters themselves (see foot- note 14), Langacker (1991b: 266) suggests that there is schematization (i.e. abstraction) across clusters, and that some of these senses may be more schematic than others, but also that there may be a "superschema" (1991b: 267) that accounts for all of the senses that compose the conceptual network. He calls such a network a *schematic network*. He discusses, for instance, the schematic network of the verb *run*, as shown in Figure 2.4.

Like in the radial network, this network is composed of different clusters or senses, one of which is more central than the others (box in bold). Other senses are seen as semantic extensions from this more central sense (broken arrows). In addition to the radial network, however, some senses are seen as schematic

---

[15] Note that this figure is a relatively simple representation of the radial category that is associated with the verb *play*, which in reality is probably more complex. This figure was drawn on the basis of the definitions provided by the online *Cambridge Dictionary*, available at: http://dicti onary.cambridge.org/fr/dictionnaire/anglais/play (last accessed: May 31, 2023).

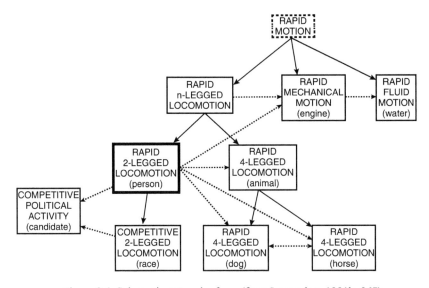

Figure 2.4 Schematic network of *run* (from Langacker, 1991b: 267)

relative to other senses (plain arrows), and one of them is schematic to all these senses (broken box). In the next chapter, I will try to show how this perspective can help to shed some light on different issues that concern the semantics–pragmatics interface, and in particular in relation to the ideas developed in Relevance Theory (see Section 3.4). For now, in order to avoid possible misunderstandings, a few points concerning these representations are worth mentioning. It is true that the different clusters identified correspond to different senses of the construction to which the network is associated, e.g. the verb *run* in Figure 2.4. In CxG, conventional polysemy (a network of interrelated senses) is the norm rather than the exception (Goldberg, 1995: 31, 2019: 20). However, it is necessary to understand, as mentioned before, that this polysemy is neither predetermined nor fixed, and that these senses are not context-free packages. First, these conceptual networks are gradually acquired via exposure to actual exemplars and emerge from this experience. As a consequence, within and across languages, not every individual will share exactly the same conceptual structure (although speakers of the same speech community most certainly have very similar ones). As Langacker (1991b: 267) himself points out, English speakers may not all have within their conceptual structure of *run* clusters of knowledge as specific as some that can be found in Figure 2.4 (e.g. the "bottom" *dog* and *horse* type of running senses). Similarly, not everyone will necessarily abstract the (same) superschema, in this case *rapid motion*. In other words, the categories that individuals possess are relatively flexible, and constantly change depending on their experience. Second, and directly related to this last observation, it is interesting to note that this usage-based approach easily explains language change and grammaticalization (Bybee, 2010; Traugott and Trousdale, 2013), since it is usage that determines the shape of these categories and how they gradually develop.

2.1.2.3 The Pragmatics of Constructions   It will now have become clear that meaning in CxG is to be understood in terms of rich conceptual structures that emerge via our experience of the world and which are constantly evolving and changing. In the next section, I will discuss the interaction between different constructions and, therefore, between different conceptual structures. Before doing so, I will address one last point, which can also explain why the terms *meaning* and *function* are preferred to the term *semantics* in CxG.[16] In this section, I will briefly look at how the notion of *pragmatics* has been discussed in relation to constructions in CxG. It is essential to understand that constructionists, although primarily focusing on what constitutes our linguistic knowledge, do not ignore the role of pragmatics. Ideally, CxG tries to account for all of "the rich semantic, pragmatic, and complex formal constraints" that somehow regulate the use of individual constructions (Goldberg, 2003: 220). However, there has so far been little attention paid to pragmatics in CxG (cf. Cappelle, 2017; Finkbeiner, 2019a; Leclercq, 2020). Furthermore, pragmatics in this framework is understood and approached in a way that differs from how it is generally discussed in the literature on the semantics–pragmatics interface. This is a potential source of confusion.

This particular approach is best illustrated in Goldberg (2004), who distinguishes between *non-conventional* pragmatics and *conventional* pragmatics (Goldberg, 2004: 428). The former kind of pragmatics has to do with online computations of contextual effects such as are usually discussed in (post-/neo-) Gricean pragmatics. The latter, *conventional* type of pragmatics is concerned with "the conventional association of certain formal properties of language with certain constraints on pragmatic contexts" (p. 428). It is this latter type of pragmatics that constructionists are mostly interested in (cf. Kay, 2004; Nikiforidou, 2009; Lee-Goldman, 2011; Cappelle, 2017; Kuzai, 2020). Yet, by virtue of being conventional, one may wonder to what extent this type of 'pragmatics' really is 'pragmatics' rather than semantics, and what exactly the term is meant to capture. This question is the focus of this section.

It is generally considered in CxG that "some constructions have pragmatic content built into them" (Cappelle, 2017: 116). Some of this pragmatic content follows from the usage-based nature of meaning representation. As Bybee

---

[16] See Leclercq (2020) for a critical discussion of the use of the terms 'semantics' and 'pragmatics' in CxG.

(2010) points out, because semantic structures are gradually acquired via repetition, "frequently made inferences from the context can become part of the meaning of an expression or construction" (Bybee, 2010: 52). An often-discussed example in CxG is the *What's* X *doing* X? (or WXDY) construction, illustrated in (25).

(25)   a. What's it doing in the box? (COCA, written)
         b. What's THAT book doing in the library? (NOW)
         c. And what's he doing in my kitchen? (COCA, written)

All of the sentences in (25) express a notion of incongruity (or disapproval) regarding a specific situation (Kay and Fillmore, 1999: 4). In (25b), for instance, the speaker seems to disapprove of a given book being available in a specific library. Although Kay and Fillmore recognize that this meaning most probably originated as a conversational implicature, "the semantics of incongruity is now CONVENTIONALLY associated with the special morphosyntax of WXDY constructs" (p. 5, original emphasis). That is, this part of the communicated meaning is not (re)calculated each time the hearer comes across the WXDY construction but is accessed as part of their knowledge of the construction. In this case, a previously pragmatic aspect has become conventional and is now part of the meaning of the construction itself. It is for this reason that Kay and Fillmore refer to it in terms of *semantics* rather than in terms of *pragmatics*.

Cappelle (2017: 118) points out, however – and this seems to have been the underlying reason for Goldberg to discuss the notion of *conventional pragmatics* – that it is not necessarily clear to what extent a conventionalized pragmatic aspect necessarily becomes a semantic aspect of a construction. The functional pole of a construction, it is argued, may actually be composed of both semantic and conventional pragmatic aspects of meaning (and hence the preference for using the words *meaning/function*). I will discuss the case of the *let alone* construction to explain this view. In their oft-cited paper, Fillmore, Kay and O'Connor (1988: 514) discuss the use of *let alone* and its communicative function in sentences such as in (26) to (28) (original emphasis).

(26)   I don't even want to read an article ABOUT, let alone a book written BY, that swine.

(27)   Max won't eat SHRIMP, let alone SQUID.

(28)   He wouldn't give A NICKEL to his MOTHER, let alone TEN DOLLARS to a COMPLETE STRANGER.

In these sentences, the *let alone* construction (or rather, the X *let alone* Y construction) is argued to introduce each of the two conjoined elements in terms of "contrasted points on an implicational scale" (Cappelle, Dugas and Tobin, 2015: 72). In the sentence in (27), for instance, Max's eating squid is understood as being less probable than his eating shrimp (which is itself already very unlikely). This aspect is argued to be the semantic contribution of the construction. In addition, it is argued that the construction is also used to indicate to the hearer that the second conjunct (e.g. that there is no chance that Max is going to eat squid) provides the most relevant – in the Gricean sense – piece of information to the context at hand (Cappelle, Dugas and Tobin, 2015: 72). In this case, the construction therefore conventionally provides the hearer with the tools that they would otherwise have had to work out in context. Yet according to Fillmore, Kay and O'Connor (1988: 532), in spite of being conventionally associated with the *let alone* construction, this later contribution is argued not to be purely semantic but is instead pragmatic (see also Cappelle, Dugas and Tobin, 2015: 73).

Note that in addition to the 'pragmatics' of examples such as the WXDY construction and the X *let alone* Y construction, a number of other pragmatic functions associated with particular constructions have been identified, such as in (29) to (30).

(29)   Can you pass the salt? (Stefanowitsch, 2003: 108)

(30)   It's not pretty, it's gorgeous. (Kay and Michaelis, 2012: 2286)

The construct in (29), for instance, is argued to instantiate the *Can you X?* construction, which is conventionally associated with a *request* indirect speech act (Stefanowitsch, 2003: 109). That is, this indirect speech act is not calculated online, but is accessed by the hearer as part of their knowledge of the construction. From the perspective of CxG, this part of the function of the construction is not purely semantic (since it is non-propositional) but is instead a pragmatic convention. Similarly, in the construct in (30), it is argued that the adverb *not* is used here not to negate the proposition itself but as a metalinguistic device to cancel a specific quantity implicature (cf. Kay and Michaelis (2012: 17), and references cited therein). That is, in constructional terms, this function is not semantic but pragmatic.

The previous paragraphs show that there is no clear agreement as to what counts as purely 'semantic' or 'pragmatic'. As discussed in Leclercq (2020), though CxG initially considers the semantics–pragmatics distinction "more or less obsolete" (auf der Straße, 2017: 61), two opposite views can be distinguished: one that considers that semantics is the domain of conventional meaning while pragmatics pertains to contextual inference (e.g. Kay and Fillmore's 1999 analysis of the WXDY construction), and one that views semantics as contributing to propositional (i.e. truth-conditional) content and pragmatics to non-truth-conditional content (e.g. Fillmore, Kay and O'Connor's 1988 analysis of the X *let alone* Y construction). It has to be understood that as much as CxG does not define meanings in terms of truth-conditions, and sees meaning as a very dynamic object (see previous section), constructionists still primarily seem to think of the notion of *semantics* as being propositional in nature (although it is not clear exactly what their position on the matter really is, e.g. Kay and Michaelis, 2012: 2277). This assumption is in particular defended by Cappelle (2017: 122), who argues that it is "useful to make a distinction between lexical or propositional semantics ... and pragmatic information." From this perspective, the information provided for example by the *let alone* construction about the second conjunct in terms of its particular relevance to a given discourse is indeed not semantic since it is non-propositional. This assumption is also central to Goldberg's (2004) distinction between conventional and non-conventional pragmatics, both of which concern non-truth-conditional aspects of meaning. As mentioned in Leclercq (2020), one might argue that this view comes into direct contradiction with the approach presented in Section 2.1.2.2, in which it was argued that truth-conditions do not define the meaning of a construction. As I see it, there is no necessary contradiction, however: "[o]ne can maintain the view that meaning is not restricted to truth conditions and at the same time argue that there is a level at which some aspects of meaning (more than others) will eventually contribute to establishing the truth value of the proposition expressed" (Leclercq, 2020: 232). Indeed, as Gärdenfors (1999) puts it, "the truth of expressions is considered to be secondary, since truth concerns the relation between the mental structure and the world. [...] Meaning comes before truth" (p. 21). So it is possible for CxG to preserve a clear semantic/pragmatic distinction and to treat as purely *semantic* those (conventional) aspects of meaning that are eligible to contextual truth values and as *pragmatic* those that are not. We will see in Chapter 4 how this question relates to the conceptual/procedural distinction established in Relevance Theory.

Now, regardless of how semantics and pragmatics are understood in CxG, it is relatively explicit that non-conventional pragmatics (Goldberg, 2004: 428), i.e. conversational pragmatics as discussed in the (post-/neo-)Gricean tradition, is not the focus of interest in CxG. Rather, the interest remains to a large extent centered on knowledge itself. Nevertheless, because of CxG's usage-based approach to language, as mentioned before, it does recognize the role of pragmatics during verbal communication. Unfortunately, constructionists sometimes leave some room for ambiguity concerning their exact stance on the question. For instance, the title *What's pragmatics doing outside constructions?* in Cappelle (2017) is a bit surprising. It might seem as though the author is rejecting the possibility for pragmatics to exist outside of constructions. The *What's X doing Y?* construction used here, which Cappelle himself discusses, indeed introduces a notion of incongruity and disapproval for the relation between X and Y. Does this mean that Cappelle (and constructionists more generally) rejects the role of conversational, non-conventional pragmatics?

No. Although this is what his title could suggest, this is not the position of CxG. Cappelle himself acknowledges the major role of (non-conventional) pragmatics during the interpretation of an utterance (Cappelle, 2017: 117). The aim of Cappelle (2017) is only to show that pragmatics can also be part of constructions, and that it does not only take place outside of constructions.[17] Of course, the aim of CxG is only to describe an individual's linguistic knowledge, and therefore it could be argued that it does not need to explain the ins and outs of conversational pragmatics. In this case, however, CxG on its own is not enough to fully explain how linguistic communication works and succeeds. In order to do so, one needs an account of how non-conventional pragmatics operates. Goldberg (2006) argues that

[a] focus on form to the neglect of function is like investigating a human organ such as the liver, without attending to what the liver does: while this is not impossible, it is certain to fail to be explanatory. (p. 168)

Similarly, one might argue that focusing on semantics without looking at pragmatics, although not impossible, has little explanatory power. As Gonzálvez-García (2020: 112) puts it, "the treatment of semantic and/or pragmatic facts in [Cognitive Construction Grammar] is at best somewhat inconsistent with the theoretical premises invoked." This is why an approach along the lines of Relevance Theory is necessary.

2.1.3   Constructions in Interaction: Coercion

There is one more aspect of the theory that I will now discuss and which will prove particularly relevant when comparing CxG with Relevance Theory. This has to do with the interaction between various constructions that are used in an utterance. As mentioned before, utterances result from the complex combination of a number of different constructions, all of which contribute to this utterance in terms of both form and meaning. Goldberg (2003: 221) nicely captures this complexity in Figure 2.5, for instance.

Figure 2.5 illustrates the constructionist view according to which one utterance (in (a), *What did Liza buy the child?*) results from the combination of various constructions, identified in (b). Interestingly, Figure 2.5 is but one illustration of the generativity of language which can be explained by the infinite combinatorial possibilities that constructions offer (Goldberg, 1995: 7; Fried and Östman, 2004: 14). The aim of this section is to understand more specifically the scope of these possibilities and the ways in which

---

[17] A similar observation can be made about Bergs and Diewald's (2009) *Contexts and Constructions* volume. Although some chapters do address non-conventional pragmatics, most are concerned with how pragmatics can be part of constructions.

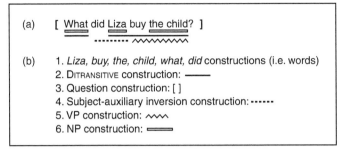

Figure 2.5 Constructing an utterance (adapted from Goldberg, 2003: 221)

constructions, and in particular lexemes, may (or may not) interact with other constructions. Consider for instance the use of *fly* in the following examples.

(31)   The pilot announced that geese were *flying* in the sky. (COCA, written)

(32)   Our son was just three months old when we first *flew* him across the Atlantic. (COCA, written)

(33)   It was a breathtaking experience to fly over the beautiful valley of Palampur. Why walk, when you can *fly* your way down! (NOW)

Example (31) contains a rather prototypical use of the verb, in both form and meaning. The uses of *fly* in (32) and (33), however, are comparatively more unusual. In (32), *fly* is interpreted in terms of a caused motion, whereby the parents have taken their son on a flight across the Atlantic at three months of age. In (33), there is a particular focus placed on the specific *manner* of motion which is encoded by the verb *fly*. In CxG, it is considered that these interpretations actually result from their being used inside another construction, the CAUSED-MOTION construction and the WAY construction respectively. We can see indeed that these sentences differ from (31) not only in meaning but also in form. In (32), the form [SUBJ V OBJ OBL] can be easily identified. As mentioned in Section 2.1.1, this form is associated with the meaning X *causes* Y *to go* Z to form the CAUSED-MOTION construction. It is understood in CxG that the interpretation of *fly* in (32) follows from its being used in that construction. Similarly in (33), the form [SUBJ V *one's way* OBL] is argued to be associated with a particular manner of motion interpretation to form the WAY construction, and it is the use of *fly* in this construction that provides its particular interpretation in (33). So the interpretation of the verb *fly* here depends as much on the semantics of the constructions in which it is used as on its own lexical meaning.

In the example just discussed, it could be argued that the verb *fly* readily combines with the semantics of the two constructions in which it occurs.[18] This naturally follows because there is *semantic coherence* and *semantic correspondence* (cf. Goldberg, 1995: 50) between the lexical item and the two constructions, i.e. the semantic features of the lexical item that is used closely correspond to those of the constructions in which it occurs and therefore can combine (or *fuse*) with each of them. The verb *fly* indeed refers to a specific motion event which is a central aspect of both the Caused-Motion and the Way constructions. Sometimes, however, a lexeme and the construction in which it occurs are not semantically (and morphosyntactically) coherent and compatible. Consider the sentences in (34) to (36).

(34)   He drank three *beers* hoping that would help. It did not. (COCA, written)

(35)   I just *Google Mapped* my way to an exam because I didn't know where Engineering South was. #senioryear (Twitter, @Brittany_N_Lee, 21 apr. 2016)

(36)   The doc (...) had *happied* himself to death on his own laudanum two months before. (COCA, written)

In (34), the noun *beer* is a mass noun that should not be specified for number, i.e. it should neither be inflected with the plural *-s* suffix nor with the number *three*, and which is prima facie incompatible with the morphosyntactic context in which it occurs.[19] Nevertheless, instead of the mass reading (i.e. the liquid), *beer* is here interpreted in accordance with its morphosyntactic context in terms of a countable portion of beer (given our world knowledge of how beer is usually served, most probably three bottles or pints). That is, its interpretation is somehow inherited from the semantics of the construction in which (and with which) it occurs. Similarly in (35), the noun *Google Maps*, which usually refers to a GPS application, is here used as a denominal verb to refer to a particular means of motion. That is, the speaker communicates that they used Google Maps in order to arrive at the location of their exam. CxG has a specific explanation for the origin of this interpretation. This interpretation is argued to be inherited from the Way construction (Subj V *one's way* Obl) in which it occurs. The lexeme *Google Maps* is originally neither a verb nor does it encode means of motion (which is expected in that position of the Way construction). At first sight, there is a semantic (and morphosyntactic) mismatch between the noun and the Way construction. Nevertheless, it is interpreted as a means of motion verb in accordance with the position it occupies in that construction. Finally, in (36), the adjective *happy* is also used creatively as a de-adjectival

---

[18] This will be discussed more fully in Chapter 4.
[19] Hilpert (2019: 17) discusses a similar example.

verb. In this case, it is not used to refer to the doc's mental state, but to the (metaphorical) act of leading himself to his own death by using drugs. This can once again be explained in terms of the larger construction in which it occurs: in this case the CAUSED-MOTION construction (SUBJ V OBJ OBL). Although *happy* is neither a verb nor encodes caused-motion (as required by the CAUSED-MOTION construction), it is so interpreted in accordance with the larger construction in which it occurs.

The examples just discussed show that sometimes a lexeme can be used in a construction with which it is seemingly incompatible, i.e. there can be a mismatch between the semantic and morphosyntactic properties of the lexeme and those of the construction in which it occurs. In these cases, the lexeme is systematically reinterpreted in accordance with the semantics of that construction. This resolution process has been discussed in CxG in terms of *coercion* (Goldberg, 1995: 159; Michaelis, 2003a, 2003b, 2004; Lauwers and Willems, 2011; Hilpert, 2019: 17; Leclercq, 2019). The term *coercion* was first used outside the framework of Construction Grammar. The terms 'coerce' and 'coercion' were initially used in programming languages (Aït-Kaci, 1984) and artificial intelligence (Hobbs, Walker and Amsler, 1982; Hobbs and Martin, 1987; Hobbs et al., 1993) and were soon adopted and developed by formal semanticists interested in aspectual meaning (Moens and Steedman, 1988: 17; Pustejovsky, 1991: 425, 1995: 106, 2011: 1401; de Swart, 2000: 7, 2011: 580). It is from this work on aspect that Construction Grammar has borrowed the term *coercion*. In particular, Michaelis (2004) took up the notion and adapted it to the needs of the theory. The term has been used to describe a variety of phenomena in the different frameworks just mentioned. Nevertheless, they all share the view that coercion is concerned with the resolution of an incompatibility between a selector (e.g. argument structure construction) and a selected (e.g. lexeme) whereby the latter adapts to the former. This has been referred to by Michaelis (2004) as the "override principle":

The override principle. If a lexical item is semantically incompatible with its morpho-syntactic context, the meaning of the lexical item conforms to the meaning of the structure in which it is embedded. (p. 25)

The interpretations of the lexemes *beer*, *Google Maps* and *happy* as they are used in (34) to (36) precisely follow from such coercion effects: they are interpreted in accordance with the semantics of the different constructions in which they occur. As mentioned before, the same coercion effect is involved in example (13), repeated here:

(37)   Lyn crutched Tom her apple. (Kaschak and Glenberg, 2000: 512)

The interpretation of the denominal verb *crutch* in terms of transfer (whereby Lyn used the crutch to give Tom her apple) is inherited from the DITRANSITIVE construction in which it occurs (SUBJ V OBJ1 OBJ2). Although there is originally a semantic (and morphosyntactic) mismatch between the noun *crutch* and the verb position it occupies in the DITRANSITIVE construction, the noun is reinterpreted in accordance with the semantics of the construction.

There are three further points concerning coercion that I wish to address. First, it has to be understood that the notion of coercion has been widely discussed in a number of different frameworks and that it is perceived and described in slightly different ways in each of them (see Audring and Booij (2016) for an interesting discussion). For instance, in the tradition of formal semantics (cf. Pustejovsky, 1991, 1995, 2011; de Swart, 2000, 2011; Jackendoff, 1997), on the basis of which Michaelis has elaborated her own account, coercion seems to be understood as an autonomous linguistic process whereby language itself coerces (or shifts) the meaning of a particular lexeme. Lauwers and Willems (2011: 1224) point out that these approaches have indeed given very little attention to the role of language users and context during the interpretation process. Such a position somehow seems to resonate in Michaelis' own work in any case, and in particular in the way the override principle has been stated. Because of CxG's usage-based approach to language, however, I believe that most construction grammarians view coercion as involving a process whereby the language users themselves have to solve the mismatch between the lexeme and the morphosyntactic context in which they occur. Such a perspective has been nicely captured by Langacker (1987):

Putting together novel expressions is something that speakers do, not grammars. It is a problem-solving activity that demands a constructive effort and occurs when linguistic convention is put to use in specific circumstances. (p. 65)

This particular point of view will be addressed more fully in Chapter 4 and I will take into account other arguments when relating the notion of coercion to some of the work developed in Relevance Theory, for, as we will see, this notion raises a lot of questions. In particular, and this is my second point, one of these questions has to do with how the "problem-solving activity," i.e. the mismatch resolution, is actually accounted for. After all, as Yoon (2012) points out, although coercion in CxG is seen as a process carried out by language users, "the psychological process toward the resolution [is] not dealt with" (Yoon, 2012: 7). This question will also be addressed in Chapter 4.

Finally, it is also worth mentioning that there is a limit to coercion. Coercion is possible because of the productivity of the constructions that speakers use (Lauwers and Willems, 2011: 1224), i.e. the possibility for a construction to produce novel forms and combine with new lexemes. However, this productivity is constrained (cf. Cappelle, 2014), that is, it is not possible for any construction to combine with any new lexeme and for coercion (i.e. mismatch resolution) to take place. This restriction is often discussed in terms of *partial productivity, coverage, competition* and *statistical preemption* (Goldberg, 1995: 120, 2019; Boyd and Goldberg, 2011; Goldberg, 2011; Suttle and Goldberg, 2011). That is, as productive as constructions may be, there are systematic constraints that limit the range of possible coinages. Given the focus of this book on lexical meaning, however, I will not delve into the specific constraints on constructional productivity but only focus on those cases where novel forms (such as in (34) to (37)) are possible and give rise to coercion effects (see also Bergs, 2018; Hoffmann, 2018; and references cited therein).

2.1.4   *Construction Grammar: Summing Up*

Construction Grammar is a cognitively grounded theory of language that mostly focuses on knowledge. As a functionalist approach, it assumes that all forms that a language is composed of are essentially meaningful. From this perspective, meaning should be at the very heart of linguistic analysis. In particular, construction grammarians often discuss the semantics (or rather *function*) that is associated with any given construction. Due to its particular appeal to usage, we have seen that CxG has a particular understanding of the notion of semantics. As mentioned in Section 2.1.2.2, meaning is discussed in terms of encyclopedic knowledge. It therefore rejects the traditional division between semantics (as purely linguistic knowledge) and pragmatics (in terms of encyclopedic knowledge), but rather believes in a more gradual distinction from more to less conventional aspects of encyclopedic knowledge. As a result, it is assumed that the functional pole of constructions is rather rich and that polysemy is almost systematic. In the next chapter, this view will be compared to the relevance-theoretic approach, and I will discuss whether or not the two are compatible. What is particularly interesting in CxG is that it considers all different forms of a given language to be systematically associated with different functions. As discussed in the case of the dative alternation, even small differences in form are related to differences in function. This therefore provides the analyst – whether it be a semanticist or a pragmaticist – with a relatively clear agenda. Constructions indeed provide a solid source of information in order to identify the speaker's intended interpretation. Hence, trying to identify a speaker's meaning should always involve looking carefully at the particular form of an utterance, from which a number of specific functions can be recovered and to which pragmatic principles can apply. As we will see in Chapter 3, however, this multifaceted strategy is not always adopted in Relevance Theory.

The difficulty with Construction Grammar is to pin down exactly its view on pragmatics. On the one hand, it has been shown that much pragmatic content is considered to be part of a construction's function. This was referred to as conventional pragmatics. On the other hand, it is less clear how non-conventional (i.e. conversational) pragmatics generally fits in with the general enterprise of CxG, which gives rather little space to these facets of 'meaning'. Of course, constructionists may argue that CxG aims only at providing a framework for linguistic knowledge and that (non-conventional) pragmatics falls outside its scope. However, it is not clear why this should necessarily be the case. CxG assumes that linguistic knowledge results from one's experience with language. From this perspective, the experience itself – which involves non-conventional pragmatics – should be as much an aim of study as the resulting knowledge. It has been shown, however, that construction grammarians tend to focus on the result itself (i.e. on knowledge) more than they do on the experience. This is the reason why, for instance, speakers are sometimes credited with too much knowledge (e.g. Sandra and Rice (1995) on prepositions, see also Sandra (1998: 368)) that instead should probably be attributed to pragmatics. In order to arrive at a cognitively more accurate description of linguistic knowledge and language more generally (which was earlier stated as being one of CxG's main goals, CxG may therefore have to integrate principles of pragmatics more explicitly in its framework.

2.2   Relevance Theory

Relevance Theory is a theory of cognition and cognitive processes which has mostly been applied to verbal communication. In this framework, much focus is placed on the semantics–pragmatics interface and the processes involved during the interpretation of an utterance. It was originally developed by Dan Sperber and Deirdre Wilson and was first fully spelled out in their seminal book *Relevance* ([1986] 1995). Relevance Theory grew out of Sperber and Wilson's desire to make sense of our capacity to understand the world, and in particular our capacity to communicate effectively. As such, it had a direct impact on the field of pragmatics. Indeed, Paul Grice – whose work provided a major incentive for the development of pragmatics – had already addressed some of the most central issues discussed in Relevance Theory (Grice, 1989). Yet, although sharing a number of Gricean assumptions, Sperber and Wilson developed Relevance Theory as an alternative account to that of Grice (and other post- and neo-Gricean theories) and thus challenged traditional perspectives on pragmatics. In Relevance Theory, the success of verbal communication is not attributed to a number of maxims, or rules, that interlocutors follow, but to a single cognitive mechanism referred to as the *principle of relevance* (see Section 2.2.1).

Since the publication of *Relevance* in 1986, the theory has been extensively revised and extended to address many of the issues discussed in the pragmatics literature (cf. Carston, 2002a; Wilson and Sperber, 2012; Clark, 2013a; Wilson, 2017; Allott, 2020). The length of Francisco Yus' up-to-date online bibliography (http://personal.ua.es/francisco.yus/rt.html), which gathers almost all of the research embedded in a relevance-theoretic perspective, bears witness to this. The variety of contributors to the development of the theory has naturally led to diverging points of view within the framework itself. Nevertheless, relevance theorists have remained relatively united and, for that reason, I will continue using the general term Relevance Theory (and its acronym RT) in spite of individual differences across some of its advocates.

2.2.1   Principle(s) of Relevance

The reason Relevance Theory has remained a stable framework for so many years is most probably the fact that in spite of internal differences among relevance theorists, the underlying assumption responsible for the development of the theory has never changed and still inspires many researchers. This assumption I referred to earlier as the *principle of relevance*. This principle was first introduced in *Relevance* (Sperber and Wilson, [1986] 1995) and remains today the most central element of the theory around which other ideas have been developed. It is already worth noting that although a number of relevance-theoretic notions will be challenged in this book, the *principle of relevance* will not be one of them. This principle offers key answers to some of the questions that Construction Grammar fails to address, and this is why it deserves a section of its own.

2.2.1.1 Defining Relevance   Understanding the term *principle of relevance* in RT can be a challenge for at least two reasons. First, part of the difficulty lies in the ambiguity of the term used, for there are actually not one but two principles of relevance: the first (or cognitive) principle of relevance and the second (or communicative) principle of relevance (Sperber and Wilson, 1995: 261). In the literature, however, it is common to refer to the second principle as *the* principle of relevance (see Section 2.2.1.2).[20] Second, another difficulty concerns the meaning of the term *relevance* itself. This notion is used in RT in a very technical sense, which differs both from the everyday perception of 'relevance' and from Grice's understanding of the notion. Yet, in order to understand the two principles of relevance (i.e. how and to what phenomena

---

[20] This is most probably because the second/communicative principle of relevance was originally the only one discussed in the 1986 edition of *Relevance*. Claims about cognition were only turned into a principle in the second edition of the book in 1995.

the notion of relevance applies), it is essential to define exactly what is meant by *relevance* in the first place.

As mentioned before, RT is first and foremost a theory about cognition. In particular, it aims at explaining, in cognitively realistic terms, information processing, and notably how inferential processes are constrained (Wilson and Sperber, 1991: 586; Sinclair and Winckler, 1991: 13; Sperber and Wilson, 1995: 32, 66; Clark, 2013a: xv). The notion of relevance therefore does not apply only to language but to all possible types of cognitive stimuli: visual, auditory, kinesthetic, etc. The perspective developed in RT was originally based on Jerry Fodor's *language of thought* and modularity of mind hypotheses (Fodor, 1975, 1983).[21] The term *cognition* is understood in RT as having "to do with 'thinking'" (Clark, 2013a: 91). Like Fodor, RT assumes that thoughts are language-like mental (or conceptual) representations and that thinking (i.e. cognition) is the computation of these mental representations (Sperber and Wilson, 1995: 71). External stimuli are taken as input by specialized modules (or input systems) which transform the type of information they receive (visual, linguistic, etc.) into mental representations of the same format: *logical forms* (p. 72). These mental representations are then used as input information by central cognitive systems which perform computations over them. The information provided by the various input systems is integrated with information stored in memory and various inferential tasks are then performed (p. 71). These inferential tasks form the basis of comprehension processes and belief fixation. It is such processes, for instance, that enrich the often-incomplete logical forms into full-fledged assumptions (i.e. fully propositional conceptual structures). As we will see in the next section, most linguistic logical forms provided by a given utterance need to be enriched. More generally, the inferential tasks performed by the central cognitive systems enable an individual to keep their representation of the world, their belief system, as accurate as possible by comparing the newly formed assumptions with those already stored in memory (Clark, 2013a: 96).

According to Fodor, the computations that take place within the central systems are primarily inferential and require different types of pragmatic abilities (Fodor, 1983: 110). He argues, however, that it is not possible to describe exactly how these inferential tasks are carried out and how all of the information that comes into somebody's central systems is actually processed in order to keep their belief system up to date (p. 112). Sperber and Wilson disagree with Fodor, however, and they introduced the notion of *relevance* as an attempt to provide such an explanation (Sperber and Wilson, 1995: 66).

---

[21] Note that RT has since moved away from Fodor's (1983) original ideas and now adopts a slightly different view of the modularity of the mind (see, for instance, Sperber, 1994, 2001, 2005; Carston, 1997a, 2006; Wilson and Sperber, 2004; Wilson, 2005). Issues related to this debate will not be addressed in this book.

According to Sperber and Wilson, not all information is equally worth processing. Information worth processing is *relevant* information. First introduced as a lawlike generalization, the notion of relevance has laid the foundations of RT.

Relevance is not an either/or property of a given input but, rather, is a matter of degree (Sperber, 2005: 63). The relevance of an input is defined in terms of a balance between cognitive effects and processing effort (Wilson and Sperber, 2004: 609):

(38)   **Relevance of an input to an individual**
         a. Other things being equal, the greater the positive cognitive effects achieved by processing an input, the greater the relevance of the input to the individual at that time.
         b. Other things being equal, the greater the processing effort expended, the lower the relevance of the input to the individual at that time.

The first part of this definition makes it clear that the more positive cognitive effects a stimulus provides to an individual in a particular context, the more relevant it is. A stimulus has cognitive effects whenever, once integrated with information already stored in memory, it causes a change in an individual's set of assumptions (their *cognitive environment*, Sperber and Wilson, 1995: 38). According to Sperber and Wilson (1995: 109), there are in particular three ways in which a given stimulus can have such cognitive effects. First, a new stimulus achieves cognitive effects if it strengthens an already existing assumption. This happens, for instance, if you suspect two of your friends might be dating, yet do not have much proof. Then one day, you see them walking in the street holding hands. This new information achieves cognitive effects by strengthening your assumption that they are dating. Second, a new stimulus also achieves cognitive effects if it contradicts an already existing assumption. For instance, you might think that your husband is out working in the garden, but then you suddenly see him in front of the computer checking his email. This new information achieves cognitive effects by contradicting a previously held assumption. Finally, a new stimulus also has cognitive effects if, when integrated with older assumptions, it leads to the derivation of a new assumption (called a *contextual implication*, Sperber and Wilson, 1995: 107). For instance, you have been informed that the concert will be canceled if it rains. A few hours before the event, as you walk back home, a storm hits town. This new information achieves cognitive effects since you derive the contextual implication that the concert will be canceled (and therefore you can stay at home, etc.). According to Wilson and Sperber (2004: 608), the derivation of contextual implications provides the most important type of cognitive effects.

The relevance of a given input is not a specific quantitative notion that can be easily measured but is, rather, comparative (Sperber and Wilson, 1987: 742,

1995: 132). The relevance of an input indeed varies depending on the number of cognitive effects it provides in a specific context. The same input may be more or less relevant depending on the context or the strength[22] of the assumptions that are manifest to an individual at a given time. More importantly, as the definition in (38b) clearly indicates, the relevance of an input is also a function of the mental effort spent on processing it (Sperber and Wilson, 1995: 124). The amount of effort required depends on a number of different factors such as "recency of use, frequency of use, perceptual salience, ease of retrieval from memory, linguistic or logical complexity and size of the context" (Clark, 2013a: 104; see also Allott (2013: 66) and references cited therein). The more processing effort is needed by a given stimulus, the less relevant it is.

2.2.1.2 Principles of Relevance   It will have become clear from the preceding section that various sources of information can be more or less relevant depending on the mental processing effort they require as well as the number of cognitive effects they achieve. A central claim within RT is that we do not pay equal attention to these different inputs. Rather, it is claimed that we tend to allocate cognitive resources only to those inputs that are maximally relevant. This is referred to as the first (or cognitive) principle of relevance (Wilson and Sperber, 2004: 610):

(39)   **Cognitive Principle of Relevance**
        Human cognition tends to be geared to the maximization of relevance.

This means that both our specialized input systems (which compute external stimuli) and the central systems (which compute internal stimuli) tend to devote cognitive resources to inputs that provide as many cognitive effects as possible for as little processing effort as possible (Sperber and Wilson, 1995: 261). This tendency, it is argued, results from a biological evolution caused by the systematic pressure towards relevance (Sperber, 1996: 114, 2005: 67; Sperber and Wilson, 2002: 13; Wilson and Sperber, 2004: 110). Of course, it is important to understand that, in and of themselves, most natural stimuli do not provide any indication of their potential relevance. As a consequence, the selection of maximally relevant information is said to follow from a specific heuristic that involves "local arbitrations, aimed at incremental gains, between simultaneously available inputs competing for immediately available resources" (Sperber and Wilson, 1995: 261; cf. also Sperber, 2005: 63). How exactly such heuristics apply to language will be

---

[22] The strength of an assumption refers to the extent to which an assumption is accepted as true by an individual (Sperber and Wilson, 1995: 75; see also Wilson, 2022 on the strength of communicated propositions).

discussed in the next section. According to Sperber and Wilson (1995: 156), however, some stimuli do provide an indication of their own potential relevance to an individual: *ostensive* stimuli. This hypothesis forms the basis of the second (or communicative) principle of relevance (Wilson and Sperber, 2004: 612):

(40)   **Communicative Principle of Relevance**
        Every ostensive stimulus conveys a presumption of its own optimal relevance.

A stimulus is ostensive whenever it indicates an individual's intention to communicate and to be informative (Sperber and Wilson, 1995: 54–64). Utterances are probably the paradigm case of ostensive stimuli (hence the focus on language in RT), but other types of stimuli can also be ostensive (e.g. gesture). In RT, it is argued that ostensive stimuli – such as a speaker's utterance – systematically communicate a presumption of their own optimal relevance, as described in (41) (from Wilson and Sperber, 2004: 612).

(41)   **Presumption of optimal relevance**
        a. The ostensive stimulus is relevant enough to be worth the audience's processing effort.
        b. It is the most relevant one compatible with the communicator's abilities and preferences.

From this perspective, ostensive stimuli are systematically expected to provide an individual with enough cognitive effects to justify the amount of effort required to process them. The consequences of this presumption are twofold. First, because of this expectation, an individual systematically processes ostensive stimuli in such a way as to optimize their relevance. In addition, it also follows from this presumption that individuals who intend to communicate a given assumption need to make sure the ostensive stimulus they use can be optimally processed by the addressee (Sperber and Wilson, 1995: 157).[23] Both these corollaries have been tested and have received support from experimental evidence (cf. Sperber, Cara and Girotto, 1995; Girotto et al., 2001; van der Henst, Carles and Sperber, 2002; van der Henst, Sperber and Politzer, 2002; van der Henst and Sperber, 2004; van der Henst, 2006; Gibbs and Bryant, 2008). More generally, it has to be understood that the communicative principle of relevance is not meant as a specific rule that individuals need to follow (and could therefore violate) but is introduced in RT as a lawlike generalization about what the human mind does whenever it is faced with ostensive stimuli (Sperber and Wilson, 1995: 162). In the next section, we will see how this principle applies to linguistic stimuli and in particular how it is relevant to the field of lexical pragmatics. Note

---

[23] This second consequence has in fact recently led Park and Clark (2022) to aptly argue that there is a *relevance-focused production heuristics.*

that in order to facilitate the discussion, I will generally refer to the second (communicative) principle of relevance as *the* principle of relevance. Given the focus on language and lexical pragmatics, this is the most relevant of the two principles for our discussion.

2.2.2   Meaning, the Underdeterminacy Thesis and Comprehension Heuristics

The notion of relevance has been primarily applied to linguistic communication. As mentioned above, the use of language is indeed a paradigm case of an ostensive stimulus (see discussion in Assimakopoulos, 2022) and therefore raises expectations of optimal relevance. Speakers are thus expected to make their contribution worth the hearer's processing effort and, concurrently, hearers tend to look for an interpretation that provides enough cognitive effects to justify the amount of effort invested in the process. This observation has been used in RT in particular to explain the pragmatics of linguistic communication.[24] In RT, the term *ostensive-inferential communication* is in fact generally preferred to the term linguistic communication (Sperber and Wilson, 1995: 50). It is a central assumption in RT that linguistic communication does not only consist in the ostensive use of linguistic conventions. Rather, in order for linguistic communication to be effective, and for the speaker's meaning to be fully recovered, much inferencing also needs to take place. Inference is needed, for instance, for the derivation of *implicatures*, this latter term having been introduced by Paul Grice (1989: 24). Consider the following dialogue:

(42)   LAURA: Would you like some more chicken?
        PETER: I'm full, thanks.

Here, in order to understand Peter's answer and act in accordance with the information it conveys, Laura needs to derive the implicature that Peter does not want any more chicken. Implicatures are textbook examples of what an individual needs to infer and what requires good pragmatic competence (Zufferey, Moeschler and Reboul, 2019). It is clear for relevance theorists, however, that much more than just implicatures actually need to be inferred in order for communication to be successful. It was noted earlier that linguistic logical forms often need to be enriched into full-fledged (i.e. fully propositional) assumptions. It is indeed argued in RT that a linguistic input often fails to provide all of the information that is being explicitly communicated by an

---

[24] In RT, the term *pragmatics* refers to inferential processes and inferred meanings and the term *semantics* usually refers to the encoded meaning of an expression (Wilson, 2011: 9).

individual. This is usually discussed in terms of the *underdeterminacy thesis* (Carston, 2002a: 19):

(43)   **The underdeterminacy thesis**
         Linguistic meaning underdetermines what is said.

That is, it is assumed in RT that there is a gap between the meaning of the words that we use (i.e. *linguistic* meaning) and the content of the proposition that is explicitly expressed (i.e. *what is said* in Gricean terms (Grice, 1989: 25)). The communicated propositions are systematically richer than the meaning of the linguistic conventions used to convey those propositions. According to this view, much inferencing is therefore also needed at the explicit level of communication in order to derive a speaker's intended interpretation. There are various sources of linguistic underdeterminacy. Carston (2002a: 28) identifies six such sources. The examples given in (44) to (49), and in particular the italicized items, illustrate each of these sources.

(44)   Multiple encodings (i.e. ambiguities)
         a. Give me my *bow.* (COCA, written)
         b. Both of them really get to every *ball.* (COCA, spoken)

(45)   Indexical references
         a. *She* pointed out some consequences of not wearing the correct shoe. (NOW)
         b. Some of the wealthiest people in the world live *there.* (NOW)

(46)   Missing constituents
         a. I was just wondering if you were good *enough.* [for what?] (BNC, written)
         b. Chelsea are a *better* bet for trophies. [than whom?] (BNC, written)

(47)   Unspecified scope of elements
         a. Everyone is*n't* perfect. (COCA, written)
         b. We need 103 Canberrans to bake *a* cake. (NOW)

(48)   Underspecificity or weakness of encoded conceptual content
         a. What it comes down to is trying to give *children* a better Christmas. (BNC, spoken)
         b. Let's be more efficient and make the tax payers' *money* be used wisely. (BNC, spoken)

(49)   Overspecificity or narrowness of encoded conceptual content
         a. It's so *empty* I can hear the tick of a wristwatch from three rows away. (NOW)
         b. That's exactly what it was. I feel that I loved a – a *teddy bear* for 15 years, and suddenly I've met this young man who – who has everything I wanted my son to have. (COCA, spoken)

Prior to Carston, Grice had already acknowledged the types of underdeterminacy identified in (44) and (45), for which disambiguation and reference assignment are required (Grice, 1989: 25). He does not explain, however, how these processes are carried out (Carston, 2002a: 21). Utterances such as in (46) are said to be missing a constituent (and therefore underdetermine what is said) since no truth value can be attributed to them without this constituent.[25] In (46a), for instance, one needs to know exactly what quality or skill is being referred to in order to be able to evaluate whether 'you' is good enough. The sentences in (47) are typical examples of scopal ambiguities, whereby the scope of a given linguistic item needs to be contextually worked out in order to understand the speaker's intended interpretation. In (47a), for instance, it is not clear whether the speaker is communicating that not everyone is perfect or that no one is perfect. In (48) and (49), the different examples used more directly fall within the field of lexical pragmatics, the focus of this book. In (48a), the encoded content of the noun *children* underspecifies what is actually being communicated since not just any children are being referred to but only children in need. In (49a), the encoded content of the adjective *empty* over-specifies what is explicitly expressed given that the room was not literally empty, but only sufficiently so that the speaker could hear the ticking of someone else's watch. In both cases the content of the word used is either too specific or not specific enough (with regard to the speaker's intended interpretation) and needs to be pragmatically adjusted. More examples will be discussed in the next section.

It is argued in RT that the interpretation of the utterances in (44) to (49) involves a single inferential process. As mentioned before, the aim of RT is to explain how this inferential process is constrained on the basis of the principle of relevance. This approach will be introduced in the rest of this section. First, however, it is important to note that it is clear from the relevance-theoretic perspective that inferential processes are not only required for the derivation of implicatures and implicated content. Rather, pragmatic inference is also involved at the explicit level of communication, whereby the conceptual material provided by the linguistic logical form of an utterance also needs to be pragmatically enriched into a fully propositional assumption (Sperber and Wilson, 1995: 181; Carston, 1988: 41, 2002a: 107, 2016a: 614). For this reason, Sperber and Wilson (1995) coined the term *explicature* (by analogy with the term implicature) to refer to the pragmatically enriched explicit content of an utterance (Sperber and Wilson, 1995: 182; see also Carston, 1999, 2004, 2009, 2010).[26] It follows from this perspective that RT draws the line between semantics and pragmatics somewhere at the explicit level of communication (cf. Carston and Hall, 2012). While an implicature is purely the product of

---

[25] Perry (1993: 206) uses the term *unarticulated constituents* (see also Bach, 1994a: 269).

[26] Similar terms have been used elsewhere in the pragmatics literature (see, for instance, Recanati's (1989: 297–302) use of the phrase *what is said* and Bach's (1994b: 125) notion of *impliciture*).

pragmatic inference, an explicature is a "semantic-pragmatic hybrid" (Carston, 2004: 819) since it is a pragmatic development of a linguistic logical form.

One of the goals of RT is to explain exactly how the inferential derivation of explicit and implicit content is constrained. It will have become clear from the previous sections that in RT the principle of relevance is considered as being the main driving force behind interpretation processes. Ostensive stimuli come with a presumption of their own optimal relevance. As a consequence, speakers need to optimize the relevance of their utterances, and hearers, whether for the recovery of explicatures or implicatures, need to look for an interpretation that provides them with enough cognitive effects to justify the amount of effort they put into the interpretation process. In this sense, inferential processes are constrained by the search for relevance, which is systematically expected given the ostensive nature of utterances. Still, it remains to be spelled out exactly how hearers actually proceed to recover the speaker's intended interpretation. The principle of relevance specifically indicates that the more cognitive effort, the less relevance. As a result, hearers do not consider all possible interpretations and then choose the most relevant one. This would require too much processing effort and therefore be self-defeating (see Sperber, 2005: 64). Rather, it is argued in RT that the principle of relevance naturally lays the foundations for the following comprehension procedure (Sperber and Wilson, 2002: 18; Wilson and Sperber, 2004: 613):

(50) **Relevance-theoretic comprehension procedure**
   a. Follow a path of least effort in computing cognitive effects. In particular, test interpretive hypotheses (disambiguations, reference resolutions, implicatures, etc.) in order of accessibility.
   b. Stop when your expectations of relevance are satisfied.

That is, for a given utterance, hearers do not process all possible interpretations but only focus on those that are most salient and which they test (for optimal relevance) in order of accessibility. Once an interpretation provides them with enough cognitive effects to justify the amount of processing effort involved, they stop searching and consider this interpretation to be the one intended by the speaker.[27] From a relevance-theoretic perspective, this comprehension procedure does not involve complex conscious computations. Rather, it is understood as an unconscious and intuitive process that involves "fast and frugal heuristics" (Wilson and Sperber, 2004: 624; see also Gigerenzer et al., 1999). In other

---

[27] As Wilson and Sperber (2004) point out, this naturally requires that "a speaker who wants her utterance to be as easy as possible to understand should formulate it (within the limits of her abilities and preferences) so that the first interpretation to satisfy the hearer's expectation of relevance is the one she intended to convey" (Wilson and Sperber, 2004: 614).

words, it is computationally the simplest procedure possible (cf. Allott, 2002: 80). Consider the following exchange:

(51)   PETER: I just thought we could put the sofa in Tom's car.
         RICHARD: It's too big!

In order to understand Richard's answer, Peter first needs to recognize the ostensive nature of Richard's behavior. The recognition of Richard's ostensive behavior creates an expectation of optimal relevance, whereby Peter is to allocate cognitive resources in such a way as to optimize the relevance of the logical form provided by Richard's utterance. Peter therefore derives the explicature by assigning a referent to the pronoun *it* (i.e. the sofa) as well as enriching the adjectival phrase *too big* (i.e. too big to fit in Tom's car). This is the most relevant explicature that Peter can derive, and he stops at this interpretation, since it enables him to infer the implicatures that they cannot put the sofa in Tom's car and that they need to find another solution. These implicatures are directly relevant to Peter since they contradict (at least) one of his assumptions and thus modify his cognitive environment. As such, this interpretation provides Peter with enough cognitive effects to justify the effort invested in processing Richard's utterance, and therefore he stops looking for other interpretations. Note that, from the relevance-theoretic approach, the derivation of explicatures and implicatures is not treated as sequential. In the example just discussed, for instance, Peter does not first derive the explicature *The sofa is too big to fit in Tom's car* and then the implicature *We cannot put the sofa in Tom's car*. Rather, the derivation of explicatures and implicatures is coordinated and both are gradually derived on the basis of contextual assumptions in order to optimize relevance. This is referred to by Wilson and Sperber (2004: 617) as a process of *mutual parallel adjustment*.

In the next section, I will focus particularly on how this comprehension heuristics has been applied to lexical meaning and will therefore mostly discuss the derivation of explicatures. It is first important to understand why exactly this comprehension procedure is possible in the first place. Following Grice (1989: 213–223), it is argued in RT that inferential communication is primarily possible because of our ability to attribute particular mental states (such as beliefs, desires and intentions) to our interlocutors and vice versa (Sperber and Wilson, 1995: 24, 2002: 3; Carston, 1999: 103). This mind-reading ability is usually discussed in terms of the *theory of mind* hypothesis (see Carruthers and Smith, 1996; Goldman, 2012). According to Sperber and Wilson (1995), ostensive-inferential communication is possible notably because of our capacity to recognize someone's communicative and informative intentions (Sperber and Wilson, 1995: 50–64). From this recognition follows a presumption of relevance that systematically constrains the inferential processes that are required to derive a speaker's communicated content and to build mental representations about an individual's thoughts and desires as well as specific attitudes.[28] The relationship between mind-reading abilities on the one hand (and in particular intention recognition) and pragmatic abilities on the other has been widely discussed in the pragmatics literature (cf. Haugh, 2008; Haugh and Jaszczolt, 2012). Unlike other pragmatic theories, however, RT has more systematically integrated theory of mind into its framework, which naturally leads to the development of new ideas within the theory. One such development concerns the type of information that hearers actually recover when interpreting a given utterance. On the basis of their mind-reading abilities, it is argued in RT that hearers do not only recover a speaker's communicated assumptions (be they *explicatures* or *implicatures*), but also recover a speaker's commitment and attitude towards those. That is, hearers also recover speakers' meta-representations of their communicated assumptions (Wilson, 2000). One particular kind of meta-representation that hearers are said to recover is called a *higher-level explicature* (Wilson and Sperber, 1993: 4; Sperber, 2000b: 6; Ifantidou, 2001: 80; Carston, 2004: 825). Consider the following example (from Wilson and Sperber, 1993: 4):

(52) a. PETER: Can you help?
      MARY (SADLY): I can't.
   b. Mary says she can't help Peter to find a job.
   c. Mary believes she can't help Peter to find a job.
   d. Mary regrets that she can't help Peter to find a job.

In order to understand Mary's answer in (52a), Peter will derive the explicature *Mary cannot help me to find a job* on the basis of his expectation of optimal relevance. In addition, it is argued in RT that Peter will also embed this explicature within a higher-level representation (i.e. a meta-representation) such as in (52b) to (52d). This higher-level explicature includes either the representation of a particular speech act (as in (52b)) or the representation of a propositional attitude (as in (52c) and (52d)) (cf. Carston, 2004: 825). Exactly which of these higher-level explicatures are derived by Peter naturally depends on the context and therefore on which assumptions are manifest to him when interpreting Mary's utterance. Note that from the relevance-theoretic stand-point, however, "hearers always infer at least one higher level of embedding for

---

[28] In cognitive psychology, it is argued that our mind is equipped with a specific "theory-of-mind module" that enables mind-reading inferential processes (see Leslie, 1992, 1994; Baron-Cohen, 1994, 1995; Scholl and Leslie, 1999, inter alia). Within RT, Sperber and Wilson argue that pragmatics (and in particular the search for optimally relevant interpretations) is a specific type of mind-reading ability and even suggest that it constitutes a specialized submodule: the *comprehension* (or *Relevance*) module (Sperber, 2000a: 129; Wilson, 2000: 42; Sperber and Wilson, 2002: 5). Whether or not this is actually the case will not be discussed here. However, it is worth noting that according to Zufferey (2010), the relevance-theoretic approach "seems to offer the best model to account for the role of theory of mind in verbal communication" (Zufferey, 2010: 25; see also Zufferey, 2015: 91).

any proposition we express" (Clark, 2013a: 209). The systematic derivation of higher-level explicatures therefore makes them an integral part of the interpretation of an utterance. Carston (2004: 825) in fact argues that sometimes the relevance of an utterance is to be found precisely in higher-level explicatures.[29]

Note that the notion of higher-level explicatures is directly relevant to our discussion because of the particular way in which they can be derived. In the example in (52) above, their derivation seems to be entirely pragmatic. Yet it has been suggested in RT that, in precisely the same way as some words provide rich clues about the speaker's intended interpretations, there must be linguistic items whose sole function is to help the hearer recover higher-level explicatures (cf. Wilson and Sperber, 2012: 166). This will be discussed more fully in Section 2.2.3.2. For now, it is worth noting from the relevance-theoretic perspective that questions of semantics and pragmatics pervade linguistic communication. For this reason, RT prefers to talk about ostensive-inferential communication.

In this section, the focus was placed on the pragmatics of linguistic communication. Any good theory of pragmatics, however, necessarily rests upon a particular theory of semantics, and vice versa. Exactly what approach to semantics is adopted in RT will be addressed in the next section. This will enable us to identify explicitly the similarities and differences between RT and CxG and how compatible they are in terms of theoretical description. Before doing so, I wish to make a small observation. It was shown previously that CxG mostly focuses on the semantic (i.e. conventional) side of linguistic communication without much consideration for (non-conventional) pragmatics. As we have seen in this section, however, much of what is actually communicated by an individual is inferred in context and not provided by the linguistic items that they use. From this perspective, CxG alone can therefore not explain exactly how linguistic communication succeeds. This is the reason why CxG needs to be combined with a theory of pragmatics such as RT to be fully explanatory. At the same time, integrating RT and CxG can prove to be a real challenge for the following reason: the relevance-theoretic approach to pragmatics is actually based on a view of semantics that radically differs from that adopted in CxG.

---

[29] As Reboul (2001) rightly points out, this notion "also enables [relevance theorists] to propose a solution to *Moore's paradox*" (Reboul, 2001: 46; emphasis mine), which has to do with the absurd nature of sentences like "I called you and I don't believe I did." In RT, when a speaker asserts a proposition P, her interlocutor usually derives the higher-level implicature that she believes P to be true.

2.2.3   Semantics in Relevance Theory

RT is particularly well known as a theory of pragmatics that tackles issues related to non-conventional aspects of linguistic communication. Yet RT also offers a specific understanding of the nature of linguistically encoded content, i.e. of semantics.

As mentioned in Section 2.1.2.2, in a purely terminological sense, Relevance Theory and Construction Grammar share a similar view since both frameworks discuss the notion of semantics in terms of *concepts*. It is argued in RT that the (optimally relevant) assumption communicated by a speaker forms "a structured set of concepts" (Sperber and Wilson, 1995: 85). From a theoretical standpoint, however, the perspectives developed in RT and CxG are fundamentally different since they are based on two opposite understandings of the nature of concepts. Indeed, relevance theorists follow Jerry Fodor's hypothesis (Fodor et al., 1980; Fodor, 1998), which postulates that concepts are *atomic* (Sperber and Wilson, 1995: 91, 1998: 187; Carston, 2002a: 321). This specific approach is categorically rejected in the constructionist approach. In addition, concepts in RT are only discussed in relation to lexical items: "the 'meaning' of a word is provided by the associated concept" (Sperber and Wilson, 1995: 90). Unlike in CxG, however, comparatively little attention is paid to the semantics of larger linguistic patterns (see below).

The RT-specific approach to 'concepts' is explained in the next section. In particular, I will try to show how RT's commitment to atomism has heavily influenced its analysis of lexical pragmatics, which results in theoretical (in)compatibility with CxG. However, it is worth first mentioning that RT discusses the notion of semantics not only in terms of concepts but also in terms of *procedures*. On the basis of the work of Blakemore (1987, 2002), more recent developments of RT consist in arguing that the encoded content of some linguistic expressions might best be described in terms of *procedural* meaning. What the term procedural meaning exactly captures (and why it is relevant to our discussion) will be explained in Section 2.2.3.2.

2.2.3.1   Concepts and Ad Hoc Concepts

In their seminal book *Relevance*, Sperber and Wilson (1995) discuss the encoded content of linguistic items in terms of their associated concepts (Sperber and Wilson, 1995: 90). In particular, following Fodor, Sperber and Wilson adopt an atomic, non-decompositional approach: "the meaning of a word such as 'yellow', 'giraffe' or 'salt' is an *irreducible* concept" (p. 91; emphasis mine). RT's commitment to conceptual atomism becomes explicitly clear in Carston (2002a):

I follow Jerry Fodor in assuming that concepts encoded by (monomorphemic) lexical items are atomic and so not decompositional; they don't have definitions (sets of necessary and sufficient component features) and they are not structured around prototypes or bundles of stereotypical features (for the arguments, see Fodor et al., 1980; Fodor, 1998; Laurence and Margolis, 1999). (p. 321)

It will have become clear that this approach to concepts is in direct opposition to that adopted in CxG, in which concepts are precisely understood in terms of encyclopedic knowledge organized in a network of related bundles around a prototype (see Section 2.1.2.2). The aim of this section is to spell out explicitly what the atomic account adopted in RT consists of. In addition, I will introduce the relevance-theoretic approach to lexical pragmatics and show how this perspective is directly influenced by the atomic approach to lexical semantics (and as a result cannot be easily integrated into a framework such as CxG). It is important to note here that the notion of *concept* represents a real issue in RT and that, within the theory itself, there are at least "three different possible views of what constitutes the content of concepts" (Groefsema, 2007: 139). In this section, I will introduce what I consider to be the more traditional approach to concepts in RT, as well as some of the issues that it raises for the semantics–pragmatics interface. A more comprehensive analysis of the relevance-theoretic perspective on concepts is given in the next chapter.

From a Fodorian point of view, the information provided by an atomic concept does not consist of a set of specific features, and even less so of a particular definition. Rather, conceptual information is said to consist of a nomological mind–world relation, i.e. a lawlike mind–world dependency (Fodor, 1998: 12).[30] The information provided by the concept CAT, for instance, consists of a necessary relationship between that concept and a specific instantiation of a cat in the real world. From this perspective, the argument goes, it is impossible to define what the word *cat* actually means: *cat* simply means CAT (p. 67). This lays the foundations for Fodor's (1998: 55) *disquotational lexicon* hypothesis, which RT largely adopts. In order to discuss a given lexical concept, relevance theorists disquote the word and put it in capitals: *love* means LOVE, *happy* means HAPPY, etc. This formalization serves to highlight the hypothesis that words and concepts belong to two different types of lexicon (see Sperber and Wilson, 1998). When the linguistic item directly contributes to a particular sentence (public lexicon), the conceptual counterpart systematically feeds the language of thought (mental lexicon). This is one of the two functions of lexical concepts: they directly appear in the linguistic logical forms that form the basis of the thoughts that we communicate (Sperber and Wilson, 1995: 86).

In addition, atomic concepts also perform another function which appears to be essential within RT. In addition to contributing to the language of thought, atomic concepts also serve as an address (i.e. a point of access) to a variety of

[30] More simply, Carston (2010) says that the content of an atomic concept consists in "its denotation – what it refers to in the world" (Carston, 2010: 265).

information stored in memory. Specifically, there are three types of information that a concept gives access to: lexical, logical and encyclopedic (Sperber and Wilson, 1995: 86). The lexical entry of a given concept provides details about the linguistic item used to express that concept. This ranges from the phonological and morphosyntactic properties as well as co-occurrence possibilities. The logical entry of a concept provides information about the logical implications of that concept and consists of "a set of deductive rules which apply to logical forms of which that concept is a constituent" (Sperber and Wilson, 1995: 86). That is, for instance, the logical entry of the concept CAT includes inference rules such as {CAT → ANIMAL} and {CAT → MAMMAL} which enable an individual to compute the logical form in which the concept occurs and to derive new assumptions. From this perspective, the logical entry does not provide representational information about the concept but only computational information about how to use that concept (p. 89). In opposition, the encyclopedic entry precisely consists of representational information. The encyclopedic entry includes all of the real-world knowledge and assumptions that an individual stores in association with a specific concept and which provides a rich contextual background for the derivation of new assumptions. In the case of the concept CAT, this includes assumptions such as:

General knowledge about the appearance and behaviour of cats, including, perhaps, visual images of cats, and, for some people, scientific knowledge about cats, such as their anatomy, their genetic make-up, or their relation to other feline species, etc., and, for most people, personal experiences of, and attitudes towards, particular cats. (Carston, 2002a: 321)

Sperber and Wilson (1995: 88) observe that "such notions as *schema, frame, prototype* or *script*" are often used to discuss encyclopedic knowledge and in particular how the encyclopedic entry is internally structured and organized. Sperber and Wilson commit to none of those views, however (Sperber and Wilson, 1995: 88). In fact, unlike the different theoretical models that introduce these notions, RT is generally not inclined to explain how encyclopedic information is structured. To be precise, the encyclopedic entry is actually viewed as a "'grab bag' of encyclopaedic information" (Hall, 2017: 94). The only type of structure which is discussed is "in terms of the degree of accessibility of the items of information it contains, which implies that the internal structure of this entry is in constant flux" (Wałaszewska, 2011: 316; see also Carston, 2002a: 321). In comparison to the different networks discussed in Section 2.1.2.2, RT's notion of encyclopedic knowledge is therefore relatively structureless. This can be easily explained due to the status attributed to encyclopedic information in RT.

From the relevance-theoretic standpoint, the types of information stored in the logical and encyclopedic entries of a given concept only serve to compute the logical form in which that concept occurs. It is often argued, however, that they do not directly contribute to the semantics of the lexical item that is associated with that concept. Here, RT and CxG therefore provide opposite analyses. While in CxG encyclopedic knowledge is considered a central element of conceptual content, and is particularly structured, in RT it is only perceived as "contextual information" (Ribeiro, 2013: 104; see also Sperber and Wilson, 1995: 89; Carston, 1997b: 119). Note that it is not always clear, though, what the status of logical and encyclopedic information actually is in RT. Groefsema (2007: 139) convincingly shows how the relevance-theoretic perspective on concepts developed in Sperber and Wilson (1995) leaves room for various interpretations, some of which would actually consist in viewing encyclopedic and/or logical information as being content-constitutive. This will be discussed at length in the next chapter. Nevertheless, there is a general tendency to consider that the logical and encyclopedic information that a concept gives access to does not constitute its content:

Neither the encyclopaedic nor the logical information associated with a concept can be thought of as constitutive of the concept or as being its content. (Reboul, 2008: 522–523)

[Logical and encyclopaedic] properties are clearly not internal components of the lexical concepts themselves. (Carston, 2010: 249)

None of the information – logical or encyclopaedic – is constitutive of the concept. (Hall, 2011: 4)

The fact that the logical and encyclopedic entries are not content-constitutive is often supported, in addition to Fodor's own arguments (see Fodor et al., 1980; Fodor, 1998), by a number of observations within RT. First of all, some concepts may not have both of these entries. Sperber and Wilson (1995: 92) argue, for instance, that the concept to which the lexical item *and* is associated "may lack an encyclopaedic entry," i.e. it is not itself associated with real-world knowledge. Similarly, it is argued that concepts associated with proper names may not trigger inferential rules and therefore lack a logical entry (p. 92). In addition, relevance theorists appear to share the assumption that only a limited set of inferential rules can occur in the logical entry of a concept. (They never discuss more than one or two inference rules for each concept they look at.) Why this should be the case is not necessarily clear, but this motivates relevance theorists to assume that the logical entry "generally [falls] short of anything definitional" (Carston, 2002a: 321). This is further supported by the observation that different concepts may share similar inferential rules, which therefore cannot be used to distinguish between them. The concepts CAT and DOG, for instance, both contain the inferential rule {ANIMAL OF A CERTAIN KIND} (p. 322). Ultimately, it is argued that – unlike logical information – encyclopedic knowledge varies a lot across individuals and time

(Sperber and Wilson, 1995: 88) and is therefore too unstable to possibly be content-constitutive.

In spite of not being content-constitutive, the information stored in the logical and encyclopedic entries is argued to play a significant role during the interpretation process of an utterance. As will become clear in the rest of this section, they are key elements in the relevance-theoretic account of lexical pragmatics.

A central assumption in RT is that the words we use underdetermine the actual content of the thoughts that we communicate. In Section 2.2.2, this was referred to as the underdeterminacy thesis. In the sentence in (48a), repeated here in (53), the word *children*, for instance is used to express not the concept CHILDREN with which it is originally associated but the unlexicalized (atomic) concept CHILDREN-IN-NEED.

(53)   What it comes down to is trying to give *children* a better Christmas.

It is argued in RT that, as the example in (53) illustrates, most of the concepts that we actually communicate are not lexicalized, i.e. they lack a lexical entry (Sperber and Wilson, 1998: 189). In order to convey these concepts, speakers therefore use the lexical entry of the most resembling concept, on the basis of which hearers recover the communicated concept in accordance with their expectations of relevance and following the comprehension procedure discussed in Section 2.2.2. Consider the sentences in (54) and (55). These examples nicely show that, in different contexts, the same lexical item (here *man*) may be used to express a variety of different concepts and not necessarily the one to which it is originally associated.

(54)   A: I need a man to love me. (COCA, spoken)
         B: Your dad loves you.
         A: Dad, come on, you know what I mean.

(55)   A: I need a man to love me. (COCA, spoken)
         B: Tom loves you.
         A: I said a man.

In neither of the examples does the speaker use the lexical item *man* to refer to the atomic concept MAN, say 'a male human being'. In (54), assuming that the speaker is a heterosexual woman, she probably means to communicate a concept such as 'heterosexual bachelor ready to commit to a long-lasting relationship'. In (55), she could intend the concept 'heterosexual bachelor with prototypically masculine features'. These two concepts are not lexicalized in English. In order to communicate these concepts, the speaker therefore uses the lexical entry of another, similar (enough) concept on the basis of which the hearer should be able to infer the intended ones in accordance with their expectations of relevance and, therefore, by following the relevance comprehension procedure. How exactly the intended concepts are recovered by the hearer is a major concern to relevance theorists. Naturally, as will have become clear, it is argued in RT that the recovery of these unlexicalized concepts is largely constrained by the search for optimal relevance which is triggered by the ostensive nature of the speaker's utterance. Precisely how the content of these concepts is actually established still calls for specification, however. Relevance theorists propose a specific account to explain the underlying mechanisms of lexical pragmatics, i.e. the meaning-construction process of lexical items.

The relevance-theoretic account of lexical pragmatics is generally based on the work of Lawrence Barsalou and his notion of *ad hoc categories* (Barsalou, 1983, 1987, 1993). According to Barsalou, conceptual categories (i.e. concepts) are never just retrieved from memory. Rather, we systematically construct ad hoc *categories*, i.e. occasion-specific categorizations (or conceptualizations), that are tailored to the specifics of each situation in which they occur.[31] (See references cited in footnote 31 for empirical and experimental evidence.) Following Barsalou, RT argues that utterance comprehension systematically requires the creation of ad hoc *concepts*. From this perspective, in spite of their being associated with a specific atomic concept, it is argued in RT that "all words behave as if they encoded pro-concepts: that is . . . the concept it is used to convey in a given utterance has to be contextually worked out" (Sperber and Wilson, 1998: 185). The interpretation of the sentences in (53) to (55), for instance, does not consist first in testing (for relevance) the concepts CHILDREN and MAN associated with the lexical items *children* and *man* and then in deriving the intended concept. Rather, their interpretation directly requires the contextual construction of the ad hoc concepts CHILDREN* in (53), MAN* in (54) and MAN**

---

[31] Already, it is important to note that this theoretical choice is unfortunate since it is inconsistent with the atomic approach to concepts adopted in RT. Barsalou et al. (1993: 57) note that:

[Barsalou] has been fairly schizophrenic in his definition of *concept*. Barsalou (1987, 1989, 1993) argues that concepts are temporary representations in working memory; Barsalou (1992a) and this chapter argue that concepts are bodies of knowledge in long-term memory; Barsalou (1992b) argues that concepts determine categorization. From this paper on, the following terminology will be followed: *Concepts* are the underlying knowledge in long-term memory from which temporary *conceptualizations* in working memory are constructed.

This quote shows that it is quite a challenge to pin down exactly what Barsalou considers to be a concept. I will come back to his view in the next chapter. For now, suffice it to say that his view of concepts is indisputably not atomic and neither is his view of ad hoc categorization (cf. Barsalou, 2000: 247, 2012: 239, 2016: 11; Yeh and Barsalou, 2006: 352; inter alia). Therefore, although relevance theorists generally discuss lexical semantics (i.e. concepts) in atomic terms, their approach to lexical pragmatics is based on a non-atomic approach. As I will try to show in the rest of this section and in particular in the next chapter, this naturally leaves a number of questions unanswered and results in many inconsistencies within RT.

in (55).[32] As I will show in the next chapter, this view naturally raises a number of fundamental questions. For instance, it is no longer clear what the role of the lexically encoded concept actually is. As Recanati (2004: 97) points out, lexical concepts therefore seem to be "communicationally irrelevant." This is rather inconsistent with the general claim that human cognition is geared towards relevance. In addition, the challenge is to know exactly what the nature of these ad hoc concepts is and how they are derived. These questions are at the origin of much debate within RT (see Chapter 3). Concerning the nature of ad hoc concepts, the traditional approach in RT considers that, like lexical concepts, they are atomic (e.g. Carston, 2010: 250). As for the way they are derived, the rest of this section will describe the underlying assumption developed in RT.

In RT, the derivation of ad hoc concepts is argued to result from a single inferential process often called *'free' pragmatic enrichment* (Carston, 2004: 830, 2010: 218). This pragmatic process is *free* in the sense that it is not directly required by the linguistic item which is used to express that concept. Nevertheless, it will have become clear that "free" pragmatic enrichment remains constrained (or guided) by the search for optimal relevance in order to develop the logical form into a full-fledged explicature. In RT, this process of pragmatic enrichment is said to result in three possible outcomes: a narrower concept, a broader concept, or both a narrower and broader concept (Carston, 1997b: 121, 2002a: 334; Wilson and Carston, 2006: 409, 2007: 231; Sperber and Wilson, 2008: 92).

There is conceptual narrowing whenever the sense (or denotation) of the ad hoc concept is more specific than that of the lexical concept from which it is derived (Wilson and Carston, 2007: 232). The interpretations of *children* and *man* above involve such conceptual narrowing. Consider also the following examples:

(56)   a. I have a *temperature*. (Sperber and Wilson, 2008: 91)
        b. Either you become a *human being* or you leave the group. (Wilson and Carston, 2007: 240)
        c. I'm not *drinking* tonight. (Wilson and Carston, 2007: 232)

In (56a), the noun *temperature* is not used to communicate the context-free concept TEMPERATURE (i.e. 'some degree of heat') which it originally encodes. That someone has a particular temperature is a simple truism that achieves no relevance to an individual since it provides them with no cognitive effects. Rather, what is communicated in (56a) is the more specific, narrower ad hoc concept TEMPERATURE*, 'abnormally high temperature', which is argued to be

---

[32] It is conventional in the relevance-theoretic literature to use the * symbol to differentiate ad hoc concepts (e.g. CHILDREN*) from context-independent lexical concepts (e.g. CHILDREN). When different (but related) ad hoc concepts are being referred to, such as in (54) and (55), a number of stars may be added to distinguish between them (e.g. MAN*, MAN**, MAN***, etc.).

inferentially derived following the comprehension procedure. A similar truism can be found in (56b). It can but only be mutually manifest to the interlocutors that the hearer (already) is a human being, and the latter must therefore infer a more specific ad hoc concept HUMAN-BEING*, e.g. a 'well-mannered person'. A similar narrowing process is also said to occur when interpreting (56c). Depending on the context, the speaker can be taken to communicate either that they will not be drinking any alcoholic drinks at all (DRINK*), or that they will not drink themself drunk (DRINK**). Both these interpretations are more specific than the encoded concept DRINK (i.e. 'absorption of liquids') and have to be inferentially derived by the hearer.

The derivation of ad hoc concepts, as mentioned above, may also provide an interpretation which is broader than that of the lexical concept from which it is derived. In this case, it is argued that the sense (or denotation) of the ad hoc concept is more general than that of the lexical concept (Wilson and Carston, 2007: 234). Consider the following sentences:

(57)   a. Holland is *flat*. (Sperber and Wilson, 2008: 91)
         b. This policy will *bankrupt* the farmers. (Wilson and Carston, 2007: 234)
         c. This steak is *raw*. (Carston, 2002a: 328)

In (57a), the adjective *flat* is not used to convey the concept FLAT, i.e. that Holland is literally even. Rather, the word is loosely used to communicate the broader ad hoc concept FLAT* whereby Holland is simply understood as not being mountainous. In (57b), the verb *bankrupt* can be understood literally. But there might also be some contexts in which it is loosely used to communicate that farmers will in fact lose a great amount of money (but yet not go bankrupt). This interpretation therefore requires the derivation of the broader ad hoc concept BANKRUPT*. Finally, the sentence in (57c) may be used literally to communicate that the steak is not cooked at all. It can also be used more loosely, however. For instance, you might use (57c) when you are not pleased with the cooking of your steak in a restaurant, in which case interpreting *raw* requires the derivation of the less specific ad hoc concept RAW*, i.e. not cooked enough.

Finally, ad hoc concepts can also be both narrower and broader than the encoded lexical concept from which they are derived. In this case, the sense of the ad hoc concept merely overlaps with that of the lexical concept (Carston, 1997b: 114).

(58)   a. Robert is a *computer*. (Wilson, 2009: 44)
         b. Caroline is a *princess*. (Wilson and Carston, 2006: 406)
         c. Sally is an *angel*. (Wilson, 2009: 44)

In (58a), *computer* is used to communicate the ad hoc concept COMPUTER*. This concept is narrower in the sense that it only refers to the quality of fast computation, and broader in that the category is extended to include individuals other than physical objects. Interpreting (58b) requires the derivation of the ad hoc concept PRINCESS* which is also both narrower and broader than the lexical concept PRINCESS. It is broader since it is extended to non-royal individuals and narrower since it only selects (for instance) the particularly good physical properties often attributed to princesses. Similarly, the interpretation of *angel* in (58c) is argued to be both narrower and broader than the lexical concept ANGEL. It is narrower since it only includes good angels, and broader given that it extends beyond celestial creatures.[33]

It will have become clear that all of these cases of conceptual narrowing and/ or broadening are said to be derived following the relevance comprehension procedure discussed in Section 2.2.2. The challenge here is to understand exactly what constitutes the content of ad hoc concepts. It was mentioned earlier that, like lexical concepts, ad hoc concepts are also considered to be atomic. If such is the case, it is very unclear in what way ad hoc concepts can be narrower/broader than lexical concepts. The notions of narrowing and broadening necessarily require some internal structure that can be exploited in different ways (cf. Assimakopoulos (2012: 23), and references cited therein). By virtue of being atomic, however, concepts in RT do not provide such structure. The reason why the terms *narrower* and *broader* are used follows from the way the content of these concepts is said to be determined. Ad hoc concepts are derived not solely on the basis of the atomic (lexical) concept itself, but primarily on the basis of the information stored in the logical and encyclopedic entries that the concept gives access to. Carston (1997b) explicitly says that, in order to derive ad hoc concepts

the hearer decodes the lexically encoded concept, thereby gaining access to certain logical and encyclopedic properties; he treats the utterance as a rough guide to what the speaker intends to communicate, and, in effect, sorts through the available properties, rejecting those that are not relevant in the particular context and accepting those that are, as reflections of the speaker's view. (p. 107)

---

[33] As the sentences in (58) illustrate, ad hoc concepts that are both narrower and broader than the lexical concepts often include examples of metaphorical use. Within RT, the interpretation of (lexical) metaphors is argued to follow from exactly the same process of conceptual development as cases of loose and hyperbolic use. The only difference concerns the extent to which the denotation of the ad hoc concept actually overlaps with that of the lexical concept from which it originates. For this reason, the notion of a "literal–loose–metaphorical continuum" has been introduced within RT (Sperber and Wilson, 2008: 93, see also Wilson and Carston, 2007). In comparison, cognitive linguists (and, therefore, construction grammarians) usually give a different treatment to metaphors (cf. Grady (2007) for a detailed overview). I will not address this issue here. For some work on the compatibility between the relevance-theoretic approach to metaphors and that elaborated in cognitive linguistics, see Tendahl and Gibbs (2008), Tendahl (2009), Wilson (2009, 2022), Stöver (2010) and Gibbs and Tendahl (2011).

That is, the content of ad hoc concepts is argued to be determined on the basis of the information stored in the encyclopedic and/or logical entries of the context-free lexical concept (Carston, 2002a: 347). From this perspective, it is easier to understand how ad hoc concepts can be narrower/broader than the lexical concepts from which they are inferentially derived. It is the set of information stored in the logical and encyclopedic entries that is narrower/broader (p. 347). As will become clear in the next chapter, this approach to the construction of (lexical) meaning provides a solid basis for the understanding of lexical semantics and pragmatics that I will explore in more detail and put in relation to the (not so different) constructionist perspective. Nevertheless, as far as meaning is concerned, there still seems to be a contradiction within RT (cf. Mioduszewska, 2015). On the one hand, it is argued that both lexical and ad hoc concepts are atomic and that it is this atom that constitutes the content of the lexical item used. At the same time, the difference between lexical concepts and ad hoc concepts is located at the level of the logical/encyclopedic entries, in particular in terms of how the information stored in those entries actually overlaps. In a sense, this suggests that the information stored in the logical/encyclopedic entries is therefore content-constitutive, unlike what is often argued in RT. Given this dichotomy, there can be only one of two outcomes. One possibility is to keep arguing that the content of lexical items (i.e. lexical semantics) must be the atomic concept itself. In this case, the challenge is to know exactly what the nature of ad hoc concepts actually is. This is explicitly what Carston (2010) points out:

The questions in the domain of relevance-theoretic lexical pragmatics that strike me as most interesting and most in need of some long hard thought concern the nature of ad hoc concepts. Are ad hoc concepts the same kind of entity as lexical concepts (apart from not being lexicalised)? Are they atomic or decompositional (perhaps even definitional)? . . . This is a research programme with most of the work yet to be done and I do not have much to offer here but a few hunches, hopes, and intuitions. (p. 249)

Although Carston (2010: 250) argues that these questions still "remain to be answered," however, she considers that there is no reason to think that ad hoc concepts are not atomic. Alternatively, it has been suggested that ad hoc concepts, unlike lexical concepts, are not atomic but decompositional/definitional (e.g. Vicente and Martínez Manrique, 2010; Allott and Textor, 2012). The other possibility consists in abandoning the general atomic commitment to concepts and in considering that both lexical and ad hoc concepts are decompositional/definitional (e.g. Assimakopoulos, 2012). As might have become clear from the previous discussion, I will suggest an analysis along these lines in the next chapter.[34] Please note, of course, that the two possibilities

---

[34] It is important to note that the focus of this book is on linguistic meaning and not conceptual format. I will therefore not argue in favor of or against conceptual atomism. This debate requires more space than is possible here and has already resulted in a considerable body of research.

just discussed both rest on the initial assumption that lexical items must encode concepts. In the next chapter, I will show that more recent developments of RT also consider an alternative possibility whereby (context-free) lexical meaning might not be conceptual at all (see Section 3.3.2).

It is crucial to understand that this discussion of the nature of lexical semantics is indispensable. The perspective on concepts adopted in RT has serious theoretical consequences. I will discuss two of them here.

One of the consequences of the relevance-theoretic approach to concepts/ lexical semantics concerns its understanding of the notions of monosemy and encoded polysemy. There is a general tendency in RT to assume that lexical items are monosemous, i.e. that they only encode one concept. The different analyses of the sentences in (56) to (58) have already pointed in that direction. It is argued that the interpretation of the items *temperature* in (56a), *drink* in (56c) and *angel* in (58c), for instance, are all pragmatically inferred from context following the relevance-theoretic comprehension procedure. From a constructionist perspective, however, these senses are already encoded by the lexical items which are used to communicate them.[35] Of course, it can be argued that the analyses of the sentences in (56) to (58) are purely rhetorical and are only meant to explain the relevance-theoretic approach to lexical pragmatics, and that relevance theorists are well aware that these particular senses might already be part of the speaker's knowledge. In fact, relevance theorists readily recognize that some of the senses they discuss in inferential terms might be stored by speakers of English (e.g. Wilson, 2003: 277; Wilson and Carston, 2007: 238, Carston, 2016a: 618, 2019: 152, 2021: 122). Strictly speaking, encoded polysemy is therefore not rejected in RT. Yet, monosemy is still preferred to polysemy. As I have shown in Leclercq (2023), for instance, the various relevance-theoretic accounts of modal meaning in English all adopt (and strongly argue for) a monosemous account (cf. Walton, 1988; Haegeman, 1989; Groefsema, 1992, 1995; Klinge, 1993; Berbeira Gardón, 1996, 1998, 2006; Nicolle, 1996, 1997a, 1998a; Papafragou, 2000; Kisielewska-Krysiuk, 2008). More generally, Carston (2002a) says:

I am uneasy with the assumption that a monosemous analysis is always to be preferred to a polysemous one, though the "if at all possible, go pragmatic" strategy that it entails is one that I generally follow myself, as it makes for much more elegant analyses and because, for the time being, we lack any other strong guiding principle. (p. 219)

Rather, my aim is to argue that, regardless of whether concepts are atomic or not, the encoded meaning (i.e. semantics) of lexemes must contain the encyclopedic information that a concept gives access to.

[35] It is worth noting that the senses discussed earlier for the item *temperature*, *drink* and *angel* actually all have an entry in different dictionaries (e.g. Cambridge Dictionary, last accessed November 29, 2017, https://dictionary.cambridge.org/dictionary/english/temperature).

It is not clear why the notion of *elegance* is used as a (defining) criterion when conducting a scientific investigation, especially if one is to be descriptively accurate. (That is, one should be careful not to aim for elegance at any cost.) Beyond concerns of elegance, the relevance-theoretic appeal to monosemy is primarily grounded in a number of assumptions on which the theory was developed.

First, encoded polysemy might be dispreferred simply because it does not fit well with Fodor's atomic view of conceptual content and in particular with the disquotational lexicon hypothesis (cf. Fodor and Lepore, 2002: 116–117; see also Carston, 2010: 276). Fodor (1998: 53) explicitly argues that "there is no such thing as polysemy." Of course, not all relevance theorists share Fodor's view. Falkum (2011), for instance, very explicitly argues that "contrary to Fodor, I believe that there is such a thing as polysemy" (p. 61). Yet the kind of polysemy that Falkum has in mind is not *encoded* polysemy but some sort of *pragmatic* polysemy: words can be used to communicate different concepts in different contexts, the actual content of which has to be systematically inferred (p. 61). In other words, there is still no room given to encoded polysemy. I believe this is largely due to another theoretical commitment within RT.

Encoded polysemy might be eschewed by relevance theorists simply because it is at odds, in spite of what could be argued, with the relevance-theoretic approach to ad hoc concepts. (This will be discussed at more length in the next chapter.) Even though relevance theorists claim that they are not particularly interested in encoded polysemy, they do argue that their pragmatic approach to lexical meaning can explain its origin (see Falkum, 2011: 147, 2015: 96; Carston, 2013: 187, 2016a: 619, 2019: 152, 2021: 123, inter alia). The repeated derivation of an ad hoc concept will lead to its conventionalization alongside the original lexical concept. This is a point of view I share. As Assimakopoulos (2012: 19) points out, however, the notion of ad hoc concepts was originally developed within RT as a rejection of the "encoded first" hypothesis.[36] It is argued in RT that the lexically encoded concept is not simply retrieved from memory and tested first for optimal relevance but that an ad hoc concept is systematically constructed following the relevance-theoretic comprehension procedure. In this case, as mentioned before, the question is to know what the role of the encoded concept actually is. Intuitively, it seems more *relevant* (since relatively effortless) to test this concept first for optimal relevance and then to try and derive an ad hoc concept. In the next chapter, I will discuss some of the issues that this approach raises and some of the solutions that have been suggested. The point to be made here is that monosemy might be

---

[36] Assimakopoulos (2012: 19) actually refers to the '*literal* first' hypothesis, in keeping with the relevance theoretic tradition. However, this hypothesis does not relate to literal versus non-literal (e.g. metaphorical) types of meaning but to encoded versus inferred types of meaning. This is why I prefer to use the term *encoded* here.

generally preferred within RT because it is hard to see how relevance theorists could explain the relevance (in the technical sense) of having several encoded senses when they cannot explain the relevance of having even just one. That is, in a sense, since the encoded senses are argued not to be tested first, then why bother storing them in the first place? This kind of thinking seems to be underlying the latest development in Wilson (2011, 2016) and Carston (2013, 2016b), which I will discuss at length in the next chapter.

This perspective comes in direct opposition to the view adopted in CxG, according to which polysemy is the norm and monosemy the exception. I tend to sympathize with the constructionist approach, especially since I doubt that the 'if at all possible, go pragmatic' strategy can achieve descriptive accuracy. In the next chapter, one of my aims will be to show that there is no necessary incompatibility between arguing both for polysemy as well as against the "encoded first" hypothesis. One only needs, as Carston herself points out, specific guiding principles. I will attempt to provide such principles.

There is another, less direct, consequence of the relevance-theoretic approach to concepts that also needs mentioning. The main aim of relevance theorists is not so much to describe linguistic competence as it is to explain the pragmatics of linguistic communication. Yet in order to provide an accurate account of linguistic pragmatics, it is essential to know exactly what constitutes an individual's linguistic knowledge and how this knowledge actually contributes to different communicative acts. In RT, considerable attention is given to lexical concepts, their nature and how they are used in context. Unlike in CxG, however, comparatively little attention is given to other (larger) elements of the language. Only a few relevance-theoretic studies mention the possibility for larger (non-lexical) patterns to be meaningful and to contribute to the understanding of an utterance. This includes, for instance, work on sentence types (e.g. Clark, 1991), prosody (cf. Scott, 2017, 2021, and references cited therein for a detailed overview) and clefts (e.g. Jucker, 1997). More generally, however, most of the work conducted from a relevance-theoretic standpoint focuses strictly on aspects of lexical semantics/pragmatics.[37] As a result, it is argued, for instance, that interpreting the creative use of *flick-knife* and *wrist* in (59) and (60) consists of a purely pragmatic process, whereby the ad hoc concepts FLICK-KNIFE* and WRIST* are derived in accordance with the principle of relevance.

(59)   Handguns are the new *flick-knives.* (Wilson and Carston, 2007: 236)

(60)   She *wristed* the ball over the net. (Wilson and Carston, 2007: 237)

The interpretation of *flick-knives* as metonymically referring to a bigger category (e.g. favorite weapon of choice) is said to result from "a single pragmatic

---

[37] This is clear from the topics addressed in references in Francisco Yus' detailed online bibliography (http://personal.ua.es/francisco.yus/rt.html).

process of lexical adjustment" (Wilson and Carston, 2007: 236). Similarly, interpreting *wristed* as a particular caused-motion verb solely depends on one's background knowledge "about the various arm movements of competent tennis players" (p. 237). That is, in order to explain the interpretation of these lexemes, no linguistic elements other than the lexemes themselves are discussed. As a consequence, relevance theorists once more have to turn to pragmatics to explain their interpretation. From the constructionist perspective, however, this strategy can sometimes be avoided. It is clear in CxG that it is not only lexemes that are meaningful but also larger (syntactic) units of the language. The interpretation of the sentences in (59) and (60), for instance, does not depend only on the lexemes that are used but also on the meaning of the larger constructions in which they occur: in (59) the X *is the new* Y construction and in (60) the CAUSED-MOTION construction. In (59), the metonymic interpretation of *flick-knives* is required by the slot it occupies in the X *is the new* Y construction. Similarly, in (60), the caused-motion interpretation of *wristed* is already part of the CAUSED-MOTION construction in which it occurs. Exactly how the lexeme inherits its meaning from the construction will be discussed in greater detail in Chapter 4.

Naturally, it must be understood that relevance theorists do not necessarily reject constructionist ideas. Yet there remains a general tendency not to view larger patterns of language as meaningful units. (After all, RT generally adopts a Chomskyan formal approach to language, against which CxG was precisely developed. See Carston, 2000: 87; Clark, 2013a: 346.) Because of the relative absence of such insights into linguistic structures, however, relevance theorists once more have to play the "all pragmatics" strategy, an option which – although (arguably) theoretically appealing – may not always be descriptively accurate. For this reason, I believe instead that RT can benefit from the constructionist insights.

Exactly how the various lexemes inherit their meanings from the construction in which they occur will be discussed in more detail in Chapter 4, where I will show that combining insights from RT and CxG is necessary because neither account on its own can explain the interpretations of (59) and (60).

2.2.3.2 Procedural Meaning   It is a central assumption in RT that communication depends on inference more than it does on language. From this perspective, language is only "subservient to the inferential process" and in particular to *relevance* (Sperber and Wilson, 1995: 176). Language indeed provides the most cost-efficient way to achieve optimal relevance. In the previous section, we saw that lexical concepts for instance provide rich clues for the recovery of the intended interpretation which is inferentially constructed. That is, lexical concepts provide a solid basis for where relevance is to be sought and found. Given this particular approach to linguistic communication, referred to in RT as ostensive-inferential communication, the challenge is to know exactly how language contributes to the comprehension process. It is argued in RT that in addition to specific mental representations (i.e. concepts), language might also be used to provide information about how to compute these mental representations and directly constrain the inferential process involved during the search for optimal relevance. This type of information is often referred to as *procedural*, and was first introduced in RT in the work of Diane Blakemore (1987, 1990, 2002). As a result, it is argued that lexical items may have either conceptual or procedural semantics, each contributing differently to the interpretation of the utterance in which they are used.

What exactly constitutes the nature of procedural expressions is not clear (cf. Groefsema, 1992; Bezuidenhout, 2004; Curcó, 2011; Wilson, 2011, 2012, inter alia). This issue will be taken up in Chapter 4. It is generally argued, however, that unlike lexical concepts, procedural expressions do not map onto mental representations but are instead used to convey specific *instructions* for the processing of conceptual elements. Blakemore (1992: 151) explicitly describes procedural expressions as items that "encode instructions for processing propositional representations." The aim of these procedures is to guide the hearer towards optimal relevance by constraining the inferential process and by limiting the range of possible inferences. That is, they act as semantic constraints on inferential processes. In order to illustrate this observation, Blakemore originally discussed the use of discourse connectives in English in such procedural terms:

(61)   Tom can open Ben's safe. *So* he knows the combination. (Blakemore, 2002: 79)

(62)   Tom can open Ben's safe. *After all*, he knows the combination. (Blakemore, 2002: 79)

According to Blakemore, the use of *so* and *after all* in (61) and (62), respectively, is only meant to provide the hearer with an instruction about how to connect the two propositions and guide the hearer towards optimal relevance. The markers do not contribute to these propositions but only to their computation: their use directs the hearer towards the particular consequential/causal relationship intended by the speaker and which they have to infer. Without these markers, hearers may either fail to recover the speaker's intended interpretation or simply spend too much effort deriving it (hence making it less *relevant*). Hence, procedural expressions are primarily used to facilitate the optimization of relevance.

Since the work of Blakemore, the conceptual/procedural distinction has been extended and applied to various expressions within RT (cf. Escandell-Vidal, Leonetti and Ahern (2011) for a detailed overview). Although this has raised a number of issues within RT (see Carston, 2016b), there are two observations that need to be mentioned with respect to procedural meaning.

The first observation is that, given that inference occurs both at the explicit and implicit level of communication in RT (see Section 2.2.2), procedural meaning can be used to constrain the derivation of both implicatures and explicatures. In the case of discourse markers, it is often argued that they put a constraint on the derivation of implicatures. In Grice's (1989: 25) famous example *He is an Englishman; he is, therefore, brave*, the discourse marker *therefore* is used to constrain the derivation of the implicated premise *Englishmen are brave*. Expressions with procedural meaning can also constrain the derivation of explicatures and higher-level explicatures, however. At the level of explicatures, it is argued, for instance, that pronouns and demonstratives provide semantic constraints for the recovery of a specific referent and therefore have procedural semantics (Wilson and Sperber, 1993; Scott, 2011, 2013, 2016). Procedural meaning can also constrain the derivation of higher-level explicatures. Clark (1991) argues, for instance, that sentence types (i.e. imperatives, exclamatives and interrogatives) provide the hearer with an instruction for how to reconstruct the speaker's attitude towards the communicated proposition, i.e. to reconstruct how the proposition is mentally represented by the speaker.

The second observation concerns the actual nature of procedural meaning. Although it is not necessarily clear what constitutes the semantics of procedural expressions, a number of criteria are often used to distinguish concepts from procedures. Carston (2016b: 160–161) lists five properties that define procedural encoding: (i) introspective inaccessibility, (ii) non-compositionality, (iii) rigidity, (iv) not susceptible to nonliteral use, and (v) not polysemous. These properties will be discussed in Chapter 4. As we will see, they may not be completely unerring. However, it is worth mentioning that rigidity is often perceived as being the best defining feature of procedural expressions (cf. Escandell-Vidal and Leonetti, 2011). The rigidity of procedural meaning has to be understood in comparison with the relative flexibility of conceptual meaning. Whenever there is an incompatibility between a lexical concept and a procedural expression, the semantics of the procedural expression always wins out over the lexical concepts, which has to be adjusted to fit with the procedural semantics. Consider the following example:

(63)   John is being silly. (Escandell-Vidal and Leonetti, 2011: 93)

The authors argue that, although the stative feature inherent to the concept SILLY is incompatible with the dynamic nature of progressive aspect in English, it is the procedural nature of progressive marking (i.e. "procedural information about how to construct the internal representation of the state of affairs," p. 92) that forces a dynamic representation of the situation. This type of description, whereby the meaning of an expression adjusts to that of another linguistic item, is described in Construction Grammar in terms of coercion. Interestingly, it is exactly in those terms that Escandell-Vidal and Leonetti describe the difference between conceptual and procedural meaning.[38] They argue that lexical concepts are coercible but procedural expressions are not: they only have a coercive force (2011: 86). This observation will prove very useful in Chapter 4 when discussing the notion of coercion. I will show that the notion of coercion as discussed in CxG might help shed new light on the actual nature of procedural encoding.

2.2.4   Relevance Theory: Summing Up

Relevance Theory is a cognitive theory of communication. It is based on the assumption that our mind is equipped with the capacity to treat only those pieces of information that provide us with enough cognitive effects to justify the amount of effort involved to process them, i.e. *relevant* information. This 'principle of relevance' in particular makes it possible to explain exactly how linguistic communication can succeed in spite of the fact that most of the words we use often fail to determine exactly the thoughts we intend to communicate. Ostensive acts of communication raise a specific expectation of relevance. As a result, understanding an utterance simply consists in optimizing the relevance of its interpretation. This involves a particular comprehension procedure which leads to the derivation of both explicatures (enriched explicit content) and implicatures (inferred implicit content). In particular, we have seen that RT puts forward a specific account of how conceptual content is adjusted in context and how ad hoc concepts – context-specific concepts – are derived in order to meet this expectation. This approach to lexical pragmatics will prove particularly useful in the next chapter, for, as mentioned previously, CxG lacks a detailed account of pragmatics and RT provides one of the most developed accounts of pragmatics in the literature.

The challenge with Relevance Theory is not to understand how pragmatics works but to pin down the extent to which it is actually involved in linguistic communication. Relevance theorists largely adopt a broad Fodorian perspective on semantics according to which lexical concepts are atomic. Yet this perspective is not completely compatible with how they account for the derivation of ad hoc concepts. As a result, the question is left open as to what actually constitutes the content of both lexical concepts and ad hoc concepts. This

---

[38] In order to explain example (63), Escandell-Vidal and Leonetti (2011) explicitly refer to the literature on *aspectual coercion*. It is worth noting that they are, to my knowledge, the only ones in RT to use the term *coercion*.

ambiguity about the nature of concepts, however, has led relevance theorists to play the "all pragmatics" strategy. As a result, words are almost systematically considered to be semantically monosemous, and ad hoc concepts systematically have to be inferred. But also, the meanings that words are used to convey are often analyzed independently of the particular constructions in which they occur. Yet, from the perspective of CxG, a number of aspects that are considered to belong to pragmatics in RT are often viewed as semantic properties. In the next chapter, the aim will be to try and combine these two approaches to conceptual content and show that a combination of them might be more psychologically real as well as more descriptively accurate.

2.3   Conclusion

Construction Grammar and Relevance Theory are currently two of the most discussed frameworks in their respective domains. Construction Grammar has put forward a specific account of linguistic knowledge, and Relevance Theory presents a detailed perspective on communication more generally. It will have become clear, however, that the strength of one of these two frameworks often corresponds to the weakness of the other. Where CxG provides a detailed account of linguistic forms and semantics, Relevance Theory still seems to be looking for specific guidelines on what constitutes the content of linguistic expressions. At the same time, where Relevance Theory proposes a very thorough understanding of pragmatic inference, Construction Grammar fails to integrate such principles into its framework. The aim of this book thus consists in drawing a theoretical bridge between these two frameworks and to show that the two frameworks nicely complement each other. Integrating the two frameworks is more easily said than done, however, as they are based on radically opposite ways of understanding what constitutes not only meaning but even language more generally. Clark (2013a) explicitly says that Relevance Theory "is based on a broadly Chomskyan approach to language and on Fodorian assumptions about modularity" (Clark, 2013a: 95). Construction Grammar, however, is one of the early functional approaches to grammar that was developed in opposition to these two traditions. Nevertheless, the aim of the next chapters is to show that in spite of these differences, Construction Grammar and Relevance Theory are not de facto incompatible.

Most recently, the need for CxG and RT to interact and be integrated has become more and more apparent. As mentioned in footnote 33, some recent work in the field of lexical metaphors aims to combine the two approaches. In a recent (concluding) chapter, Billy Clark (2017) points out that:

One example which has often occurred to me and which has not been much considered, if at all, is the possibility of adopting ideas about the pragmatic principles which constrain interpretation from one approach and connecting them with ideas about the nature of semantics and pragmatics from other approaches. . . . It might be possible, for example, for construction grammarians to adopt only the central relevance-theoretic principles and consider how they might constrain interpretations within a construction grammar approach. Once again, it seems that there are significant benefits from bringing together researchers from different backgrounds. (p. 352)

More recently, Finkbeiner (2019b) edited a special issue that precisely focused on how ideas from Construction Grammar can be combined with perspectives from post-/neo-Gricean approaches to pragmatics. So it generally appears that there is a desire to bring together these two frameworks (see also Xue and Lin, 2022). The aim of this book, which builds on ideas developed in previous research (cf. Leclercq, 2019, 2020, 2022, 2023), is precisely to spell out some of the directions in which this integration can be operated.

3   Redefining Lexical Semantics and Pragmatics

The aim of this chapter is to arrive at a better understanding of lexical semantics and pragmatics. The main challenge addressed in this book is that of pinning down exactly what constitutes the content of lexical items and how this content is exploited in context. While the notion of *concept* is often used, its complex nature is at the origin of debate across and within different theoretical frameworks. Construction Grammar and Relevance Theory, for instance, have been developed on the basis of opposite understandings of what concepts are and how they contribute to the interpretation of an utterance. Yet more recent developments in RT lead me to believe that the two approaches might not be incompatible. In fact, I intend to show that combining insights from the two frameworks provides an interesting view of the semantics and pragmatics of lexical elements.

The perspectives on semantics adopted in CxG and RT have long been diametrically opposed (e.g. Fodor, 1998; Levine and Bickhard, 1999). On the one hand, RT rests on the Fodorian assumption that concepts are necessarily atomic, whereas in CxG it is argued that concepts are encyclopedic in nature. When combining the two theories, this divergence need not (arguably) be a challenge, however. One could simply decide to focus on those distinctive aspects of each theory for which the other crucially lacks an explanation (for instance, lexical pragmatics in CxG, and constructional semantics in RT). Yet I am strongly convinced it could be a mistake to do so. Indeed, the more you look into each of the two frameworks, the more you realize that internal developments have been greatly influenced by their respective approaches to semantics, especially in RT. It is therefore essential to address this question of lexical semantics so as to pave the way for a genuine integration of RT and CxG.

The notion of concepts adopted in CxG has been relatively unchallenged within the theory itself, and remains rather stable (see Section 2.1.2.2). In comparison, the status of concepts in RT is more controversial. As pointed out, the picture painted in the previous chapter is a simplified version of a much more complex situation. There is a real debate in the relevance-theoretic literature as to what exactly constitutes the nature and content of concepts and, as a natural consequence, that of ad hoc concepts. I will introduce this

66

debate in the first sections of this chapter. Eventually, I will argue that the perspective on conceptual content adopted in CxG might provide an interesting alternative to most of the approaches developed within RT. At the same time, it will be shown that the relevance-theoretic approach to lexical pragmatics can also shed new light on the actual function of conceptual content, i.e. on the actual function of lexical semantics, and how this content is exploited in context.

In this book, the terms (lexical) *semantics* and *pragmatics* will be used very regularly. Although these terms are described in different ways in RT and CxG, there is a general agreement that semantics has to do with conventional aspects of meaning whereas pragmatics refers to inferred meanings and inferential processes. This is how I will use these terms in the rest of this book (see Leclercq (2020) for an alternative view, however).[39]

3.1   On the Nature of Concepts and Ad Hoc Concepts in RT

The difficulty in understanding exactly what constitutes conceptual content in RT dates back (at least) to Sperber and Wilson's ([1986] 1995) use of the term. In *Relevance*, Sperber and Wilson originally treat "concepts as *triples of entries* … spelling out its logical, lexical and encyclopaedic content" (Sperber and Wilson, 1995: 92; emphasis mine). From this perspective, a concept consists of the combination of those three entries, as shown in Figure 3.1.[40]

In order to understand the implications of such a view of concepts, I will apply this model to the concept CAT, a representation of which is given in Figure 3.2. In accordance with the basic approach outlined in Sperber and Wilson ([1986] 1995), this concept consists of three entries. The lexical entry is composed of the word that is used to express the concept (*cat*), its phonological

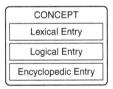

Figure 3.1 Concepts (adapted from Sperber and Wilson, 1995: 92)

---

[39] Please note that this chapter focuses only on conceptual meaning. The type of meaning which in RT is identified as *procedural* (see Section 2.3.2) will be discussed in the next chapter.
[40] See Section 2.2.3.1 for a detailed description of each entry.

```
┌─────────────────────────────────┐
│       CONCEPT CAT               │
├─────────────────────────────────┤
│ Lexical Entry                   │
│  cat  /ˈkæt/  noun  ...         │
├─────────────────────────────────┤
│ Logical Entry                   │
│  [animal] [mammal]  [...]       │
├─────────────────────────────────┤
│ Encyclopedic Entry              │
│  have whiskers / meow /...      │
└─────────────────────────────────┘
```

Figure 3.2 Concept CAT

properties and its morphosyntactic features. In the logical entry a number of inferential rules are stored that enable the use of that concept (e.g. that cats are animals, that cats are mammals, etc.). And finally, the encyclopedic entry stores all of the encyclopedic information (or world knowledge) that directly concerns cats, along with the information that individuals have gradually acquired.

With such a description, the difficulty remains to identify exactly what constitutes the semantics of the lexical item that is used to express the concept. Indeed, Sperber and Wilson argue that "the 'meaning' of a word is provided by the associated concept (or, in the case of an ambiguous word, concepts)" (Sperber and Wilson, 1995: 90). Yet, in Figure 3.2, it is clear that what constitutes the concept CAT is the sum of the information found in the lexical, logical and encyclopedic entries. This therefore suggests that the meaning of the lexical item *cat* partly consists of the lexical entry itself. It is unlikely that Sperber and Wilson endorse this view, however. Groefsema (2007: 138) also argues that this is "an undesirable conclusion."

Given this scenario, either the notion of concept or of meaning has to be redefined. According to Groefsema, there are three possible views that emerge from this observation:

1. The logical and encyclopaedic entries of a concept constitute the content of the concept.
2. Conceptual addresses are simple, unanalysable concepts whose entries do not constitute their content.
3. The logical entry of a concept constitutes the content of that concept, while information in the encyclopaedic entry does not contribute to the content of the concept. The role of the encyclopaedic entry is to contribute to the context in which an utterance encoding the concept is interpreted.   (Groefsema, 2007: 139)

In the next sections, I will introduce each of these alternatives, taking into account their respective advantages and limits. In particular, the aim is to identify how much each of these views can account for the notions of monosemy and polysemy, as well as provide a sound basis for the derivation of ad hoc concepts. It is important to note that these views do not receive equal attention in RT. Concerning the first view, for instance, only Groefsema explicitly argues in favor of it (or, at least, a version of it; see Section 3.1.3). For that reason, I will introduce the first view only after I have presented View 2 and View 3. Both these views indeed receive support from a number of relevance theorists. The aim is to try and identify which of these views is most compatible with the perspective adopted in CxG.

3.1.1   Concepts as Atoms

The first solution to the issue identified above is to consider that concepts are not, in fact, triples of entries but rather, as represented in Figure 3.3, consist of a different object (in bold) which itself gives access to the different entries (View 2). This is the perspective that was presented in the previous chapter.

According to this view, the meaning of a lexical entry consists of the atomic concept with which it is associated. The logical and encyclopedic information that a concept also gives access to only serves during the inferential phase of comprehension, and is used to derive ad hoc concepts, explicatures and implicatures (see Section 2.2.3.1). This broadly Fodorian approach to concepts[41] helps to compensate for the difficulty identified above. In this case, the lexical entry is no longer a constitutive element of the concept, and the meaning of the lexical entry can be identified explicitly: it is the atomic concept itself. As mentioned in the previous chapter, this is the view most largely adopted within RT.

Although this view solves the ambiguity inherent in the description given in the previous section, it also raises a number of issues itself, a couple of which were briefly discussed in the previous chapter and will be taken up here. One of

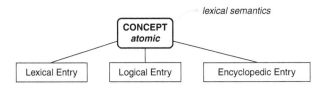

Figure 3.3 Concepts as atoms

---

[41] Fodor argues that concepts are atomic, but does not give any particular status to logical and encyclopedic information, at least originally (see, for instance, Fodor, 1998). Later he adopted a similar perspective by explicitly placing encyclopedic knowledge within "mental files" (Fodor, 2008: 94).

the very first difficulties with this view is to understand exactly what is considered to constitute the content of an atomic concept. Fodor (1998: 12) argues that the content of concepts consists of their "causal-cum-nomological" relations with the world (i.e. a lawlike causal dependency between the concept and a specific referent in the real world). In Carston's (2010) words, as mentioned before,

the content or semantics of this entity is its denotation, what it refers to in the world, and the lexical form that encodes it, in effect, inherits its denotational semantics. (Carston, 2010: 245)

From this perspective, the content of a concept is not some internal representation but consists only of the relationship between the concept and the object or property that it refers to in the mind-external world. A number of objections have been raised against this type of referential semantics, in particular by philosophers (e.g. Wittgenstein, 1958; Quine, 1960; Davidson, 1967, 1984; Chomsky, 2000, 2003; Brandom, 2000; Ludlow, 2003; Sztencel, 2012a, 2012b, 2018, inter alia). The aim of this section is not to look individually at each of these objections, especially since they have often been presented on the basis of various theoretical commitments to meaning, truth and reference. Rather, the aim is to show that such a view of referential semantics does not align with the more general picture of lexical pragmatics developed in RT (as opposed to what might be expected to be the case) and as a result challenges the relevance-theoretic commitment to conceptual atomism.

3.1.1.1 Relevance Theory and Referential Semantics: Compatible? The content of an atomic concept, according to Fodor, consists in the *necessary* (causal-cum-nomological) relationship that the concept has with a particular object in the mind-external world. One of the questions addressed by Sztencel (2012a) concerns the origins of this necessity, and in particular why it is that concepts refer to the things they do. Specifically, she nicely shows that Fodor's definition of conceptual content is relatively circular and therefore fails to be fully explanatory (Sztencel, 2012a). Given the relevance-theoretic commitment to Fodor's approach, this also becomes an issue for RT. Sztencel's (2012a) argument runs as follows: if concepts necessarily have to refer to (or *lock onto*, to use Fodor's terminology) a specific referent in the external world, then there must be something internal to concepts (and prior to reference) that forces us to select this specific referent:

The question is: what is it about any particular concept in and of itself that makes it lock onto the things it does lock onto and not other things? The problem is that if primitive concepts are to be in a non-arbitrary relation to what they "lock to" then they must have logically prior internal content independent of, but determinative of, the "locking" relation just like complex concepts. (Sztencel, 2012a: 491)

For instance, what is it about the concept CAT that *necessarily* makes it refer to cats? According to Fodor, however, the only element that composes the content of the concept CAT is the referential relation itself. This is why Sztencel argues that there is circularity in Fodor's view of conceptual meaning: in this account, what can explain reference to cats is the referential relation itself.

The reason this question is directly relevant to RT comes from the particular way in which Fodor tried to handle the issue (although he most probably did not consider it to be an issue). One of the ways in which Fodor could have simply objected to the circularity just mentioned is by arguing that, after all, he considers atomic concepts to be innate (Fodor, 1998: 124). In this case, although the circularity identified above remains, it cannot be used as an argument against Fodor any more. Concepts refer to the things they do in virtue of what they are programmed to refer to. Assuming Fodor is right, "since normal adults command a vocabulary of at least 60,000 words, it would seem that, at a bare minimum, they possess 60,000 *innate* concepts" (Laurence and Margolis, 2002: 28; emphasis mine). It is doubtful that we have (as many as) 60,000 innate concepts and I agree with Churchland (1986: 389) that it is "difficult to take such an idea seriously." Many arguments have been presented in the literature on concepts against the innateness hypothesis (see, among many others, Locke [1690] 1975; Berkeley, 1709; Hume, [1739] 1978; Wittgenstein, 1958; Johnson, 1987; Lakoff, 1988; Putnam, 1988; Elman et al., 1996; Cowie, 1998, 1999; Barsalou, 1999; Levine and Bickhard, 1999; Prinz, 2002; Tomasello, 2003; Sampson, 2005, and the references cited in Section 2.1). There is convincing evidence in the above papers, and I agree with what their authors write. For reasons of space, however, I will not elaborate on those arguments.

The questionable plausibility of the innateness argument is not the main issue here. More generally, to view concepts as innate has a direct consequence for the relevance-theoretic perspective on lexical pragmatics. It is strongly argued in RT that the concepts that are expressed in utterances are not lexically encoded but need to be pragmatically inferred by the hearer in order to derive the intended interpretation (see Section 2.2.3.1). If one considers concepts to be innate, however, it becomes doubtful whether any (ad hoc) atomic concepts have to be inferred and that such inferential mechanisms as described in RT are ever useful. Speakers simply have a number of concepts at their disposal.

Naturally, it could be argued that many of those innate concepts are non-lexicalized and still need to be contextually derived (or selected) in accordance with the principle of relevance. After all, it is often argued in RT that many (supposedly) ad hoc concepts are not purely the product of pragmatics, in the sense that they are not entirely new but consist of stored concepts that are simply not lexicalized:[42]

> The pragmatic process of inferring ad hoc concepts in utterance interpretation ... may result in a tokening of one of these stable, albeit non-lexicalised, concepts, already established in the hearer's conceptual system. (Carston, 2010: 251)

Neither Fodor nor relevance theorists have adopted exactly this view, however. On this issue, RT radically departs from Fodor's account. On the one hand, Fodor somehow argues against the possibility that there might be unlexicalized atomic concepts. According to him, there is a strict one-to-one mapping between lexical words and atomic concepts (Fodor, 1998: 55). Discussing different uses of the verb *keep* (*NP kept the money*, *NP kept the crowd happy*, etc.), he argues that the differences in meaning come from the verb's arguments but not from the verb itself: in all instances, *keep* expresses the single atomic concept KEEP (p. 52). As a result, as mentioned in Section 2.2.3.1, Fodor also considers that "there is no such thing as polysemy" (1998: 53). In this case, a theory of ad hoc concepts (and more generally of inference) is not required. On the other hand, RT takes a much more nuanced approach. First of all, it has long been argued within RT that there is not a one-to-one mapping between the public and the mental lexicon (i.e. between words and concepts), but that there is a one-to-many mapping (Sperber and Wilson, 1998). That is, individuals also store and use concepts that are not lexicalized. In fact, on the basis of the work of Barsalou, Sperber and Wilson explicitly argue that "the idea that there is an exhaustive, one-to-one mapping between concepts and words is quite implausible" (1998: 185). I also share this view. As a result, even if concepts were innate, a theory of concept inference/selection such as developed in RT is required. This is all the more true since relevance theorists seem to assume that concepts are not innate but are instead acquired or learned. This position is more or less explicit in the work of Carston (2002a) and Wilson and Sperber (2012) and becomes very explicit in the work of Wharton (2004, 2014), who specifically discusses the acquisition of lexical meaning, i.e. conceptual content.[43] It therefore also follows that many of the concepts that are communicated are considered to "be quite new" (Carston, 2010: 251) and need to be inferred pragmatically. That is, unlike what is suggested by Fodor, speakers are not innately equipped with a finite set of concepts, but there is an infinite number of concepts that they can use and gradually acquire (hence the need for the comprehension procedure developed in RT).

---

[42] In this case, however, it is no longer clear in what sense these concepts are ad hoc (cf. Mioduszewska, 2015: 87).

[43] To my knowledge, only Carston assumes that "we are born with at least some innate concepts" (2010: 250). It is unclear whether she still holds this view, however (see Section 3.3.2).

It will start to become clear why the referential approach to conceptual content proposed by Fodor does not fit well with RT, unlike what relevance theorists believe. By rejecting the innateness hypothesis, RT inevitably also has to abandon the referential approach to meaning put forward by Fodor (which they do not). Indeed, without the innateness hypothesis, there is no explanation given for the necessary relationship between a concept and its referent. Naturally, the critics will argue that scientific theorizing often consists in working with hypotheses for which we may as yet lack an explanation, and RT, therefore, does not have to abandon referentialism. Nevertheless, there are (at least) two more reasons why RT might prefer to move away from referentialism.

The first reason follows from the observation that referentialism is inconsistent with one of the most central claims put forward within RT. The notion of *explicatures* was developed within RT to account for the observation that the logical form of an utterance never fully determines the speaker's intended interpretation, which has to be pragmatically derived (see Section 2.2.2). This is referred to as the *underdeterminacy* thesis. And from this perspective, logical forms cannot be defined in terms of truth-conditions:

Various terms for this are used in the literature; the linguistic expression employed is described as providing an incomplete logical form, a 'semantic' skeleton, 'semantic' scaffolding, a 'semantic' template, a proposition/assumption schema (see, for instance, Sperber and Wilson, 1986/95; Recanati, 1993; Bach, 1994b; Taylor, 2001). What all of these different locutions entail is that the linguistic contribution is not propositional, it is not a complete semantic entity, not truth evaluable. (Carston, 2002b: 134)

In RT, it is generally assumed that only the enriched propositions that are derived pragmatically, i.e. explicatures and implicatures, can be described in such truth-conditional terms (Carston and Hall, 2012: 76; see also Moeschler, 2018). Yet, when considering that concepts have referential semantics (by locking onto a specific entity or property in the mind-external world), then they "must have truth-theoretic content" (Sztencel, 2011: 379). By extension, the logical forms in which concepts occur should also be defined in terms of these truth-conditions. Even if the concepts that occur in the logical forms do not correspond exactly to what the speaker intends to communicate, they still have truth-conditions.[44] It is therefore inconsistent for RT to argue both that concepts have referential content and that logical forms are not truth-evaluable. For this reason, "it has become unclear in what form Relevance Theory still holds the underdeterminacy thesis" (p. 376). As a result, either RT needs to

[44] Note that, outside RT, a number of researchers have precisely provided descriptions along these lines (e.g. Borg, 2004, 2016; Cappelen and Lepore, 2005, inter alia). According to them, although sentences fail to provide the speaker's intended meaning, the words that a speaker uses do have truth-theoretic content.

change its view concerning the nature of conceptual content, or it needs to revise (or abandon, even) the underdeterminacy thesis (cf. Burton-Roberts, 2005). Some might want to stick with the Fodorian assumption that concepts are necessarily referential. In this case, the difficulty is to determine exactly in what sense logical forms underdetermine the speakers' intended interpretation. It is most likely that relevance theorists will prefer to keep the underdeterminacy thesis as it is currently formulated, and which provides a strong basis on which the rest of the theory has been developed (see, in particular, Section 2.2.2), and rather to reconsider the nature of lexical concepts. I also believe this is the most preferable option. From this perspective, concepts do not have truth-theoretic content, but truth values are only accessible once the explicatures have been derived (and which relevance theorists call *real* (as opposed to *linguistic*) semantics, cf. Clark, 2013a: 299).[45] Naturally, this requires the explicit spelling out of what constitutes the content of lexical concepts. As we will see in the next sections, there have been a few suggestions in RT.

There is a second important argument against a purely referential account of conceptual content: Fodor himself seems to be aware of the difficulties that such an account of meaning faces. Sztencel (2018) aptly captures the reason why concepts must have some internal content:

> If concepts do actually lock onto things in the world, we want to say that they do so non-arbitrarily – in other words, that there is something about the concept itself (some property of the concept, which I am calling its internal content) that determines that it locks onto the things it does lock onto and not anything else. The question is then: should we align 'semantics' with (internal) content or with (external) reference? Having so distinguished between content and reference, it seems reasonable to say that content is metaphysically prior to and a precondition for reference. Insofar as 'semantics' is referential at all, such semanticity derives from, is parasitic on, internal conceptual content. It is arguable, then, that it is internal content that is fundamentally 'semantic'. (Sztencel, 2018: 14)

It appears that Fodor is not a complete stranger to this line of argumentation. After all, he once argued "(a) that the *content* of a linguistic expression should be distinguished from such of its semantic properties as its truth conditions; and (b) that content *is* – though truth conditions are not – a construct out of the communicative intentions of speaker/hearers" (Fodor, 1982: 105–106; original

---

[45] Although 'meaning' in CxG (as in cognitive linguistics more generally) is not defined in truth-conditional terms, which is a perspective I largely endorse myself, this second view (i.e. an approach in terms of 'real' semantics) is closer to the approach generally adopted in CxG. Indeed, the way RT relocates truth-values at another, pragmatic, level does not radically differ from the perspective (most probably) adopted in CxG (which, as mentioned earlier, cannot entirely get away without truth-conditions), according to which truth-values are secondary to meaning and are evaluated in context.

emphasis). From this perspective, meaning is in the head and not purely referential.[46] As mentioned in the previous chapter, the idea that meaning is *in the head* is a view that cognitive linguists in general and construction grammarians in particular have largely adopted. In fact, Chomsky himself also subscribes to this view. He explicitly argues that "the semantic properties of words are used to think and talk about the world in terms of the perspectives made available by the resources of the mind" (Chomsky, 2000: 16). Moreover, Fodor also understands that reference alone (and, with it, truth-conditions) cannot distinguish between the meaning of different lexical items, especially those that are co-referential (e.g. *Superman* and *Clark Kent*; Fodor, 2008: 86). He specifically argues that to distinguish between the two, one also has to associate with the lexical items different *modes of presentation* (Fodor, 1998: 15).[47]

Unfortunately, in spite of these observations, Fodor still clings to the idea that concepts must be atomic, referential items. According to him, as far as conceptual *content* (i.e. meaning) is concerned, neither the mode of presentation nor the mental files (cf. footnote 41) that he introduces are actually relevant: "all that matters is the extension" (Fodor, 2008: 87). Relevance theorists do not have to comply with Fodor, however. It will not be the first time that they part company from him (e.g. on how modular the mind is, on the acquisition of concepts, on inference rules). RT could be stronger as a theory if it were to change its view of conceptual content and adopt a non-referential approach to lexical meaning. The challenge in this case, of course, is to identify exactly what constitutes this content. Is it the inference rules located in the logical entry? This is a possibility that some relevance theorists entertain and which will be introduced in Section 3.1.2. Or is the content of a concept determined by the information stored in the encyclopedic entry? In Section 3.1.3, we will see that Groefsema (2007) favors this position. As mentioned in the previous chapter, this is also a view that is strongly defended in cognitive linguistics and, therefore, in CxG. In fact, it is also worth noting that some philosophers have argued that the information stored within Fodor's mental files (which more or less correspond to RT's encyclopedic knowledge) should be considered to be the content of those concepts (e.g. Lee, 2017). In Section 3.4, I will also argue in favor of such a perspective on conceptual content.

3.1.1.2 Ad Hoc Concepts and Atomism: Problems It is important to understand the immediate relevance of the previous section to the question addressed

---

[46] Arguing against Hilary Putnam, Fodor (1982: 110) says that he finds "unattractive" a position whereby "meaning is not in the head."

[47] Fodor's modes of presentation closely resembles the notion of construal/vantage point put forward (in different ways) in cognitive linguistics.

in this chapter. In the previous chapter, it was conceptual atomism, and not referentialism, that was considered to be the main issue for RT. Conceptual atomism does not (arguably) presuppose referentialism, or vice versa. It could therefore be argued that, having rejected referentialism, one could still maintain atomism. According to Fodor, however, referentialism and atomism are necessarily related. (As we will see in this section, this is also the case for Carston.) Fodor actually calls himself a "referential atomist" (Fodor, 2008: 99). It has been shown in the previous section, however, that referentialism is generally incompatible with the relevance-theoretic enterprise. One is therefore also entitled to question the necessity (and, even, the possibility) for RT to argue that concepts are atomic. The aim of this section is precisely to show that atomism is also incompatible with the relevance-theoretic approach to lexical pragmatics and that alternative perspectives have to be considered.[48]

Conceptual atomism and the relevance-theoretic approach to pragmatics are incompatible for a number of reasons, all of which are closely related. One of them, however, particularly stands out from the others and seems to be the most problematic case for RT. This issue was briefly addressed in the previous chapter and will be elaborated on here. The difficulty for RT is to explain, on the basis of atomic concepts, how hearers manage to derive ad hoc concepts.[49] Take the following examples:

(64)   It's clear that *stress* can contribute to chronic disease, but fixing stress is not as simple as taking a deep breath or an occasional yoga class. (NOW)

(65)   During the adoption process in 2015, Avinash told the court that he loves his Taya and Tayi (uncle and aunt) who are now his *parents* and they too love him. (NOW)

---

[48] As mentioned several times already, it is important to note that the focus of this book is 'meaning'. Therefore, when arguing against atomism, I only mean to argue that conceptual content (i.e. the meaning of lexical items) is not atomic. I make absolutely no claim regarding the *form* that concepts take when occurring in thoughts, however. They may well be atomic (say, a conceptual address, or Fodor's 'file name'), but I challenge the view that their content consists of this atom.

[49] The systematic derivation of ad hoc concepts in itself is not at issue here. Barsalou indeed provides solid evidence that individuals systematically create ad hoc categories (cf. footnote 31 for references). This view is also very much in line with most approaches developed in cognitive linguistics, such as Langacker's notion of conceptualization which he uses to refer to the dynamic nature of conceptual content:

Rather than being fixed, the values of linguistic elements are actively negotiated; and rather than being static, the meanings of complex expressions emerge and develop in discourse. ... Meaning is not identified with concepts but with **conceptualization**, the term being chosen precisely to highlight its dynamic nature. (Langacker, 2008: 30; original emphasis)

The only issue being tackled in this section is the apparent incompatibility between the particular way ad hoc concepts are said to be derived and the atomic commitment to the nature of concepts and ad hoc concepts.

There are various ways in which the lexemes *stress* and *parent* can be understood depending on how they are used by the speaker. It is theoretically possible (in the required contexts, of course, not here) that their interpretation will lead to the recovery of the encoded concepts STRESS and PARENT (whatever these are). This scenario is relatively unproblematic, since in this case the intended interpretation (and therefore the content of the communicated concept) equals that of the lexical (encoded) concept. Difficulties emerge, however, if the hearer has to infer an ad hoc concept. This is the case for the interpretation of the sentences in (64) and (65). In the sentence in (64), the word *stress* can be understood as communicating the more specific (i.e. narrower) concept STRESS*: 'high/undue levels of stress'. In the sentence in (65), hearers have to infer the more general (i.e. broader) concept PARENT* in which the biological aspect of parenthood is dropped. From the relevance-theoretic standpoint, these two examples illustrate cases of conceptual narrowing and broadening, respectively (see Section 2.2.3.1).

As mentioned in the previous chapter, the difficulty here is to understand how RT can argue in favor of both conceptual atomism and the systematic narrowing and/or broadening of conceptual content. Considering that lexical concepts and ad hoc concepts are atomic, it is unclear in what sense exactly ad hoc concepts can be narrower/broader than lexical concepts. Somehow, these notions necessarily require some form of internal structure that our minds can exploit in different ways (in accordance, of course, with the comprehension procedure). The notion of ad hoc concepts is often introduced in the relevance-theoretic literature in direct reference to the work of Barsalou on 'ad hoc categories'. Yet, looking carefully at what Barsalou himself argues, it is relatively clear that concepts are not atomic, and that the process of conceptual adjustment is possible only because concepts are considered to be "bodies of knowledge in long-term memory" (Barsalou et al., 1993: 57). Interestingly, in some specific accounts of RT, one could also be led to believe that a similar view is adopted by relevance theorists themselves. After all, they often argue that the derivation of ad hoc concepts crucially depends on the information stored in the encyclopedic entry:

On this approach, *bank* ... might be understood as conveying not the encoded concept BANK but the ad hoc concept BANK*, with **a more restricted encyclopedic entry** and a narrower denotation. (Wilson and Sperber, 2004: 618; emphasis mine)

In another utterance situation, **different items of encyclopaedic information** about children might be more highly activated making most accessible such implications as that Boris doesn't earn his keep, expects others to look after him, is irresponsible, etc., resulting in a distinct ad hoc concept CHILD** in the explicature. (Carston, 2012: 613; emphasis mine)

In this case, the information stored in the encyclopedic entry provides the structure on the basis of which ad hoc concepts can be derived. In other words, the content of ad hoc concepts more or less resembles that of lexical concepts depending on the degree of overlap between the information stored in their respective encyclopedic entries. Naturally, this strongly suggests that encyclopedic information must be content-constitutive. Yet, this is incompatible with RT's commitment to atomism. This incompatibility has already been pointed out by a number of relevance theorists, among whom is Anne Reboul:

> Relevance Theory rests on a Fodorian account of concepts according to which concepts are atomic, hence not definitions. Ad hoc concepts, however, are supposed to be formed by modifying the definition of the original concept by deleting features or introducing them in the definition. This directly contradicts a Fodorian view of concepts. (Reboul, 2014: 20)

In addition to Reboul (2014), this contradiction has also been discussed, among others, by Vicente (2005: 190), Burton-Roberts (2007: 106), Groefsema (2007: 146), Vicente and Martínez-Manrique (2010: 49), Allott and Textor (2012: 198), Assimakopoulos (2012: 23), and Mioduszewska (2015: 83). As a result, either RT has to change its approach to the formation and nature of ad hoc concepts, or it needs to rethink exactly what it considers conceptual content to consist of. From the perspective outlined above, the information stored in the encyclopedic entry (and the logical entry) is a good candidate. In the rest of this chapter, I will strongly argue in favor of this option. Before doing so, it is worth investigating a bit further this incompatibility between atomism and the relevance-theoretic notion of ad hoc concepts.

In spite of the demonstration just made, Carston maintains that she has been "unable to find any arguments supporting the alleged incompatibility" (Carston, 2010: 247) and argues that the underlying thinking that points towards this incompatibility "is quite wide of the mark since the account of ad hoc concept formation is not semantic and not internal to the linguistic system" (p. 247). This last statement has long puzzled me for a number of reasons. First of all, it is doubtful whether anyone (among relevance theorists or not) has ever considered the process of conceptual adjustment to be a purely semantic process. But more importantly, it is unclear why the fact that this is indeed a pragmatic process can be used as an argument against the incompatibility discussed by many. If it were so obvious, then presumably the apparent incompatibility would have been raised less often. Furthermore, regardless of whether one considers conceptual adjustment to be a semantic or a pragmatic process, the type of conceptual narrowing/broadening discussed in RT requires some internal structure to be exploited which the atomic approach does not offer. For this reason, although the incompatibility between the atomic view of concepts and the relevance-theoretic approach to ad hoc concepts formation strikes many as blatant, it is important to take a closer look at the reasons why Carston assumes that there is no such incompatibility.

In order to understand Carston's comment, one needs to take into account all of her theoretical commitments. Of all relevance theorists, Carston is probably the most Fodorian in her approach to meaning. She is in particular very faithful to the referential approach that he advocates. This is particularly clear from the way in which she uses the term *denotation* (see, for instance, Carston, 1997b, 2002a, 2010, 2012). It is most probably this commitment to referential semantics that can explain Carston's surprise (and rightly so). It is clear to Carston that the information stored in the encyclopedic entry is not content-constitutive but only provides contextual information about concepts, i.e. about their denotation. Although this stored encyclopedic knowledge is indeed exploited during the comprehension phase to recover the intended concept, it does not eventually form the content of this ad hoc concept either. The content of ad hoc concepts is determined, like lexical concepts, solely by their denotation. The encyclopedic and logical information that a lexical concept provides only serves in context to recover the denotation of the communicated ad hoc concept. According to Carston, the level at which conceptual narrowing/broadening matters is not the encyclopedic level (which is not content-constitutive) but the level of the denotation itself. Ad hoc concepts can be said to be narrower/broader than the lexical concepts from which they are derived depending on the degree of overlap between the set of items that fall within their denotation (Carston, 2002a: 353). This is why, according to Carston, it is not incompatible to argue both that ad hoc concepts are atomic (since they consist of a referential relation) and that they can be narrower/broader than the lexical concept from which they are formed (depending on their denotational overlap).[50]

Carston's perspective seems internally coherent and therefore appears to solve the incompatibility mentioned above. The question is whether this view is theoretically and descriptively accurate, however. There are two crucial points that need to be addressed here. First, Carston's account is flawed since it ignores a basic constraint imposed by referential atomism. According to Hall (2011), the atomic account requires that neither the logical nor the encyclopedic types of information made accessible by a concept be "constitutive or reference-determining" (Hall, 2011: 7). Yet, as was just explained, it is clear in Carston's account that the logical and encyclopedic entries directly contribute to establishing reference. As a result, her view suggests (in spite of what she argues) that these two types of information *are* content-constitutive (since content determines reference).[51] This is why her approach to concepts and ad

---

[50] That is why Carston (2010: 247) argues that the derivation of ad hoc concepts takes place outside the linguistic system.

[51] That content determines reference seems to be implicitly assumed by those who discuss the incompatibility identified above (see, for instance, Reboul, 2000: 60).

hoc concepts runs counter to the atomic view of conceptual content, which compromises the coherence of her account. Second, Carston's approach is all the more problematic in that her defense of conceptual atomism rests primarily on the assumption that concepts are referential. Besides the issue of determining how reference is established, it was shown in the previous section that referential semantics is incompatible with some of the core notions developed within RT (e.g. the one-to-many mapping between words and concepts, the difference in truth-conditions between the logical form and explicatures, etc.). So Carston advocates for a referential account, but there are a number of critical questions that she fails to address (see Section 3.1.1.1), which further threatens the coherence of the account sketched in the previous paragraph. It is therefore highly questionable whether conceptual atomism can be maintained in RT. Rather, it is preferable to drop conceptual atomism, together with referentialism. It was shown in the previous section that in order to be able to establish reference, one must have some internal content (prior to reference) which itself can be considered to constitute the content of that concept. Carston assumes that the recovery of an ad hoc concept's denotation is largely made possible by the encyclopedic entry made accessible by the lexical concept with which it is associated. From this perspective, the information stored in the encyclopedic entry once more seems to be the best candidate for what constitutes conceptual content. This view, which will be adopted later in this chapter, is further supported by the observation that the account of ad hoc concepts presented in RT was developed on the basis of Barsalou's work on (ad hoc) categories which, as mentioned above, he conceives of as bodies of information (and not as atoms).

It is worth noting that Carston finds Fodor's arguments for conceptual atomism "unassailable" (Carston, 2010: 245) and argues that "the most compelling of these, perhaps, is that no-one has been able, despite centuries of trying, to give adequate definitions for any but a tiny group of words" (p. 245). This viewpoint will be discussed in more detail in Section 3.5. Suffice it to say that it remains dubious why Fodor's arguments are unassailable, in particular the one Carston mentions and which actually seem to be the most inconsequential argument Fodor puts forward.[52] That no one has ever been able to provide specific definitions for most of the words we use is not bulletproof evidence that conceptual content is necessarily atomic. It might, however, tell us something about how the mind works, as I will suggest in Section 3.5. But Fodor's own skepticism about definitions cannot be used as an argument for atomism.

---

[52] As far as the content of concepts is concerned, there is quite a large amount of evidence (see Section 2.1.2.2), starting from the work of Barsalou himself, that shows that conceptual content consists of a structured network of information rather than an atom. Therefore, Fodor's arguments are, in fact, assailable.

The difficulties that an atomic view of conceptual content involves go beyond the challenge represented by the derivation of ad hoc concepts. One further difficulty concerns how conceptual content can be argued to be acquired. If, like Fodor, one assumes concepts to be innate and to be in a one-to-one mapping with the lexicon, then there is no such issue. As mentioned in the previous section, however, relevance theorists tend not to view concepts as innate objects and consider that there are more concepts than just those that are lexicalized. In this case, it is unclear exactly, given the variety of atomic concepts that a lexeme could lock onto, which of those it should actually be associated with.[53]

Directly related to this issue is the question of monosemy and polysemy. If one considers concepts to be atomic, then it is also not straightforward how polysemy can possibly be represented in one's mind. As mentioned in the previous chapter, indeed, Fodor himself assumes that there is no such thing as polysemy since he considers there to be a one-to-one mapping between words and concepts. Relevance theorists, however, do not adopt such isomorphism. They admit that some words might be (conventionally) polysemous. Yet, considering that concepts are atoms, only two outcomes for the representation of meaning are possible, polysemy not being one of them. In the first case, if one assumes that conventional polysemy exists (although it is obvious to construction grammarians, it is much less so in the pragmatics literature), then the identified meanings cannot be distinguished from cases of homonymy. Indeed, in this case it is opaque how one mentally represents the assumed relationship between the different atoms. It is doubtful, however, that the senses of the lexeme *wood* (e.g. 'material' and 'geographical area') are unrelated in the same way as the senses of the lexeme *bank* are (e.g. 'financial institution' and 'land alongside a river'). Considering that conventional polysemy exists, it is preferable to keep the notion distinct from cases of homonymy. Yet, viewing concepts as atoms does not make this possible. The alternative option is to consider that although lexemes can be used to convey different concepts in different contexts, only one of those concepts is actually encoded by the lexeme which is used to express them. This is what Carston (2013: 187) calls *pragmatic* polysemy, which is a view also defended by Falkum (2011, 2015). Here, although lexemes are considered to be pragmatically

---

[53] Given the aim of this book, I will not go into the detail of this issue here. Nevertheless, it is worth noting that this question has led to quite diverging opinions among the relevance theorists who try to answer the question. On the one hand, for instance, Tim Wharton is "very much into nativist accounts of concept acquisition, in the sense of Bloom 1996, Dehaene 1997 and Margolis 1998" (Tim Wharton, p.c.). In comparison, Sandrine Zufferey argues that frequency must have a key role in the acquisition of concepts (Zufferey, 2010: 146, 2015).

polysemous, they are assumed to be semantically monosemous. I have expressed strong doubts about such a perspective in the previous chapter. In Section 3.3, I will elaborate on these doubts.

3.1.1.3 Concepts and Atomism: Conclusions Conceptual atomism provides an interesting solution to the challenge identified above in terms of what exactly constitutes the meaning of a lexical item. The meaning comes from the referential relation made accessible by the atomic concept. I have argued that this perspective – which is the most adopted in RT – faces a number of problems. The first difficulty concerns the referential nature of this concept. Referential semantics, beyond its own limits, is not compatible with some of the most central tenets of RT. In addition, conceptual atomism does not seem to be compatible with the account of ad hoc concept formation largely discussed within RT. Instead, it has been suggested that an account whereby concepts have internal content is better equipped to face the different challenges that referential atomism faces. Before introducing such an account, it is worth looking at the other accounts of conceptual meaning that have been argued for in RT.

3.1.2   Conceptual Content and the Logical Entry

Another way of dealing with the issue identified at the beginning of this chapter is to consider that the content of concepts, regardless of whether or not they are atomic, (also) consists of the information stored in the logical entry that the concept gives access to. This view is the third possibility discussed by Groefsema (2007) and is illustrated in Figure 3.4.

This possibility can be more or less explicitly found in the work of a number of relevance theorists. Sperber and Wilson (1987), for instance, specifically argue that they "see [the semantic properties of a word] as provided by the logical entry filed at the same address" (Sperber and Wilson, 1987: 741). Later, Carston (2002a) adopts a similar view. She argues that logical information is a defining property of concepts, i.e. it is

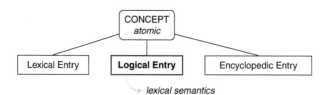

Figure 3.4 Logical entry as conceptual content

content-constitutive, and that conceptual narrowing and broadening is located at the level of the logical entry:

An ad hoc concept formed by strengthening a lexical concept seems to involve elevating an encyclopaedic property of the latter to *a logical (or content-constitutive) status* ... an ad hoc concept formed by the loosening of a lexical concept seems to involve dropping one or more of the *logical or defining properties* of the latter. (Carston, 2002a: 339, emphasis mine)

This view quite explicitly suggests that the logical entry made accessible by a concept provides the meaning of a lexical entry. Yet this comes in complete opposition to (and again seems incompatible with, see Section 3.1.1.2) Carston's strong atomic commitment to conceptual content. More recently, she argues that:

A decompositional view might also seem to have been implied by my talk (Carston 2002a: 339) of the dropping of logical properties (in the case of loose uses) and the promoting of encyclopaedic properties (in the case of narrowing), although this does not strictly follow, since these properties are clearly not internal components of the lexical concepts themselves and need not be taken that way for ad hoc concepts either. In fact, it was my aim then, as now, to maintain a consistently atomic view of concepts if at all possible. (Carston, 2010: 249)

The opposition between these two quotes quite clearly shows the tension that can be found in Carston's own work and more generally within RT. Carston is aware of this tension and explicitly points out (in Carston, 2010) that she should not be understood as arguing that the logical properties are content-constitutive. Nevertheless, this post-hoc clarification may not be entirely convincing for it generally seems that she is struggling to explain the different facets of her approach. Indeed, a few pages before denying that this is the perspective she adopts, Carston (2010) repeats that the inference rules found in the logical entry of a concept "are, crucially, taken to be content constitutive" (Carston, 2010: 246).

Elsewhere in the relevance-theoretic literature, Falkum (2011) writes that logical properties "are thought to be content-constitutive of a concept" (Falkum, 2011: 118). This view is in particular strongly defended by Horsey (2006).

This approach to conceptual content provides, like the first view discussed previously, an interesting solution to the issue identified at the beginning of this chapter when trying to pin down exactly what Sperber and Wilson consider to be the content of a concept. In this case, the meaning of a lexical item consists of the information stored in the logical entry.[54] Like in the previous scenario,

---

[54] After the first publication of *Relevance*, Macnamara (1987: 724) is probably the first to have noticed the difficulty of identifying exactly what Sperber and Wilson consider the content of a concept to consist of. It is interesting to note that it is when responding to Macnamara that Sperber and Wilson (1987) argue that the information stored in the logical entry constitutes the content of a concept.

the information stored in the encyclopedic entry only serves during the inferential phase of comprehension to derive explicatures and implicatures. However, although this perspective does not share the limits of the atomic view, it also faces a number of issues.

Unlike the atomic account of conceptual content, this view can capture more easily in what sense exactly conceptual narrowing and/or broadening is possible. As described by Carston above, it is the set of inference rules that one stores in the logical entry that provides (together with encyclopedic information) the necessary structure on the basis of which narrowing/broadening can occur. Somehow, this view is also equipped to answer the challenge that referentialism represents. In this case, one has internal content from which a specific reference can be established. And yet, this view does not entirely solve the issue of how to determine reference. First of all, the content of the logical entry of some concepts is not sufficient to justify exactly why they refer to the entity/object they do and not to another. Consider, for instance, the concepts ROTTWEILER and DOBERMANN. In order to be able to establish reference, the internal content must be sufficiently detailed to enable us to pick the right referent. When using the two concepts ROTTWEILER and DOBERMANN, one refers to two distinct kinds of dogs even though they (arguably) look quite similar. Yet it is not clear in RT whether the logical entry associated with each of these two concepts provides enough (in the sense of *distinguishing*) information to determine the right reference, i.e. reference to rottweilers and to dobermanns respectively (and not the other way round). As mentioned in the previous chapter, it is often argued in RT that the information stored in the logical entry never fully defines a concept. Sperber and Wilson (1995) argue that:

Our framework allows for empty logical entries, logical entries which amount to a proper definition of the concept, and logical entries which fall anywhere between these two extremes: that is, which provide some logical specification of the concept without fully defining it. (p. 92)

Such a view is problematic if we assume that the information stored in the logical entry is content-constitutive and should, therefore, be reference-determining. It is unclear how one can accurately establish reference if the concepts one uses are not fully defined (and sufficiently distinct from other concepts). As a result, either RT needs to argue that the logical entry always fully defines a concept, or it needs to consider that the content of a concept is not (only) determined by the information stored in the logical entry, for otherwise reference cannot be established. The latter option is preferable, and as we will see in the next section, the information stored in the encyclopedic entry once again seems to be a good candidate.

Now, in spite of the latter observation, let's assume for a moment that the logical entry fully determines the content of a concept. In this case, the meaning of a concept is clearly identifiable, it is prior to reference, enables conceptual narrowing/broadening, and makes reference assignment possible. There are two reasons why this option still remains relatively problematic, however. The first reason comes from the observation that this perspective faces exactly the same limits as "classical" (Aristotelian) definitions in terms of necessary and sufficient conditions.[55] Indeed, if the logical entry of a concept fully defines that concept, then it will inevitably consist of a set of necessary and sufficient inferential rules which can be used to compute (Sperber and Wilson, 1995: 89) the logical forms in which these concepts occur. Yet there are a number of issues with this view. One of them follows from the observation that concepts are not mentally represented in such rigid terms, but are more flexibly organized (around a prototype) and have fuzzy boundaries (see, for instance, Rosch 1975).[56] This explains why, for instance, both eagles and ostriches can be described as birds even though the feature 'fly' (which could be argued to be central to the concept BIRD, i.e. common to all birds) applies to eagles but not to ostriches. As a result, if one still wants to argue, on the one hand, that (like eagles) ostriches are birds and, on the other, that concepts are defined in terms of inferential rules, then the property {BIRD → FLY} needs to be dropped from the list. The difficulty for a theory of concepts is that this might result in concepts that possess very few inferential rules and that, as a consequence, fail to be fully defined since they are not sufficiently distinguishable from one another. That is, whether we like it or not, the logical entry cannot fully define a concept. In that case, this leads us back to the challenge identified above. Directly related to this issue is the observation that for some concepts, in particular abstract ones, it is quite hard to understand exactly what inferential rules can possibly make up their logical entry. For instance, it is unclear what rules are attached to the concept FREEDOM, and in particular in what sense these rules enable us to distinguish it from another abstract concept such as LIBERTY.[57] Generally, then, inferential rules alone cannot possibly define the content of concepts, which strongly suggests that other elements associated with concepts (e.g. encyclopedic information) must constitute their content.

There is a second reason why it is problematic to view the logical entry of a concept as being its content. If one is to define concepts in terms of inferential rules, then one must at least have some idea of what these rules actually consist of. Yet the relevance-theoretic perspective faces a number of limits which

---

[55] As Lewandowska-Tomaszczyk (2007: 146) points out, issues with classical definitions have in particular been addressed by Quine (1953, 1960), Wittgenstein (1958), and by Rosch (1973, 1975).

[56] It is worth noting that Barsalou himself considers that concepts are not defined by strict common features but are composed of a graded structure (Barsalou, 1985, 1987).

[57] This observation receives support from experimental evidence. On the basis of property-generation tasks, Wiemer-Hastings and Xu (2005) show that "abstract concepts tend to be more schematic in nature, involving a larger proportion of unspecific features than concrete concepts" (p. 733).

greatly weaken the role of the logical entry as a distinct entity. The approach developed in RT will be discussed in the rest of this section.

When Sperber and Wilson (1995) establish the distinction between the information stored in the logical and encyclopedic entries, they argue that the main difference is one of mental representation:

> The information in encyclopaedic entries is representational: it consists of a set of assumptions which may undergo deductive rules. The information in logical entries, by contrast, is computational: it consists of a set of deductive rules which apply to assumptions in which the associated concept appears. (Sperber and Wilson, 1995: 89)

From this perspective, logical information consists of deductive rules of the type {CAT → MAMMAL}. These rules help to compute (i.e. draw inferences from) the logical forms in which a lexical concept occurs. This view is problematic, however. First, when they distinguish between encyclopedic and logical information, Sperber and Wilson explicitly argue that the distinction between the two generally corresponds to the philosophical analytic–synthetic dichotomy (Sperber and Wilson, 1995: 88). That is, by virtue of defining a concept, the logical information must necessarily be true of that concept (i.e. analytic), while the (non-defining) information stored in the encyclopedic entry is only true in virtue of one's experience in the world of that concept (i.e. synthetic). Sperber and Wilson explicitly argue, however, that the analogy only means to capture the observation that knowledge can be stored in different ways (cf. quote above) but not that it necessarily entails different types of truth (p. 88). This is convenient since the analytic/synthetic distinction is rather controversial. Quine (1953, 1960) in particular believes that it is not possible to distinguish between different types of truth and specifically argues against analyticity (i.e. necessary truth). More recently in the relevance-theoretic literature, a similar view is adopted by Horsey, who argues that the information stored in the logical entry is not analytic in the traditional philosophical sense (Horsey, 2006: 74). Rather, he argues that the truth of information is subjective and may be different across individuals (p. 25), and that whether an individual chooses to place a specific piece of information in the logical or encyclopedic entry crucially depends on whether that person takes this piece of information to be content-constitutive (p. 75). Sperber and Wilson adopt a similar perspective when they argue that the same piece of information can function "now as part of the content of an assumption [i.e. logical entry], now as part of the context in which it is processed [i.e. encyclopedic entry]" (Sperber and Wilson, 1995: 89). In this case, however, it means that the distinction between the logical and the encyclopedic entry is only a "psychological distinction" (Carston, 2010: 275), i.e. a perceptual difference that may not translate into different cognitive processes. As a consequence, one could question the necessity both to distinguish between the two entries and, in particular, to argue that only the information stored in the logical entry constitutes the content of a concept. Carston (2002a) explicitly doubts that there is "really a clear logical/encyclopaedic distinction" (Carston, 2002a: 322). The necessity to distinguish between the two kinds of information seems to originate from a particular intuition. As Horsey (2006) points out, for Quine the distinction is meant to capture "intuitions of centrality" (Horsey, 2006: 13), i.e. intuitions about which pieces of information are more central to a concept than others. A similar intuition can be found in the work of Sperber and Wilson when they say:

Intuitively, there are clear-enough differences between encyclopaedic and logical entries. Encyclopaedic entries typically vary across speakers and times .... Logical entries, by contrast, are small, finite and relatively constant across speakers and times. (Sperber and Wilson, 1995: 88)

In other words, it is assumed that individuals classify as content-constitutive (i.e. logical) those pieces of information that are more central (and therefore stable) to a concept and as contextual (i.e. encyclopedic) those that are less central (and therefore less stable). This perspective is highly problematic, however. From a theoretical standpoint, apart from the philosopher's intuition, there is nothing that justifies the view according to which less stable, more peripheral aspects of concepts do not directly contribute to their content too. From a more psychological viewpoint, it is unclear why individuals should so categorically treat less central elements as necessarily not being content-constitutive, especially since it is not clear in this case how individuals even manage to decide when a given piece of information is central to a concept or not. Horsey (2006: 75) himself admits this is a challenge. That is, the distinction is not straightforward. As a consequence, there is no reason to distinguish between logical and encyclopedic information: there is simply conceptual knowledge. Of course, this does not mean that individuals do not categorize this knowledge in different ways, with some aspects of it being considered more central to a concept than others. The different networks discussed in cognitive linguistics, for instance, introduce the notion of a prototype precisely so as to account for this intuition (see also Goldberg, 2019: 16). Yet the rest of the conceptual network in which a prototype occurs is also considered to be content-constitutive.

  This last observation provides a transition to the last issue concerning logical information. If one considers that only the information stored in the logical entry is content-constitutive, then it is once more unclear how exactly (conventional, encoded) polysemy can be mentally represented, if it is at all possible. In this case, the logical entry simply consists of a hodgepodge of inferential rules that can be computed once a concept appears in the logical form of an utterance. Yet, considering that polysemy is possible, then one would want to be able to distinguish between different, organized sets of logical information that can be exploited independently of one another. It is unclear how that is possible in RT.

In this section, I considered the possibility for conceptual content to be composed of the information stored in the logical entry that a concept is argued to give access to in RT. Although this view solves the ambiguity identified at the beginning of the chapter, namely that of understanding exactly what constitutes the meaning of a lexical item, it faces a number of issues itself. In particular, the difficulty is to know whether this entry alone can ever fully define a concept. This is notably supported by the observation that pinning down exactly what constitutes the nature of this entry and in what sense it differs from the information stored in the encyclopedic entry represents a real challenge. In the following sections, I will argue that there is no need to distinguish between two types of entries. Before doing so, I will introduce the last possibility identified by Groefsema (2007: 139).

3.1.3   Conceptual Content, Logical and Encyclopedic Knowledge

The third possibility to deal with the ambiguity left by Sperber and Wilson is to consider that the content of a concept is determined by the information stored in both the logical and the encyclopedic entries (see Figure 3.5). This is the first possibility that Groefsema (2007) mentions, but I have treated it as the last possibility since there are only very few relevance theorists who adopt this perspective. This is unfortunate, as will become clear, since it is the best solution for RT (or at least, a version of it).

Like the first two options discussed in the previous sections, this view can avoid a number of challenges. In this case, it is clear what the meaning of a concept is: the combination of logical and encyclopedic information. Furthermore, it is also clear how reference assignment can be established and how ad hoc concepts can be derived.

This view, although not largely adopted within RT, may seem to follow from a particular assumption in RT. Although the atomic account presented earlier is strongly defended in RT, the concept that a lexical entry is associated with is often

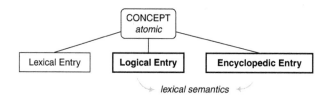

Figure 3.5 Logical and encyclopedic entries as conceptual content

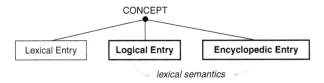

Figure 3.6 Logical and encyclopedic entries as conceptual content (2)

described simply as an address in memory, or a point of access, that enables us to retrieve the information stored in the different entries (represented in Figure 3.6).

[A concept] appears as an address in memory, a heading under which various types of information can be stored and retrieved. (Sperber and Wilson, 1995: 86)

In RT, concepts are psychological objects and each consists of a label or address. (Romero and Soria, 2010: 22)

The assumption is that a concept is a kind of 'address' in memory which provides access to three kinds of 'entry'. (Clark, 2013a: 244)

The conceptual address corresponds to the form that a concept takes in thought, while the information provided by the different entries constitutes the content of this very concept: "the distinction between address and entry is a distinction between form and content" (Sperber and Wilson, 1995: 92). As mentioned already, the lexical entry of a concept provides the linguistic counterpart used to express the concept (i.e. a specific word/sign), while the logical and encyclopedic entries can be understood here as specifying the actual content of the concept, some aspects of it being more central and stable than others.

Few relevance theorists adhere to this view, yet some have put forward very similar hypotheses. Before looking at these proposals, it is worth briefly discussing the limits of such an account of conceptual content. The main limit of this view corresponds very closely to the limit identified for the previous view with respect to the distinction between logical and encyclopedic entries. It is unclear exactly in what sense it is necessary to distinguish between logical and encyclopedic information, since this distinction may not actually reflect a cognitive reality. I will not repeat the arguments here (see page 86), but it is preferable simply to get rid of this distinction and to argue instead that there is simply conceptual content. As a result, a conceptual address does not give access to three but only to two types of entry: its linguistic form and its content. Of course, the difficulty in this case is to determine the nature of this content and whether it is more of the logical type or the encyclopedic type, as illustrated in Figure 3.7.

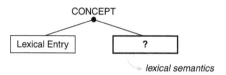

Figure 3.7 Conceptual content?

The answer to this question has to be encyclopedic knowledge. In the previous section, a number of arguments were presented against the use of inference rules to explain the nature of conceptual content. Inferential rules are hard to distinguish from other (non-deductive) inferential processes, they cannot easily account for the flexible nature of conceptual structures and therefore fail to fully define a concept. Encyclopedic knowledge does not face the same limits. First, it is not inferential in nature and thus can be distinguished from particular processes of inference involved during the comprehension phase. In addition, provided it has the right representational format (e.g. prototype theory), it can also account for the flexible nature of concepts and, therefore, fully define them (see Section 3.2). Furthermore, that conceptual content is encyclopedic in nature also seems to follow from its usage-based origin. It is rather clear when one adopts a usage-based approach to language and communication (which is the case in RT) that one primarily conceptualizes the world through one's experience with it, and in particular through the repeated exposure to particular pieces of encyclopedic information which are then organized in one's mind. This is the reason why in CxG, as in cognitive linguistics more generally, concepts are primarily described in encyclopedic terms.

It is interesting to note that the perspective on concepts just described, solely in encyclopedic terms, can sometimes be found in the relevance-theoretic literature. Having carefully considered the different options she introduces, Groefsema (2007) concludes that the only solution to the challenge she identifies is to consider that it is the encyclopedic entry of a concept that makes up its content (Groefsema, 2007: 155). This is also a view which can be found in the work of Anne Reboul. She explicitly argues, for instance, that "the distinction between *word* and *concept* is presumably nearer to that between *lexical* and *encyclopedic knowledge* than any other distinction" (Reboul, 2000: 60).[58] It also seems to be the underlying assumptions of Wilson and Sperber (2004) when they argue that "the encoded conceptual address is merely a point of access to an ordered array of encyclopedic assumptions from which the hearer is expected to select in constructing a satisfactory overall interpretation"

---

[58] See also Assimakopoulos (2008).

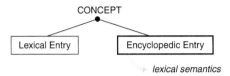

Figure 3.8 Concepts and encyclopedic content

(Wilson and Sperber, 2004: 619). This enables me to represent concepts as shown in Figure 3.8.

Already, it is worth noting that this perspective is quite reminiscent of the way in which CxG defines constructions: form–meaning pairings. Beyond this resemblance, it is interesting to note that this view faces none of the issues that the previous account does.[59] In the next section, I will try to show that this approach, which is very similar to that adopted in CxG, provides the best alternative to define lexical semantics. Before doing so, I would like to make a final observation concerning the nature of this encyclopedic entry.

As mentioned several times already, RT provides a very convincing, explicit and tangible explanation of how meaning is determined in context and, concurrently, is able to explain the origin of polysemy. Unfortunately, as pointed out by Lemmens (2017), given that the encyclopedic entry of a concept is only considered to be a "grab bag" of knowledge, it is unclear exactly how new interpretations can affect these conceptual structures in the long term and, therefore, how polysemy is assumed to be represented in one's mind. Specifically, he convincingly argues that it is "unclear how *different* modulations of one and the same lexical item will be

---

[59] Note that, in this representation, the lexical entry is still considered not to be radically distinct from the concept to which it is attached, but also part of the knowledge that one has about a concept. That is, here, lexical knowledge is conceptual knowledge. There is a debate whether or not lexical knowledge and conceptual knowledge should be distinguished (e.g. Murphy (2000), and references cited therein). This issue will not be addressed here. Nevertheless, it is worth noting that the view represented in Figure 3.8 is not unfamiliar both in RT and in CxG. Relevance Theory, in spite of its Chomskyan approach to language, assumes that concepts are made up of three entries, one of which is the lexical entry. In CxG, as in cognitive linguistics more generally, it also follows from the non-modular, usage-based approach to language that lexical knowledge is necessarily part of one's conceptual knowledge. Paradis (2003: 265) very explicitly says that:

The conventionalized routines of linguistic expression may be referred to as the lexicon. However, such a lexicon is not an encapsulated component. On the contrary, it is inseparable from conceptual knowledge and cognitive abilities in general. Lexical items evoke and are evoked by concepts, which involve all kinds of meaning specification that we use in various usage-events. I see no reason for postulating a separate non-conceptual type of lexical knowledge.

represented" (Lemmens, 2017: 104). Lemmens naturally recognizes that, when the encyclopedic entry is viewed as being content-constitutive, then the relevance-theoretic approach "is but one step away from being fully compatible with a cognitive view" (2017: 102). Lemmens' comment here is particularly relevant since it shows that arguing that conceptual knowledge is encyclopedic in nature does not suffice; one also needs to specify the particular way in which this information is structured. In the next section, we will see that the perspective adopted in CxG provides such a structure.

3.2   Lexical Semantics: A Structured Body of Encyclopedic Knowledge

The previous section shows the problem involved in pinning down the content of a concept (and, as a consequence, the meaning of lexical concepts) in RT. Following Groefsema (2007), it was shown that there are at least three views that emerge from the relevance-theoretic literature, one of which stands out particularly with respect to the others (the atomic view). The strengths and weaknesses of each of those views were presented in turn. Eventually, it was suggested that the information stored in the encyclopedic entry is the best candidate for what constitutes lexical 'meaning'. At the theoretical level it is the view that best fits the other underlying assumptions of the theory (namely, how the underdeterminacy thesis, the notion of explicatures, and the derivation of ad hoc concepts have been formulated). From a more descriptive level, and as far as meaning is concerned, this perspective does not face many of the challenges that the other views encounter. As mentioned several times already, a relatively similar view is adopted in CxG which, given its usage-based approach, also views meaning in terms of encyclopedic knowledge. In this section, I will briefly point out some of the advantages of adopting such a perspective generally, as well as discuss the ways in which the view adopted by constructionists can provide further insights into the difficult question that defining lexical semantics represents. It is on this basis that the notion of lexical pragmatics will be discussed in Section 3.4.

In order to discuss the advantages of the CxG approach, I will look in turn at all of the issues and difficulties that were identified in the previous section and show that it can handle most of them. In particular, I will focus on the way that encyclopedic knowledge is assumed to be structured in CxG and I will argue that this approach provides the required, solid basis to explain polysemy (and language change more generally).

It is traditional when discussing questions of lexical meaning, at least in philosophy, also to address the question of *reference*. In Section 3.1.1.1, it was shown that this question can sometimes represent a challenge depending on the way one defines meaning. In order to be able to establish the right reference, one necessarily needs to possess some internal conceptual content prior to reference. The perspective adopted here, according to which lexical meaning is to be defined in encyclopedic terms, precisely enables reference. This knowledge is internally stored in the minds of speakers and can be used to establish reference to a specific item/person in context. This content does not constitute the reference itself but forms the basis from which reference is possible. In this case, for instance, the reason why the concept CAT is used to refer to *cats* simply follows from what we know about cats and which enables us to refer to cats in the real world.

At the same time, unlike the different views presented earlier, this content is not considered to constitute the necessary and sufficient conditions that a concept gives access to and that are systematically used when establishing reference. That is, unlike an atomic concept or inferential rules, encyclopedic content is not taken to be necessarily and systematically true of that concept in all contexts and, therefore, is not used only to refer to items that share exactly the same properties (e.g. the concept BIRD, Section 3.1.2, can be used to refer both to eagles and ostriches, although the property 'fly' applies only to eagles and not to ostriches). This is due to the dynamic nature and graded structure of encyclopedic knowledge which individuals gradually acquire from the different contexts in which a concept occurs. As mentioned in Section 2.1.2.2, from a usage-based approach such as CxG, the conceptual structures that one has in mind emerge from one's experience with these concepts in the world. This experience involves a categorization process whereby new uses of a concept systematically affect the mental representation of that concept and new information is stored alongside old information. This process does not result in a grab bag of information, but new information is systematically placed within a conceptual network. This network is organized around a prototype, which contains the most salient features of a concept, and forms different bundles of knowledge (i.e. different *senses*) which are organized via analogy on the basis of a judgment of similarity. (The main difference between the radial network and the schematic network introduced in Section 2.1.2.2 mostly concerns the extent to which individuals actually abstract away from their experience.) A result of this process of categorization is that the different "features" that a concept makes accessible need not be necessarily activated across contexts but only get activated in the relevant contexts. That is, the conceptual network is a relatively flexible mental object that speakers and hearers can exploit in different ways. In this scenario, concepts do not make particular reference *necessary* (contra Fodor), but a given reference (and with it its truth values) is solely determined in a specific context by a particular speaker (and therefore has to be retrieved by the hearer).

This last observation provides a nice transition to the next advantage of holding an encyclopedic view of conceptual content. As mentioned above, if one considers concepts to be atomic, to consist of inferential rules or simply to be grab bags of knowledge, then it is unclear how different modulations can affect the original concept from which they are derived (and therefore, it is unclear how RT can possibly explain language change).[60] Considering instead that concepts are structured networks of acquired knowledge, this is no longer an issue. The particular way in which (old and new) information is exploited within a particular context directly impacts the conceptual network to which those pieces of information relate (either by entrenching an already existing bundle of knowledge, i.e. sense, or by creating a new one). And this perspective, together with strong pragmatic principles (such as those proposed in RT), can explain how language change actually works. I will come back to lexical pragmatics later.

In addition, and in direct relation to the previous point, this approach can also make sense of the (much-discussed) process of ad hoc concept creation. First of all, once we assume that individuals store conceptual networks, it then becomes clear in what sense we manage to derive narrower and/or broader concepts in different contexts. (Although, as we will see in Section 3.4, the terms *narrowing* and *broadening* might be slightly inappropriate.) Indeed, the conceptual network provides the necessary structure on the basis of which narrowing/broadening can occur.[61] There is conceptual narrowing when the information conveyed by a particular concept is more specific than that originally provided by the stored conceptual network; and there is conceptual broadening when the information provided by a concept is less specific than the information found in the original network. This is particularly interesting since, as mentioned above, this process also directly leaves a trace in the conceptual network, and the repeated derivation of a given ad hoc concept will lead to its entrenchment (and conventionalization) in the conceptual network from which it is originally derived. In Section 3.4, I will come back to the pragmatic process which is involved in the derivation of ad hoc concepts and how it fits in with the picture of lexical semantics presented here. As mentioned in the previous chapter, the pragmatic principles involved during meaning adjustments are often omitted in the cognitive linguistics literature, and it is not clear exactly what is meant by

---

[60] Note that in RT, although it is assumed that assumptions may be strengthened or contradicted in context (p. 37), the structure of encyclopedic knowledge is not addressed since they generally assume that concepts are atomic and that the encyclopedic entry plays only a secondary role.

[61] It is interesting to note, as mentioned several times already, that Barsalou himself (a standard reference in RT) actually develops his notion of "ad hoc categories" on the assumption that they are structured bodies of knowledge (and not atoms/inferential rules). So this perspective is also consistent with the original view from which the notion of ad hoc concepts was introduced in RT. (This is true to the extent that Barsalou only talks about narrowing processes. This will be discussed in Section 3.4.)

the words *context* and *pragmatics*. Nonetheless, it is important to point out that, regardless of how one defines pragmatics, it is largely accepted and argued within cognitive frameworks such as CxG that meaning (and therefore the conceptual networks that one stores) is not conceived of as fixed items that one simply invokes each time a specific linguistic element is used. It is a central assumption in cognitive linguistics that the meaning of a word is constantly negotiated and it is argued, like in RT, to "emerge and develop in discourse" (Langacker, 2008: 30). That is, as mentioned in Section 2.1.2.2, a crucial commitment in cognitive frameworks is that understanding an utterance does not simply consist in unpacking information but rather involves a systematic process of meaning construction (see, for instance, Taylor, Cuyckens and Dirven, 2003; Croft and Cruse, 2004; Evans, 2006, 2009; Evans and Green, 2006; Evans, Bergen and Zinken, 2007; Radden et al., 2007; Langacker, 2008; Geeraerts, 2016; Taylor, 2017; Schmid, 2020, and references cited therein). The next difficulty is of course to understand exactly how this meaning-construction process is actually carried out, since cognitive linguists often fail to make explicit the pragmatic principles involved (see Section 2.1.2.2). We will see that RT provides very interesting insights into the matter. Nevertheless, it is not because one argues that concepts are encyclopedic in nature that one therefore abandons the idea that meaning is primarily context-ually derived. Indeed, quite the opposite is true. As Lemmens (2017: 106) points out, "no one will deny the importance of contextual modulation, but this does not provide evidence that meaning should not, or cannot, be encyclopae-dic." Although this type of meaning is quite rich, it remains to be exploited and negotiated by individuals in context. How exactly this is carried out will be explained more fully later in this chapter, the aim of which is to show that although neither of the two theories provides a full account of lexical seman-tics–pragmatics, their integration precisely enables one to achieve greater descriptive accuracy.

As a matter of fact, the richness of conceptual content constitutes the last point that I want to address in this section. When one views concepts as being primarily encyclopedic in nature given that they result from one's experience, then one faces the necessary conclusion that concepts must be internally quite rich (cf. Lemmens, 2017: 106; Hogeweg and Vicente, 2020). That is, concepts are not decontextualized, abstract objects but are filled with contextual infor-mation. Two consequences directly follow from this observation. First of all, this richness can explain why encoded polysemy is considered to be the norm in frameworks such as CxG (and why it is possible in the first place). In this case, one necessarily has to organize one's knowledge, and the different nodes of the mental network that one derives represent the different senses of the lexical item associated with that concept. This view is naturally compatible with the perspective adopted in RT. Carston (2016a), for instance, very explicitly argues that "polysemy very often has its basis in pragmatics. ... Lexical meaning evolves and very often it is a (recurrent) pragmatic inference that lies at the root of new meanings" (Carston, 2016a: 621). To the best of my knowledge, no (or few) cognitive linguists would dispute Carston's claim. However, unlike the type of atomic semantics advocated by Carston, it is interesting to notice that only an encyclopedic view of conceptual content enables us to capture exactly how pragmatics can impact on the mental representation, as discussed above, and in particular how one can mentally represent the link between different modulations of the same concept and therefore make (semantic) polysemy possible. Relevance theorists are fully aware of (semantic) polysemy. Carston (2002a: 219), however, rightly suggests that postulating polysemy is not enough; one must also explain how the meaning of polysemous items is actually used and exploited in different contexts. This is an important question which will be addressed in the next sections. Before doing so, I want to discuss very briefly another consequence of assuming rich conceptual knowledge. The account of ad hoc concepts discussed in RT primarily rests on the assumption that the words we use largely fail to convey the speaker's intended interpretation (i.e. the underdeterminacy thesis). Assuming that concepts are essentially encyclopedic and, therefore, are rich representations, one could dispute the necessity to postulate the underdeterminacy thesis exactly as it is presented in RT (and strongly defended by Robyn Carston). Indeed, do the words we use always underdetermine what we want to communicate? Instead, it might also be appropriate to view the systematic derivation of ad hoc concepts (i.e. meaning construction) as resulting from some form of *indeterminacy*. Indeed, the assumption that pragmatics functions exclusively to complete the meaning of utterances that semantics fails to provide is not satisfactory. (Note that relevance theorists have never suggested that this is the case; quite the contrary since they argue for the systematic derivation of ad hoc concepts, see next section.) Rather, given the picture presented above in terms of meaning construction, semantics and pragmatics are inextricably intertwined. Yet the notion of underdeterminacy fails to capture this aspect of utterance interpretation. First, as mentioned before, it strongly suggests that pragmatics only serves to compensate for defective semantics. Yet it does not. Furthermore, it also suggests that the content provided by the words we use is quite poor. Again, as mentioned above, it is not. Rather, pragmatics and semantics are simultaneously exploited in context to derive a relevant interpretation. And in that sense, as far as polysemy is concerned, it seems preferable to argue that semantics does not (necessarily) underdetermine what a speaker wants to communicate but rather is indeterminate with respect to their intentions. This move is, of course, not meant to diminish the role of pragmatics during the process of utterance interpretation. It simply consists in giving back to semantics more room in a theory of comprehension than is often given in RT. This will be discussed more fully in the next two sections.

The encyclopedic view of conceptual knowledge such as adopted in CxG and defended here faces a major challenge: that of understanding exactly how this content is exploited in context, i.e. understanding in what sense it can fit with an account of lexical pragmatics and whether semantics and pragmatics are necessarily to be distinguished. This issue will be addressed in the next two sections. The conclusion to this section is that the encyclopedic view of conceptual content nicely resolves a number of issues that the other perspectives (discussed in the previous sections) fail to answer. These issues are primarily theoretical in nature. Moreover, the encyclopedic view nicely ties in with the accounts developed in RT and CxG. Beyond its theoretical adequacy, the encyclopedic view of concept also provides a psychologically sound assumption about concepts and is also consistent with most of the experimental research carried out in cognitive science (see, for instance, Barsalou, 2012, 2016, and references cited therein).

3.3   Concepts and Literalness: Issues of Representation or Computation?

The aim of this chapter is to provide a better understanding of lexical semantics and pragmatics. The first part of this chapter was primarily concerned with questions relating to lexical semantics. It was eventually suggested that the content of lexical items is best described in usage-based, encyclopedic terms. This view seems to be not only descriptively accurate, but it is also compatible with the views on meaning developed in both RT and CxG. The aim now is to try and position this perspective on meaning in the larger context of utterance comprehension and to understand more specifically how lexical pragmatics operates. This might seem a relatively straightforward and easy task, especially given the somewhat shared usage-based approach to 'meaning construction' adopted within both RT and CxG. However, as we will see below, this is not straightforward.

Understanding the nature of concepts and describing the manner in which they are used are, of course, two closely related issues. Precisely at the interface between lexical semantics and pragmatics, however, comes another issue that I have been careful not to mention in the first part of this chapter. It is only once this question has been addressed that I will be able to detail exactly in what sense lexical pragmatics is understood to operate.

As mentioned in the previous chapter, the account of ad hoc concepts presented in RT was originally developed on the basis of two observations. There is, of course, the underlying assumption captured by the underdeterminacy thesis that the content of the words we use often fails to fully determine what we are actually trying to communicate. But more importantly, as Assimakopoulos (2012: 17) points out, the account of ad hoc concepts developed in RT primarily rests on the rejection of the "encoded first" hypothesis (see Section 2.2.3.1). That is, in accordance with the work of Barsalou (and psycholinguists more generally), relevance theorists assume that individuals do not first test for relevance the encoded concept (or concepts) that a lexical item gives access to and then modulate this concept in context if it is not relevant enough; instead they systematically derive ad hoc concepts (i.e. systematically reconstruct a context-specific concept) across contexts. The same view is also largely adopted within CxG, in which the systematic process of meaning construction is often discussed. Within RT, however, it has recently been argued that this assumption somehow raises a dilemma concerning the nature of concepts. As we will see in Section 3.4, this does not have to be an issue, and it is not considered to be one in cognitive linguistics. The aim of this section, however, is to try and understand exactly what this issue consists of and how it has been dealt with within RT.

The issue with the "non-encoded-first" hypothesis defended in RT has in particular been discussed by Deirdre Wilson and Robyn Carston:

> Why should a hearer using the relevance-theoretic comprehension heuristic not simply test the encoded ('literal') meaning first? What could be easier than plugging the encoded concept into the proposition expressed, and adjusting it only if the resulting interpretation fails to satisfy expectations of relevance? In other words, what is there to *prevent* the encoded concept being not only activated, but also deployed? (Wilson, 2011: 12)

> However, the worry is that, given that the relevance-based comprehension heuristic explicitly licenses hearers to follow a path of least effort in accessing and testing interpretations for relevance, it seems natural to suppose that the encoded concept, which is made instantly available by the word form, would be tried first and only pragmatically adjusted if it didn't meet the required standards of relevance. (Carston, 2013: 195)

In other words, it seems more relevant (in the technical sense) to test the encoded concept for relevance before trying to derive an ad hoc concept. The question here is to know whether arguing both for the relevance-guided comprehension heuristics and against the "encoded-first" hypothesis does not lead to a theoretical contradiction. This is particularly true when one adopts, as I do in this book, a relatively rich type of lexical semantics. In Section 3.4, I will argue that the answer to this question does not concern lexical semantics but lexical pragmatics and that there is no necessary contradiction. Both Wilson and Carston, however, have treated this problem assuming that it concerns lexical semantics directly rather than lexical pragmatics, and that one therefore needs to deal with this contradiction. I will examine their views in the rest of this section.[62]

3.3.1 Deirdre Wilson's (2011, 2016) Procedural Account

Wilson (2011) is perhaps the first to have directly discussed the contradiction in adopting the relevance heuristics (*follow a path of least effort*) and rejecting the "encoded first" hypothesis. She puts forward the following solution. According to her, the reason concepts are not directly accessed but ad hoc concepts are systematically derived is to be found at the level of lexical semantics (i.e. the level of the encoded meaning of a word). She argues that the systematicity involved in the derivation of ad hoc concepts might reflect much more complex semantics than previously assumed. Specifically, she argues that, in addition to being associated with a particular concept, lexemes might automatically "trigger a procedure for constructing an ad hoc concept on the basis of the encoded [one]" (Wilson, 2011: 17). In order to explain the paradox, Wilson thus suggests that lexical words are semantic hybrids that both activate a concept and trigger a procedure to construct an ad hoc concept. (Procedures, as mentioned in the previous chapter, consist of specific instructions for the processing of conceptual information which are meant to guide the hearer towards (optimal) relevance.) In this case, it is clear how Wilson gets rid of the issue she identifies in the first place. By virtue of encoding an instruction to construct an ad hoc concept, lexemes can never simply give access to the encoded concept. We observe the instruction and do so by following a path of least effort. Paradox resolved.

According to Wilson (2011, 2016), an account in procedural terms provides an elegant explanation both for the theoretical contradiction identified earlier in this chapter and for the underpinnings of lexical pragmatics more generally. For a number of reasons, however, I share Carston's (2013) skepticism about this proposal. First, an account in procedural terms makes the derivation of ad hoc concepts not only systematic but also compulsory. Yet it is sometimes argued in RT, as Carston (2013: 196) points out, that "the encoded concept can, on occasion, be the concept communicated (Sperber and Wilson, 1998, 2008)." If the derivation of an ad hoc concept is viewed as obligatory, however, it is unclear whether or not it is ever possible to reconstruct the encoded concept (i.e. whether the procedure enables the recovery of the encoded concept). Assuming it is possible, then Wilson needs to account for the observation that reconstructing the original concept (arguably) takes more effort than simply testing it as it is, which makes the overall interpretation less relevant than it could have been (since the more processing effort, the less relevance).

---

[62] Sections 3.3.1 and 3.3.2 were published in Leclercq (2022).

Assuming it is not possible to reconstruct the original concept, the challenge is to understand how that concept (and the associated procedure) was acquired in the first place and what exactly the function of that concept is, as well as what is the relevance of storing a concept that is never actually entertained and communicated by individuals. Second, this view also suggests that words that encode a concept therefore all encode exactly the same procedure, namely that of constructing an ad hoc concept. Yet, as Carston (2013) points out, this tremendously weakens the approach to procedural meaning developed in RT. Just like no two words encode exactly the same concept, it is implicitly assumed in RT that no two words encode exactly the same procedure. Yet this assumption is seriously challenged here. (One may argue, however, that this need not directly be an issue for Wilson.) In fact, third, Wilson's proposal is all the more surprising since it assumes that all words are thus (at least partly) procedural. Yet, there is growing consensus that procedural encoding is a property of grammatical units of the language and not of lexical items (see Section 4.2.2). Finally, the challenge with Wilson's proposal also comes from the observation that the task she attributes to a particular procedure is in RT originally supposed to be taken care of by the relevance-guided comprehension heuristics (Carston, 2013: 196; Escandell-Vidal, 2017: 88). That is, individuals are said to adjust concepts in RT because of their expectations of relevance. Adding a specific procedure is quite unnecessary since it is redundant with respect to one of the central claims of the theory. Carston (2013: 193) in fact argues that this move "seems like overkill." For all these reasons, a different solution to the paradox might be preferable.[63]

3.3.2   Robyn Carston's (2013) Underspecific Content

In spite of disagreeing with Wilson's proposal, Carston shares the concern that rejecting the "encoded first" hypothesis is inconsistent with arguing for the relevance-guided comprehension heuristics. Therefore, she puts forward an alternative solution. Carston (2013: 196) suggests that, maybe, the reason encoded concepts are never tested first (and then adjusted only when they do not meet one's expectations of relevance) simply follows from the fact that words never actually encode full concepts but only conceptual schemas or templates (i.e. underspecific schematic meanings).[64] In order to recover the

---

[63] Of course, this does not mean that the interpretation of lexical items never involves procedures. Meaning is largely compositional, and I will in fact argue in Chapter 4 that the derivation of ad hoc concepts is directly guided by the procedural function of the grammatical constructions in which lexemes occur, thus sometimes giving rise to coercion effects. However, I reject the idea that *all* lexical items themselves encode the same procedure of having to create an ad hoc concept.

[64] This is a suggestion that, for other reasons, she already made in Carston (2002a: 360). Her solution thus comes across as slightly less post hoc than Wilson's.

full-fledged concepts intended by the speaker, these conceptual schemas thus have to be contextually enriched. As in Wilson's proposal, this perspective makes the construction of an ad hoc concept necessary and hence explains why, while following a path of least effort, encoded concepts are not tested first (since there is no concept to start with; see below). Unlike Wilson's proposal, however, it has the advantage of not putting any additional burden on the lexicon. Nonetheless, Carston's proposal also faces a number of crucial issues.

Carston argues that her account is as explanatory as Wilson's without sharing any of its limitations. She argues, for instance, that, unlike Wilson's account, hers "does not entail an obligatory process that is sometimes unnecessary (as when the encoded concept is the concept communicated)" (Carston, 2013: 197). Two comments can be made about this observation. First, it is not clear in what sense her account does not require an obligatory process of concept construction. By virtue of being underspecific, concept schemas necessarily have to be enriched in context in order to arrive at a specific interpretation (i.e. to derive a specific proposition). This process is therefore precisely required by the type of semantics that Carston argues for. Second, she suggests that the reason why the construction of an ad hoc concept in this account is not necessary follows from the observation that the communicated concept might be the one which is encoded. It is difficult to reconcile what seem like two opposite hypotheses. On the one hand, she argues that words do not encode concepts but concept schemas, while on the other, she argues that the communicated concept might be the encoded one. Yet either words encode full concepts or concept schemas, but the advantage of concept schemas cannot possibly be that they provide a full concept. In spite of what she might argue, Carston's account thus suffers from limitations similar to Wilson's.

The proposal that Carston develops here once more quite strikingly illustrates the tension that there is in her own work in terms of how to define concepts. If one assumes that words encode concept schemas, and not full-fledged concepts, one necessarily drops the idea according to which concepts are referential, atomic objects (a position, as mentioned before, Carston has quite staunchly defended until very recently). This is not the only issue with Carston's proposal, however. There is at least one other critical theoretical implication that needs to be discussed. The relevance-theoretic approach to the semantics–pragmatics interface was developed on the assumption, called the underdeterminacy thesis (Carston, 2002a: 19), that words alone do not suffice to recover the speaker's intended meaning and that, besides implicatures, much inferential work is also needed at the explicit level of communication. Sperber and Wilson (1995: 182) coined the term *explicature* precisely to capture the hybrid nature (semantic and pragmatic) of explicit propositions. As I understand it, though, the standard argument within relevance theory has always consisted in highlighting some form of pragmatic underdeterminacy.

That is, the sentences we use do carry a specific meaning (which occurs in the logical form of an utterance), and this meaning only has to be pragmatically enriched (e.g. disambiguation, reference assignment, conceptual adjustment) in order to derive the explicature. If one now assumes that words merely encode concept schemas, however, then one necessarily has to postulate some form of semantic underdeterminacy whereby language does not simply fail to provide the speaker's intended interpretation but altogether fails to provide any meaning at all. This seems to be Carston's underlying assumption when she says that "while sentences encode thought/proposition templates, words encode concept templates; *it's linguistic underdeterminacy all the way down*" (Carston, 2002a: 360; emphasis mine). However, this perspective is hardly plausible. For one, such a view generally seems to undermine the relevance-theoretic approach to the semantics–pragmatics interface and in particular the notion of explicatures. Indeed, from this perspective, explicatures are essentially pragmatic in nature, which means that they can never truly be explicit (cf. Sperber and Wilson, 1995: 182), which therefore adds confusion as to their role and status in utterance comprehension (cf. discussion in Borg, 2016). As will become clear in Section 3.4, I contend that individuals do have rather rich conceptual knowledge. Within relevance theory, Wilson (2011) also questions the plausibility of such an underspecification account. The idea that some words might not encode full-fledged concepts but simply act as pointers for the recovery of conceptual content can be found in Sperber and Wilson's (1998) discussion of *pro-concepts*. This notion (which is more of an assumption) only applies to a specific set of words, however (e.g. pronouns, gradable adjectives, etc.), and it is not Sperber and Wilson's intention to argue that all words encode such pro-concepts. Wilson specifically points out that "while the assumption that some words encode pro-concepts is quite plausible, the idea that all of them do is unlikely" (Wilson, 2011: 16; see also Carston, 2012: 619). Carston in fact identifies some of the limitations of her proposal herself:

Even if these abstract non-semantic lexical meanings could be elucidated, it is entirely unclear what role they would play in the account of language meaning and use. On the relevance-based pragmatic account of how ad hoc concepts/senses are contextually constructed in the process of utterance interpretation, the real work is done by the encyclopaedic information associated with a concept (a semantic entity) and there is no further constraining or guiding role to be played by a schematic (non-semantic) meaning. Nor does the schema appear to play any role in a child's acquisition of word meaning; in fact, the child's first "meanings" for a word are the (fully semantic) concepts/senses grasped in communication, so the abstract (non-semantic) meaning could only be acquired subsequently by some process of induction. Even supposing we could give an account of how this is done, what would be missing is an explanation of why it would be done, what purpose it would serve. (Carston, 2016b: 158)

There are at least two points in this quote that are worth commenting upon. First, Carston argues that the reason concepts are probably not schematic comes from the observation that these schemas would have no particular role in the comprehension procedure since it is the information stored in the encyclopedic entry that constrains the derivation of ad hoc concepts. When saying this, it is interesting to note that Carston once more gives encyclopedic information a central role in (linguistic) communication. Although it is not her intention, this view is fully compatible with the encyclopedic approach to lexical semantics introduced previously. From this perspective, it is indeed unclear what could possibly motivate the necessity of storing a single (and independent, here) schematic meaning as well as how this meaning might be used (see next section). The most convincing argument against meaning schematicism, however, comes from the second part of the quote. Carston rightly points out that the main difficulty is to understand exactly how these schemas might be acquired. These schemas can only be acquired via a gradual process of abstraction on the basis of the full-fledged concepts that one directly accesses in context. Yet the necessity for such a level of abstraction is unclear and seems rather counterintuitive (in the sense of less *relevant*, in the technical sense of the term). Abstracting away such a schematic meaning forces us to derive systematically a specific ad hoc concept in context that we might otherwise store as such and access directly. Intuitively, it could be more economical to store and organize these concepts directly in one's mind, even if some abstraction is involved (see, for instance, footnote 14 (Chapter 2) on exemplar-based and prototype models), rather than to abstract away from these concepts to such an extent that one may not even need this schematic meaning during comprehension.

Carston thus concludes that the underspecification hypothesis needs to be dropped (see also Carston, 2019, 2021). While I fully support this move, it nonetheless raises the question of whether and how Carston still intends to explain the theoretical paradox that her underspecification account was meant to resolve in the first place: if words do have specific meanings attached to them, then why aren't these tested first for relevance? Carston sketches an alternative approach:

This requires making a distinction between the kind of lexicon that features in a narrowly construed I-language, with its focus on syntactic computations and constraints, and the lexicon of the broader public language system, which is a repository of communicative devices whose conceptual contents are what the inferential pragmatic system operates on. In the narrow I-lexicon, the words (or roots) listed have no meaning, conceptual or schematic, while in the C-lexicon of the broader communicational language system, words are stored with their polysemy complexes (bundles of senses/concepts that have become conventionally associated with a word and perhaps others that are not yet fully established as stable senses). (Carston, 2016b: 159)

Carston, however, does not develop this account any further; the information in the quote only contains a basic hypothesis and is not yet developed into a full-fledged theory.[65] Unfortunately, it is not clear exactly in what sense distinguishing between I- and C-lexicon might help us deal with the issue identified above. First of all, it is unclear what is meant by *polysemy complexes* and *bundles of senses/concepts*. As mentioned several times already, there is quite a lot of tension in Carston's work as to exactly what concepts are. The terminology used, e.g. "bundles of senses," is often found in the literature on prototypes, yet this is most likely not the perspective endorsed by Carston. Importantly, placing the conceptual network at a different level of representation simply pushes the issue to a different level of analysis but does not necessarily solve it. This is particularly true because Carston argues that it is the C-lexicon that "provides input to the pragmatic processes of relevance-based comprehension" (Carston, 2019: 157). That is, it remains a challenge to understand why we should still systematically build an ad hoc concept and not try and test first for relevance any of the stored senses of the C-lexicon.

3.3.3   Concepts and Literalness: Issues of Computation

I have argued in the previous sections that adopting a schematic view of meaning is as undesirable as Wilson's procedural account, and Carston herself recognizes that this perspective is somewhat problematic. However, this means that we are left with no specific explanation for the apparent contradiction identified earlier on (namely, that of arguing for the relevance-based comprehension heuristics while at the same time arguing against the "encoded first" hypothesis). Although Carston's (2013, 2016b) proposals raise a number of issues, she asks important questions. In order to account for the dilemma identified by Wilson (2011), Carston (2013) brings into the discussion experimental work by psycholinguists so as to provide an explanation which is not only theoretically plausible within RT but generally psychologically plausible and descriptively accurate. In particular, Carston refers to Steven Frisson (and colleagues), a psycholinguist whose work precisely consists in looking at the processing of lexical items. The findings of Frisson's experiments seem to corroborate Carston's claim that meaning is underspecific (which then explains why ad hoc concepts are systematically derived). In Carston (2016b), the argument is different. She looks at the same data but this time she takes a different view and argues that meanings are not underspecific. (In this case, however, we saw above that it is unclear how the systematic derivation of ad hoc concepts is explained.) The results of these

---

[65] In more recent work, Carston (2019, 2022) shows how the distinction between I- and C-lexicon can be applied to issues in morphology (in particular in order to account for the use of cross-categorical words). However, in those papers she does not address the issue discussed here.

experiments will be reported on below. Then, in the next section, I will explain how both the results of these experiments and the dilemma identified by Wilson can be explained when adopting an encyclopedic view of lexical meaning.

The particular experiments that Carston refers to aim at a better understanding of the processing of polysemous lexemes. (She explicitly refers to the work of Frazier and Rayner, 1990; Frisson and Pickering, 2001; Pickering and Frisson, 2001; Frisson, 2009.)[66] Using eye-tracking methods, Frisson and his colleagues have tried to pin down any differences between the processing of polysemous words (which give access to distinct but related meanings) and that of homonymous terms (which give access to unrelated meanings). As polysemy and homonymy give access to more than one interpretation, one might expect that the same type of selection procedure may be involved in both cases. The results of their experiments do not confirm this hypothesis, however. Indeed, homonyms require significantly more processing time than polysemous terms (which are processed much more like monosemous items). In particular, it is shown that the different senses of polysemous items do not compete in the way that the different meanings of homonyms do. While the competing meanings of homonyms seem to be directly accessed, and therefore need to be processed, this is not the case for the different senses of polysemous terms. When interpreting the data, Frazier and Rayner (1990) argue that polysemous terms provide only an *immediate partial interpretation*, i.e. some form of common ground which can provide access to more specific senses in context. In a similar way, Frisson and Pickering argue that these results provide support for what they call the "underspecified account" (Pickering and Frisson, 2001: 567). In this case, polysemous lexemes are argued to give access not to the different senses they can be used to express but to an underspecific meaning which forms the basis from which the different senses can be arrived at in context (via some "homing in" process). This is the reason why Carston (2013) naturally sees these results as providing evidence for her claim that words might only encode underspecific meanings.

The following observations are particularly relevant given the aim of this chapter. First of all, the results of these experiments provide yet further evidence that the meanings of lexical items are not simply accessed by individuals but are instead systematically built (or constructed) in context. This is consistent with both the relevance-theoretic and the constructionist enterprises. These experiments are also particularly interesting since they directly challenge the notion of lexical semantics. On the face of it, it could seem as though individuals only store some underspecific meaning and not the rich type of

---

[66] In her Ph.D. thesis *The semantics and pragmatics of polysemy: A relevance theoretic account*, Ingrid Falkum (2011) also refers to a large set of experimental work on the processing of polysemous items, most of which provides similar results to those discussed by Carston. See Falkum (2011: 63) for specific references.

conceptual structures defended in Section 3.2. Carston (2013) specifically follows this line of argumentation, which not only provides evidence for her previous claim that words encode concept schemas (Carston, 2002a) but can also explain why the literal interpretation of a lexeme is never tested first. Carston (2016b), however, expresses strong doubts that individuals do indeed only store such underspecific meanings. I share Carston's latest skepticism, and in the next section I will show that the results of these experiments may not be incompatible with the view adopted here in terms of rich conceptual structures. It is worth pointing out that this possibility is actually mentioned by those who developed the experiments in the first place:

The underspecification model is in principle compatible with both [the radical mono-semy and the radical polysemy] views, at least as long as underspecified meanings are also part of a polysemous lexicon. (Frisson and Pickering, 2001: 166)

The idea of underspecification is perfectly compatible with a representation of all individual senses at some level, though the claim made here is that these individual senses do not play a role in the earliest stages of processing. (Frisson, 2009: 119)

The different experiments discussed by Carston therefore mostly provide evidence not against rich types of lexical semantics but in favor of relatively complex processes of lexical pragmatics. Exactly how the type of semantics adopted in this book easily accommodates the different questions addressed in this chapter is the focus of the next section.

3.4   Lexical Pragmatics: Lexically Regulated Saturation

The previous sections have highlighted the difficulty of identifying exactly what constitutes lexical semantics and how this knowledge is actually put to use in context. The aim of this section is to try and develop an approach to lexical pragmatics which addresses each of the issues identified earlier. It will have become clear that in this book I am largely arguing in favor of the type of semantics adopted in CxG in terms of rich conceptual networks of encyclope-dic knowledge (see Sections 3.1 and 3.2). The main challenge now is to understand exactly how this type of semantics can be integrated into a larger framework of lexical pragmatics and answer the different questions raised so far.

First, it is essential for me to remind the reader that, in spite of being rich, the type of semantics adopted in cognitive linguistics is not considered to provide context-free packages that hearers systematically access and necessarily take to be the speaker's intended interpretation. Rather, the conceptual material that a lexical item gives access to is by definition highly context-sensitive. As in RT, the idea that interpreting an utterance does not simply consist in the selection of a particular sense within a conceptual network but rather involves the systematic construction of meaning (or conceptualization, as Langacker puts it) forms one of the central tenets of cognitive linguistics. Adopting such a rich type of semantics, therefore, should not be perceived as a rejection of pragmatics. Quite the opposite, since cognitive linguists generally fail to see the relevance of decontextualized semantics. By comparison, as Leclercq (2022) points out, it is precisely because they adopt a rigid ('dictionary') view of meaning that proponents of RT face issues such as those discussed in Section 3.3. Yet numerous arguments have been given against such an approach to meaning (Reddy, 1979; Haiman, 1980; Fillmore, 1982; Lakoff, 1987; Langacker, 1987; Murphy, 1991; Pustejovsky, 1995). What is true, however, is that the pragmatic principles that govern the process of meaning construction, and exactly how this rich type of semantics is actually exploited in context, are largely lacking within the cognitive framework. There is, of course, a considerable body of work on metaphors. Outside this area of research, however, the domain of lexical pragmatics has generally been given little attention in cognitive linguistics and, therefore, in CxG.[67]

Lexical semantics, within both RT and CxG, is therefore the starting point on the basis of which lexical pragmatics can operate, and here is how it actually happens. The conceptual network that a lexical item provides access to is organized as a structure in which one has stored related bundles of knowledge (i.e. different senses) around a specific prototype via an analogical process of family resemblance. This network provides the basis for a process of *lexically regulated saturation*.

The term *lexically regulated saturation* was introduced by Depraetere (2010, 2014) when discussing the interpretation of modal expressions in English. In particular, she develops this notion to reconcile monosemous and polysemous approaches to modal meaning. She herself argues in favor of a polysemous analysis of modal verbs. Yet she also believes that understanding modal verbs is more complex than simply selecting one of the stored senses. Rather, she claims that the specific senses that modal verbs encode are entirely context-dependent and that they are systematically reconstructed by individuals on the basis of some context-independent layer of semantics. This independent layer of semantics forms the "semantic core" (Depraetere, 2010: 83) of modal verbs which needs to be contextually saturated by hearers in order to arrive at one of the (contextually-dependent) encoded senses. In this sense, understanding modal verbs is a *saturation* process, since the semantic cores they give access to need to be contextually enriched to provide the hearer with a specific interpretation.[68] This saturation process is, however, *lexically regulated* since

---

[67] I am of course talking about the *non-conventional* type of lexical pragmatics.

[68] The term *saturation* was first introduced by François Recanati (1989: 304). He defines saturation as a linguistically mandated pragmatic process, whereby an open variable needs to be contextually determined (e.g. reference assignment for pronouns). In Recanati's original

it is constrained not only by pragmatic principles but also by the contextually-dependent layer of semantics, i.e. by the specific senses that belong to the conceptual networks attached to modal verbs.

The aim of this section is to extend the notion of lexically regulated saturation beyond the field of modality and to argue that this process is central to lexical pragmatics more generally. In keeping with Leclercq (2023), I contend that Depraetere's original explanation remains too mechanistic, however, especially as it also seems to (implicitly) rely on a dictionary view of meaning. Not only do I reject the idea of a stable "semantic core" that needs to be enriched, I also condemn the view that speakers merely need to enrich this core into one of a set of already established senses. This leaves too little – if any – room for novel interpretations and for language variation and change. So what exactly is involved in lexically regulated saturation? One key ingredient is given to us in the cognitive linguistics literature. Metaphor (and metonymy) aside, there is a tendency to discuss the notion of "meaning construction" (or conceptualization) mostly in terms of activation (emphases mine):

An expression's meaning presupposes an extensive, multifaceted conceptual substrate that supports it, shapes it, and renders it coherent. Among the facets of this substrate are (i) the conceptions evoked or created through the previous discourse; (ii) engagement in the speech event itself, as part of the interlocutors' social interaction; (iii) apprehension of the physical, social, and cultural context; and (iv) any domains of knowledge that might prove relevant. ... Precisely what it means on a given occasion – which portions of this encyclopedic knowledge **are activated**, and to what degree – depends on all the factors cited. (Langacker, 2008: 42)

Any given word will provide a unique **activation** of part of its semantic potential on every occasion of use. This follows as every utterance, and thus the resulting conception, is unique. (Evans, 2006: 501)

Making meaning for a word like *antelope* involves **activating** conceptual knowledge about what antelopes are like. (Bergen, 2016: 143)

It is relatively clear from these quotes that (in cognitive linguistics) the conceptualization process involved during the interpretation of a lexeme mostly has to do with activating (to different degrees) parts of the conceptual knowledge associated with that lexeme.[69] Langacker mentions a few factors that are meant to explain how this activation happens. To put it simply, the

account, we are dealing with a relatively "open-ended valuation" (Depraetere, 2014: 170), since there is no predetermined set of values that one is expected to aim for. Although linguistically mandated, this type of pragmatic enrichment may therefore go in any direction. Depraetere's notion of *lexically regulated* saturation differs precisely in this regard: the stored senses provide such predetermined values that one should aim for when enriching the semantic core.

[69] In relation to the notion of meaning construction, the words *activate, activated* and *activation* are also highly frequent, for instance, both in Nick Riemer's (2016) *Routledge handbook of semantics* and in Geeraerts and Cuykens' (2007) *Oxford handbook of cognitive linguistics*.

underlying idea is that different contexts (linguistic and non-linguistic) will activate slightly different parts of our conceptual knowledge, and this motivates the claim that each (contextual) conceptualization is therefore unique. However, there are a number of issues with this approach. First, Langacker does not really elaborate on the different contextual factors that he mentions, and it is not clear in what sense these directly affect the activation process which lies at the root of conceptualization. More importantly, it is unlikely that the process of conceptualization (or, in relevance-theoretic terms, ad hoc concept creation) can be reduced merely to some activation process. Suffice it to look at language change to understand that the interpretation of a lexeme cannot simply be reduced to activating parts of the conceptual knowledge which it gives access to, for otherwise meaning would never actually change (different parts of the same conceptual network systematically getting activated). In order for language change to be possible, more than conceptual activation is required in the first place. Like relevance theorists, I assume that communication is primarily intentional, and that interpreting an utterance precisely involves taking into account the speaker's intentions. An activation account of conceptualization, however, cannot account for this important factor. Instead, one needs pragmatic (i.e. non-logical, non-deductive) inference to account for this observation (see Mazzarella (2013, 2014) and references cited therein). Within cognitive linguistics (and CxG), however, pragmatic inferences are seldom referred to in relation to lexical meaning.[70] There are basically two contexts in which the term *inference* is used in cognitive linguistics. It is often used as an umbrella term for all kinds of implicated content, i.e. for the type of content which occurs in implicatures. This is, for instance, the case in Traugott and Dasher's (2002) work on semantic change (and in particular grammaticalization), where the term *inference* seems to be equated with the notion of implicatures only. Yet it is clear in frameworks like RT that pragmatic inferences do not only concern implicatures. In addition, the notion of inference is often referred to in the literature on metaphors and metonymy (e.g. Lakoff and Johnson, 1980; Lakoff, 1987), where it is argued that lexemes that are used metaphorically inherit most of the inferences that are associated with the conceptual domain in which they are used. Yet the inferences referred to here are more of the logical type (i.e. entailments, presuppositions) rather than purely pragmatic ones. Generally speaking, the notion of pragmatic inference is barely referred to in discussion on lexical meaning in cognitive linguistics. In spite of this observation, cognitive linguists are undoubtedly sensitive to the primarily communicative function of language and, therefore, of meaning. This

---

[70] One only needs to look at how the word *inference* is used in Geeraerts and Cuykens' (2007) *Oxford handbook of cognitive linguistics*. (Talmy's contribution remains a noticeable exception.)

is very clear in Traugott and Dasher (2002), for instance, who mention the following two quotes:

As pointed out by Bartsch: "semantic change is possible because the specific linguistic norms, including semantic norms, are hypothetical norms, subordinated to the highest norms of communication (the pragmatic aspect of change)" (1984: 393). (p. 25)

We agree wholeheartedly with [Lewandowska-Tomaszczyk's (1985)] claim that meanings have "a starting point in the conventional *given*, but in the course of ongoing interaction meaning is negotiated, i.e. jointly and collaboratively constructed . . . This is the setting of semantic variability and change" (Lewandowska-Tomaszczyk, 1985: 300). (p. 26)

It is clear for Traugott and Dasher that meaning construction is primarily a collaborative communicative activity rather than the simple recovery (or activation) of conventional aspects of meaning. At least, this is what those quotes strongly suggest. And this is exactly the view I am defending here: meaning construction involves more than activating part of our conceptual knowledge; it involves the recovery of the speaker's intentions and, therefore, it requires much pragmatic inference (see Rubio-Fernández (2008) for experimental evidence).[71]

Very much in the spirit of Relevance Theory, I want to argue that lexically regulated saturation consists of an inferential process. This process is *lexically regulated* in the sense that, naturally, in different contexts, different parts of the conceptual network associated with a lexeme will be activated (and some features of a concept may be so central that they systematically get activated) and will serve as the basis for the interpretation process. These most salient features, unlike what cognitive linguists believe, only provide evidence about what particular interpretation might have been intended by the speaker, however. That is, they only raise awareness of the type of meaning that might have been intended by the speaker. (In this regard, I strongly endorse Bartsch's (1984: 393) idea that semantic norms are only "hypothetical norms," see the quote above.) It is then on the basis of those activated conceptual features that the hearer will be able to construct a relevant interpretation.[72] In that sense, it is a *saturation* (i.e. mandatory, inferential) process, since there is no meaning

---

[71] By no means do I intend to diminish the role of contextual conceptual activation. George Lakoff, for instance, has done considerable work on the role of conceptual activation (and spreading activation) in relation to metaphorical interpretations (see, for instance, Lakoff, 2014). The aim here is only to argue that activation is but the starting point of the interpretation process and not the only operation involved. Recently, Pritchard (2019) and Glynn (2022) argued that the interpretation process involves analogical (i.e. similarity-based) reasoning. My account includes, though is not limited to, analogical thinking.

[72] In a sense, this is not radically different from the relevance-theoretic perspective in which the information stored in the encyclopedic entry enables the recovery of ad hoc concepts. The main difference here is that the encyclopedic information is considered to be content-constitutive.

available to the hearer as long as a specific interpretation has not been inferred. Exactly how hearers manage to derive the speaker's intended interpretation is a question for which RT provides a very good answer: the relevance-theoretic comprehension heuristics. That is, in accordance with their expectations of relevance, individuals follow a step-by-step inferential procedure and test various interpretations for *relevance* in order of accessibility. They do so by taking into account many factors, such as the speaker's intentions, extra-linguistic factors, previous discourse contexts and stored assumptions. Once an interpretation provides them with enough cognitive effects to justify the effort put into the interpretation process, they can stop searching. The result of this saturation process may then consist in an ad hoc concept/a conceptualization that has already been derived previously in similar contexts. This will directly lead to the entrenchment (and, potentially, conventionalization) of this particular sense within a conceptual network. More importantly, this process may also lead to the derivation of relatively new ad hoc concepts which lay the foundation for semantic change. In this regard, the type of process discussed here does not radically differ from the type of acquisition process and strategies that children use when hearing a particular word for the first time. The main difference is that whereas children rely a lot (and sometimes exclusively) on extra-linguistic factors to derive the speaker's intended interpretation, adults who already possess large conceptual networks can rely on this knowledge much more and therefore (probably) more easily derive the intended meaning. Like children, however, adults also need to infer in context what the speaker actually intends to communicate, and which interpretation seems to be the most relevant. In other words, conceptual networks are never taken as given, but only provide solid evidence for the type of interpretation that the speaker may intend to communicate (and storing conceptual networks might be relevant precisely in that sense, one of their functions being that of facilitating the saturation process). Exactly how we manage to recover (or try to recover) the speaker's actual interpretation is, as argued in RT, provided by the relevance-based comprehension heuristics.

The process of lexically regulated saturation can answer many of the issues discussed previously in this chapter. First, it can account for the observation that in spite of storing rich conceptual networks, the encoded sense(s) are not tested first for relevance. Indeed, the different senses that a concept gives access to are not context-free packages that one directly has access to and from which one needs to select the most relevant sense. First of all, different parts of this conceptual network will get activated in different contexts. In addition, depending on which part of the conceptual network actually gets activated, the hearer will also have to construct a specific interpretation in accordance with their expectations of relevance. That is, the contextual activation of part of this network does not suffice to provide the speaker's interpretation (although it is most probably the case, here, that the most salient features that have been activated will be tested first for relevance). This is consistent with most of the work carried out in psycholinguistics, such as that of Barsalou (see previous sections), according to whom the construction of meaning is a complex context-sensitive process.[73] Finally, the saturation process also nicely accounts for the type of experimental evidence discussed by Carston (see Section 3.3.3), according to which "individual senses do not play a role in the earliest stages of processing" (Frisson, 2009: 119). Indeed, it will have become clear that words do not directly provide any specific sense to the interpretation process per se.

In Section 3.5, I will make final observations concerning the nature of lexical concepts and the type of pragmatic process involved during the interpretation of lexemes. Before doing so, I would like to point out one last consequence that follows from arguing for lexically regulated saturation. As mentioned in Section 3.2, this view challenges the appropriateness of using both the terms *broadening* and *narrowing* in relation to the creation of ad hoc concepts (see Bardzokas, 2023 for a similar observation). Indeed, by virtue of inferentially deriving a specific meaning on the basis of the activated conceptual features, only the term conceptual NARROWING seems appropriate. In fact, it is interesting to note that the particular way in which Barsalou himself discusses the creation of "ad hoc categories" mostly supports a NARROWING perspective (e.g. Barsalou, 1987). Yet this crucially depends on what constitutes the focus of description, and whether one is discussing the saturation process itself or the resulting ad hoc concept. It is true that only the term NARROWING seems appropriate to describe lexically regulated saturation, since the eventual conceptualization will (most often) be more specific than the set of activated conceptual features on the basis of which it has been constructed. Looking at ad hoc concepts directly, however, and comparing ad hoc concepts with the conceptual networks from which they are derived, it seems that both the terms *narrower* and *broader* can be used depending on how much their content actually overlaps. The use of these terms simply depends on whether one is focusing on the saturation process itself (a NARROWING process), or on the resulting conceptualization (which can be narrower or broader than the encoded concept).

3.5   Lexical Semantics and Pragmatics: Setting the Story Straight

The aim of this chapter was to try and define lexical semantics and lexical pragmatics. In the first part, I strongly argued in favor of a usage-based, encyclopedic approach to lexical semantics according to which individuals

---

[73] The saturation account presented here therefore provides a nice alternative to Wilson's procedural approach, since it avoids positing additional semantic constraints. While I concur with Wilson that the meaning of a lexical item is systematically (re)constructed in context, I do not attribute this mechanism to some encoded instruction but assume that it follows logically from the context-sensitive nature of the conceptual material associated with lexical items.

store complex conceptual networks. The challenge is to determine in what sense such a framework integrates lexical pragmatics. In the previous section, I have tried to show that the perspective on lexical semantics adopted here easily combines with the view of lexical pragmatics developed within RT, given that the conceptual networks are not seen as context-independent units but are instead highly context-sensitive. The aim of this section is twofold. First, I will discuss a number of assumptions about semantics which might account for the limits identified in both RT and CxG. Then, the aim is to show that, in spite of rejecting the type of lexical semantics RT generally adopts, its view of lexical pragmatics so far provides the best account of how people manage to communicate effectively.

I have shown in Sections 3.1 and 3.3 that it is difficult to determine exactly how concepts are defined within RT. Recently, the challenge of understanding why stored concepts are not necessarily tested first for relevance has in particular led to some rather peculiar hypotheses concerning the nature of lexical semantics. Generally speaking, the more RT is developed, the more room is given to pragmatics (at the cost of semantics). As explained in Section 3.1.1.2, the commitment to referential atomism has pushed relevance theorists into arguing for relatively poor semantics as opposed to increasingly more pervasive pragmatics. By contrast, in spite of recognizing the central role of usage and pragmatics in communication, there is a tendency in CxG to view the rich (semantic) networks of conceptual knowledge associated with a particular linguistic unit as sufficient: they provide most of the information communicated by an individual. In this case, much room is given to lexical semantics, and pragmatics is often marginalized to the level of implicatures.[74] Although these two analyses are in direct opposition, their respective limits originate from a relatively common assumption about the mental status of semantics. There is a tendency in the two frameworks to assume (more or less implicitly) that once a particular interpretation is entrenched and conventionalized, and becomes part of our "semantic knowledge," then this knowledge is almost necessarily consciously available to us. In RT, this seems to be one of the underlying reasons why Carston so strongly defends Fodor's atomic account (Carston, 2010: 245). She also argues, for instance, that concepts are available to consciousness and introspection (Carston, 2016b: 156). In CxG, and in cognitive linguistics more generally, we have seen that the "meaning construction" process involved during the interpretation of an utterance simply consists in the activation of parts of the network, and that inference is only involved on the implicit side of communication. As a result, semantics and (non-conventional) pragmatics are often put in opposition, with pragmatics simply bridging the gap left by semantics during the interpretation of an

---

[74] In that regard, Hoffmann (2022) is a nice exception.

utterance. This explains why, given the respective aims of the two theories, more or less room is given to lexical semantics. Relevance theorists explicitly focus on pragmatics (and hence reduce the role of semantics), whereas construction grammarians are primarily interested in linguistic knowledge (and hence reduce the role of pragmatics). In this section, I briefly want to argue that this (implicit) assumption is ill-founded. As mentioned in the previous section, semantics and pragmatics need not be put on opposite ends of some comprehension scale. Rather, they are two tightly intertwined aspects of the comprehension procedure. Therefore, it is possible to argue both for a rich type of semantics as well as for a ubiquitous type of pragmatics.

Many issues have been discussed in this chapter. If it has taught us anything, it is no doubt the observation that what is traditionally referred to as the semantics (or function) of a construction is not easily brought into consciousness and is not readily available for introspection. This observation explains why it is difficult to define exactly what lexical semantics is. For this very reason, I want to argue that it is not appropriate to discuss the function of constructions (i.e. lexemes, or larger patterns) in terms of *knowledge*. That is, the term knowledge can too easily be interpreted as though it is clear to individuals what it is that they have stored. The semantics of a particular construction, however, is (often) not consciously learned but unconsciously acquired, and the actual content is only manifest to us. Of course, in different contexts, different aspects of this content are particularly salient and accessible to an individual. But everything that is stored and composes the semantics of a particular construction can never be consciously accessed as a whole at a given time. Rather, the semantics of a particular lexeme only functions as meaning potential which is exploited in context to derive the speaker's intended interpretation.[75] (Note that the notion of meaning/semantic potential has also been used and discussed, though in different ways, by Halliday, 1973; Bezuidenhout, 2002; Allwood, 2003; Fauconnier and Turner, 2003; Croft and Cruse, 2004; Recanati, 2004; Evans and Green, 2006; Norén and Linell, 2007; La Mantia, 2018; Verschueren, 2018; Leclercq, 2022, inter alia.) That is, to put it slightly differently, we do not know concepts, but our minds make concepts

---

[75] This more or less relates to the distinction in philosophy between "knowing-that" and "knowing-how" (see Ryle, 1946; Fantl, 2017). In simple terms, knowledge-that consists in our propositional/theoretical understandings, while knowledge-how refers to the actual use of a specific capacity (mental or physical). I want to argue that (most of) the concepts we acquire originally constitute part of our knowledge-how. (I will come back to this in Chapter 4.) That is, we do not simply understand our concepts (know-that), but we actually know how to use these concepts in order to understand the world around us and engage in communication (know-how). Having and using concepts is therefore primarily a capacity of the mind. In philosophy, for instance, this perspective is defended by Robert Brandom (1998: 135). In linguistics, I believe it is a similar (although implicit) assumption that has led some linguists to describe semantics in terms of inferential rules (for instance). After all, the terms *norms* and *conventions* precisely describe practices (know-how) and not merely theoretical understandings (knowing-that).

available to us. This observation is what explains why it is possible to argue for both a rich type of semantics as well as a rich type of pragmatics. Our minds make available complex semantic structures which in different contexts will be exploited differently (see previous section).[76]

I have argued quite strongly in favor of the rich type of semantics adopted in CxG, the nature of which can be easily accommodated in a theory of pragmatics such as developed in RT. In the meantime, I have given little credit to the actual insights provided by RT on lexical pragmatics. In spite of storing complex conceptual networks, individuals still need to work out in context exactly what interpretation was intended by the speaker. Here, RT provides a very specific and detailed account of how we actually manage to do so: the relevance-based comprehension heuristics. It is important to point out that beyond making clear predictions about how we manage to communicate, these predictions have often been supported by empirical and experimental evidence (see Chapter 2). The development of experimental pragmatics is in fact largely due to the research carried out in RT when trying to test and provide evidence for the different claims of the theory (see Clark (2018) for a discussion). Of course, it will have become clear that I am not inclined to argue that inference is the main provider of meaning during the interpretation of an utterance. Nevertheless, it has been my aim to show that the underlying mechanism that RT presents concerning the interpretation process is very convincing.

3.6   Conclusion

Understanding exactly what lexical semantics and pragmatics are as well as determining how each of them actually contributes to the interpretation of an utterance is no simple task. In this chapter, I have tried to combine insights from CxG and RT to answer this difficult question. First, I tried to show the challenge involved in identifying what relevance theorists assume lexical semantics to consist of. It was shown that the commitment to referential atomism often made within RT is incompatible with some of the most central developments of the theory. I have suggested that the type of semantics adopted in CxG in terms of rich conceptual networks seems to be best suited at both the descriptive and theoretical levels. The difficulty with this perspective is to understand exactly

---

[76] More generally, one could ask whether we actually *know* a language or whether we simply *have* a language that our minds make available to us. As far as our native language is concerned, I am inclined to argue in favor of the latter option. The fallacy that we *know* a language comes from the simple fact that any use of language (i.e. linguistic performance) is directly accessible to us and often serves as the basis for introspection. Yet we do not directly have access to the linguistic system (i.e. linguistic competence). It is rather clear in most introductory textbooks to linguistics that linguists look at linguistic performance to draw conclusions about linguistic competence. This is evidence that we only *have* a language. This also seems an assumption shared by Croft (to appear) who recently argued against a focus on mental representations.

how much pragmatics is involved during the interpretation process and whether it still has a place in a theory of communication. I have strongly argued that, in spite of storing rich conceptual networks, individuals still have to reconstruct in context the intended interpretation in accordance with their expectations of relevance. From this perspective, the interpretation of a lexical construction systematically involves the complex combination of both semantics and pragmatics. On the basis of the work of Depraetere, I have suggested that interpreting a particular construction systematically requires a *lexically regulated saturation* process, whereby the rich conceptual networks that constitute its function provide the underlying structure against which the interpretation process operates. This process, however, is primarily pragmatic, and is carried out in accordance with our expectations of relevance following the comprehension procedure spelled out in RT.

4   Understanding Lexemes
The Role of the Linguistic Co-Text

Combining insights from CxG and RT might seem quite daunting for those working in the two frameworks since, in spite of their common interest in understanding human communication, they focus on different aspects of it. On the one hand, the main aim of construction grammarians is to understand language as a system and to pin down exactly what makes up linguistic knowledge. The central claim of the theory is that speakers primarily know constructions, i.e. form–meaning pairs. Goldberg (2003: 223) specifically argues that it is "constructions all the way down." On the other hand, relevance theorists mostly try to account for the cognitive principles that, in addition to the linguistic system, guarantee successful communication. This pragmatic approach to (linguistic) communication is essentially based on the observation that language alone often fails to provide us with the speaker's intended interpretation. Carston (2002a: 360) asserts that "it is linguistic underdetermi-nacy all the way down." It should therefore be clear that the two theories make radically different predictions concerning how much knowledge an individual actually has, and how this knowledge contributes to the interpretation of an utterance. In the case of CxG, individuals are credited with much more knowledge than in RT, and this knowledge is believed to play a greater role in comprehension than is assumed in RT. Contrary to what one might think, however, these two perspectives are not incompatible. We saw in the previous chapter, for instance, that understanding a lexeme is a multifaceted process that involves a complex interaction between semantics and pragmatics whereby lexemes give access to rich conceptual networks that are exploited differently in different contexts in accordance with one's expectations of relevance. The term *lexically regulated saturation* was used precisely to capture the observa-tion that understanding a lexeme is neither just a semantic nor just a pragmatic process but in fact results from the interaction of semantics and pragmatics.

The aim of this chapter is to broaden the approach to lexical semantics–pragmatics. Further insights from CxG and RT will be integrated to arrive at a more encompassing view. It might have occurred to the reader that the approach adopted in the previous chapter remains relatively lexeme-centered. Beyond the extra-linguistic environment in which lexemes are used, little attention has been given to the linguistic co-text in which they can be found and how it affects the interpretation of lexemes. Yet one of the very reasons I decided to write this book in the first place was also to assess lexemes in the broader linguistic and non-linguistic contexts and to show how this interaction affects our understanding of lexical items. (Indeed, CxG and RT focus almost exclusively either on the linguistic environment of a lexeme or on extra-linguistic factors.) The goal of this chapter is to show that an adequate appreci-ation of lexical semantics–pragmatics necessarily has to take into account the larger linguistic structures in which lexemes are embedded. It is divided into three sections. In Sections 4.1 and 4.2, two concepts will be discussed: the notion of *coercion* discussed in CxG (see Section 2.1.3) and that of *procedural meaning* introduced in RT (see Section 2.2.3.2). In Section 4.1, I will address the notion of coercion and show that the morphosyntactic environment in which lexemes occur directly affects their interpretation. At the same time, the pragmatic roots of coercion will be highlighted. In Section 4.2, I will investigate the notion of procedural meaning introduced in RT. The main aim is to try and spell out exactly what procedures consist of and to identify the types of unit that encode such (procedural) semantics. Eventually, a link will be drawn between the two notions and I will suggest that they are intimately related: constructions that have a coercive force have procedural meaning, the specific nature of which will be redefined. In Section 4.3, I will focus on more idiomatic (in the CxG sense of lexically fixed) patterns in which lexemes are found and which contribute in their own way to the interpretation of an utterance. It will be shown that while interpreting a lexeme often depends on the recognition of such sequences, the interpretation process of idiomatic patterns is also achieved pragmatically. In the end, a link will be drawn between the process of lexically regulated saturation and all of the concepts discussed in this chapter. This will enable me to show that it is lexically regulated saturation all the way down.

4.1   Coercion

The idea that understanding the meaning of a lexeme depends crucially on its morphosyntactic environment is a central assumption in CxG. It is assumed that the interpretation of a lexical construction is (almost) always a function of the larger constructions in which it occurs. Relevance theorists most probably agree with this approach. Yet, as mentioned before, there is a clear tendency in RT to focus on lexemes only when doing lexical semantics–pragmatics. As a result, the same set of sentences may be analyzed completely differently in CxG and RT. Take, for instance, the sentences in (66) and (67). In these two sentences, a lexical item receives an interpretation which includes aspects of meaning that are not originally part of its semantics. In the sentence in (66), for instance, the verb *behave* receives an unusual metaphorical 'manner of motion' interpretation. In the sentence in (67), the denominal verb *carrier pigeon* is interpreted in terms of a transfer.

(66)   You can't talk your way out of something you *behaved* your way into. You have to *behave* your way out of it. (Twitter, @DougConant, 9 jan. 2016)

(67)   They *carrier pigeoned* me an invite this morning. (Twitter, @KyleShoreBBCAN, 3 jul. 2014)

In the two frameworks, however, the origin of these interpretations is located at two different levels. According to relevance theorists, these examples represent two cases of lexical adjustment, the pragmatic nature of which leads to the derivation of a context-specific ad hoc concept. In this approach, the (re)interpretation of these lexemes is argued to be pragmatic-ally motivated by one's expectations of relevance. On the constructionist account, however, the (re)interpretation process is primarily semantically motivated. It is argued that the specific interpretation of the lexemes is due to their being used in a larger construction the meaning of which is coerced onto that of the lexical item, hence the term 'coercion' (cf. Lauwers and Willems, 2011: 1219). In (66) and (67), it is the WAY construction and the DITRANSITIVE construction, respectively, that determine the meaning of the lexemes *behave* and *carrier pigeon* (see below).

These contrasting analyses naturally have to be interpreted within the frame-work of each theory. The aim of this section is to look more deeply into the notion of coercion as well as to investigate the possibility of a more compre-hensive understanding of the concept.[77] It will become clear that the main difficulty is to pin down the nature of the process involved (semantic or pragmatic). In Sections 4.1.1 to 4.1.3, I will consider the RT approach and the CxG approach and will discuss their respective limits. It will eventually be argued, in Section 4.1.4, that the combination of the two theories provides interesting insights into coercion, which will be discussed in terms of a semantically constrained pragmatic process.

4.1.1   Relevance Theory and 'Free' Pragmatic Enrichment

Relevance theorists look at examples that constructionists have treated in terms of coercion, but the term *coercion* itself is not used in the relevance-theoretic literature.[78] As will become clear, relevance theorists generally do not distin-guish examples of coercion from other cases of lexical adjustment, all of which they analyze in terms of a single process of pragmatic enrichment. Before looking exactly at what the term coercion is meant to capture in CxG, I briefly

---

[77] Parts of this section were published in Leclercq (2019).
[78] A noticeable exception is Escandell-Vidal and Leonetti (2002, 2011). See Section 4.2.2.

want to discuss again the relevance-theoretic approach. Consider the sentences in (68) to (69).

(68)   Buying a house is easy if you've got *money*. (Wilson and Carston, 2007: 235)

(69)   I have a terrible cold, I need a *Kleenex*. (Sperber and Wilson, 2005: 370)

The sentences in (68) and (69) include a lexical item that receives an interpretation which is either narrower or broader than the encoded concept. In the sentence in (68), *money* has to be understood in the narrow sense of 'suitable amount of money'. *Kleenex*, in (69), is used in the broader sense to refer to any disposable tissue. In Relevance Theory, these specific concepts are referred to as ad hoc concepts, and are differentiated from the original (encoded) concept by marking them with an asterisk: MONEY*, KLEENEX* (Clark, 2013a: 249). What is important for our discussion is that the derivation of these ad hoc concepts is argued to be not linguistically but pragmatically motivated. That is, it is not the linguistic items that motivate this adjustment. Rather, they are created online by the hearer only to satisfy their expectations of (optimal) relevance. These concepts are therefore said to result from an inferential process of "free" pragmatic enrichment since they are the outcome of an optional process of enrichment.[79]

In this framework, examples that are treated in CxG in terms of *coercion* are analyzed in the same way as those in (68) to (69). In fact, they are generally included among other examples illustrating ad hoc concept creation, such as those in (70) to (72).

(70)   Federer is the new *Sampras*. (Wilson, 2003: 276)

(71)   He *Houdinied* his way out of the closet. (Wilson, 2003: 277)

(72)   The boy *porched* the newspaper. (Wilson and Carston, 2007: 238)

Sampras is used in the sentence in (70) not to refer specifically to the tennis player, but more generally to the category of good (or best) tennis players, to which both Roger Federer and Pete Sampras belong. In this case, it is argued that the original concept SAMPRAS made accessible by the noun is broadened and the ad hoc concept SAMPRAS* is inferentially derived by the hearer to meet their expectations of relevance. Similarly, in (71) and (72), the interpretations of the two denominal verbs *Houdinied* and *porched* are said to involve the creation of the ad hoc concepts HOUDINI* and PORCH*, where both the manner of motion interpretation of *Houdinied* in (71) and the action of throwing the newspaper to the porch in (72) are assumed to be entirely pragmatically inferred.

Within Relevance Theory, therefore, the interpretation process of the sentences in (70) to (72) is no different from that of the sentences in (68) to (69). In

---

[79] See Chapters 2 and 3 for a critical discussion of this view.

both cases it is considered to be an inferential process that is pragmatically motivated by the need for the hearer to arrive at a relevant interpretation, i.e. to arrive at an interpretation that provides enough cognitive effects to justify their processing effort. In CxG, however, the sentences in (70) to (72) receive a different treatment from those in (68) and (69). It is argued that the interpretation of the different lexemes is not pragmatically but linguistically motivated by the larger constructions in which they occur, their meanings being coerced onto the lexemes.[80]

4.1.2   Construction Grammar: Coercion

A central assumption in CxG is that it is not only morphemes, words or idioms that have construction status (i.e. conventionally associate a form with a meaning), but also the larger 'syntactic' structures in which they occur, which have their own semantic or discourse functions (see Section 2.1.1). Construction grammarians have in particular (but not only) focused on the construction status of argument structures. It is argued, for instance, that the sentences in (73) and (74) instantiate (among others) two specific constructions: respectively the CAUSED-MOTION construction (see Goldberg, 1995: 152) and the WAY construction (see Israel, 1996: 218).

(73)   a. She put the plate in front of him. (BNC, written)
        b. A child threw a stone at the horse, which bolted. (BNC, written)
        c. I moved them into a tank of their own. (BNC, written)

(74)   a. Craig made his way to the attic. (BNC, written)
        b. Annabel wormed her way into the circle around Kezia with a plate of smoked salmon sandwiches. (BNC, written)
        c. How do you navigate your way through a forest, especially if you're in a wheelchair? (BNC, written)

From this perspective, the meaning 'X causes Y to move Z' in the sentences in (73) is supposedly associated with the form [SUBJ V OBJ OBL], which together form the CAUSED-MOTION construction. Similarly, it is argued that the manner of motion meaning identified in the sentences in (74) is associated with the form [SUBJ V *one's way* OBL], which together form the WAY construction (see Chapter 1, Section 2.1.1). It is these two constructions that explain how the verb *push*, a prototypical use of which can be found in (75a), actually expresses caused-motion in the sentence in (75b) or manner of motion in (75c).

(75)   a. Excuse me, did you just *push* me? (BNC, spoken)
        b. The lieutenant *pushed* the box across the table. (BNC, written)
        c. Mike *pushed* his way into the canteen. (BNC, written)

---

[80] See Section 4.1.5 for a comparison between the RT and CxG treatments.

These interpretations follow from the use of the verb in the CAUSED-MOTION construction and the WAY construction, the respective meanings of which contribute to the understanding of *push*. In this case, given that *push* encodes a meaning similar to that of the two constructions in which it occurs (i.e. the verb *push* also semantically involves the notion of motion), it is argued that the lexeme is semantically compatible with the constructions and easily combines (or fuses) with each of them (Yoon, 2012: 3).

However, lexemes and constructions are not always semantically compatible. Sometimes the semantics of a particular lexical item does not fit the semantics of the construction in which it occurs. In the sentence in (71) for instance (repeated here in (76)), the proper noun *Houdini* is far from the prototypical manner-of-motion verb that we expect to find in that position in the WAY construction.

(76)   He *Houdinied* his way out of the closet. (Wilson, 2003: 277)

There is a semantic (and morphosyntactic) mismatch that needs to be resolved. And in this case, it is argued that the lexeme *Houdini* will be reinterpreted in accordance with the semantics of the WAY construction.[81] From this perspective, there is little overlap between the constructionist and the relevance-theoretic accounts. According to constructionists, the 'manner of motion' meaning identified in (76) is not pragmatically inferred to meet the hearer's expectation of relevance, but is provided by the WAY construction in which the noun *Houdini* occurs. That is, it is already semantically specified. The reinterpretation of the lexeme is linguistically required to solve the mismatch between the lexeme and the construction. This is where coercion occurs: in case of a semantic (and morphosyntactic) mismatch, the meaning of the construction is coerced onto the meaning of the lexeme.

As mentioned in Section 2.1.3, the term *coercion* was used in other fields of research before CxG adopted it. In those different frameworks, the notion is used to describe slightly different phenomena. Nevertheless, CxG shares with them the view that coercion is concerned with the resolution of an incompatibility between a selector (e.g. argument structure constructions) and a selected (e.g. lexemes) whereby the latter adapts to the former. In CxG, this observation has been worded by Michaelis (2004) in terms of the override principle, which

---

[81] A reviewer pointed out that examples such as in (76) might go against a CxG account since *way* doesn't seem to be crucial and can easily be replaced by *himself* (as in *He Houdinied himself out of the closet*). This example does not challenge the CxG approach, however, since it belongs to the same family of RESULTATIVE constructions as that exemplified by the example with *himself* (cf. Peña Cervel, 2017). The semantic similarity between the two examples is therefore to be expected given the respective constructions used.

states that the meaning of a lexeme accommodates to that of its morphosyntactic environment in case of a mismatch between the two (Michaelis, 2004: 25).

In the next sections, I will discuss some of the weaknesses that reduce the explanatory power of each of the two theories, and I will propose a more comprehensive understanding of coercion which merges them. In particular, the aim is to pin down the exact origin (semantic or pragmatic) of this phenomenon. Before doing so, I will illustrate the constructionist approach with a couple of other examples:

(77)   The people swarming around were clamoring for more beer, but the owner was intransigent: every three beers you had to order a *rice* with fried fish. (COCA, written)

(78)   I think Ph.D. is the new *masters*. (V. Fung, p.c., 12 dec. 2016)[82]

(79)   Ed *hammered* the metal flat. (Boas, 2011: 1272)

In each of these sentences, a lexical item receives an interpretation with which it is not conventionally associated. In the sentence in (77), *rice* receives an unusual countable interpretation. In the sentence in (78), *masters* is used metonymically to refer to the type of degree that one needs to hold in order to stand out in the job market. In (79), the denominal verb *hammered* refers to the action of using a hammer in such a way as to make the metal become flat. From the relevance-theoretic standpoint, one might want to argue that the interpretation of those lexemes involves the pragmatic derivation of the ad hoc concepts RICE*, MASTERS* and HAMMER*. From the constructionist perspective, however, their interpretation largely depends on the function of the larger constructions in which they occur. In the case of *rice*, for instance, the countable interpretation results from its being used in the INDEFINITE DETERMINATION construction (Michaelis, 2004: 27), further instances of which can be found in (80).

(80)   INDEFINITE DETERMINATION construction – [*a* NOUN]
         a. We may even rent **a hall**. (COCA, spoken)
         b. Buffer is **a word**. (COCA, spoken)
         c. Ninety-five percent of what the President says is not **a lie**. (COCA, spoken)

It is clear from these examples that this (partially schematic) construction usually selects countable nouns. Michaelis (2004: 27) argues that countability is inherent in the semantics of the construction. From this perspective, the countable interpretation of *rice* in (77) in terms of a serving of rice simply

---

[82] This sentence was used during a conversation on whether holding a masters degree still made a difference in the UK, especially in terms of attractiveness on the job market.

follows from the fact that it occurs in the INDEFINITE DETERMINATION construction, the semantics of which is coerced onto the lexeme. A similar explanation in terms of coercion holds for the examples in (78) and (79). The metonymic interpretation of *masters* in (78), for instance, takes its root in the X *is the new* Y construction (cf. Dancygier and Sweetser, 2014: 154).

(81)   X *is the new* Y construction
  a. **The garden is the new kitchen**. (COCA, written)
  b. There was a time when raising your voice was considered okay for parents to do, but now **screaming is the new spanking**. (COCA, written)
  c. In case you didn't get the message, **texting is the new talking**. (COCA, written)

The examples in (81) are typical instances of the X *is the new* Y construction. In this construction, the X and Y elements are systematically interpreted metonymically in relation to some larger category. In (81a), *garden* and *kitchen* are used to refer to that part of our houses in which we are ready to invest a lot of money. In (81b), *screaming* and *spanking* refer to parenting methods that are judged unacceptable. Finally, in (81c), *texting* and *talking* are used to talk about the main channel of communication teenagers use. The metonymic interpretation of the X and Y elements is argued to be part of the semantics of the X *is the new* Y construction (Dancygier and Sweetser, 2014: 154). From the constructionist standpoint, the interpretation of *masters* in example (78) above therefore follows from its being used inside this construction from which the (metonymic) interpretation is coerced.[83]

It is also coercion that can explain the use of *hammer* in (79), *Ed hammered the metal flat*. In this case, *hammer* is used in the RESULTATIVE construction, and it is the semantics of this construction that (in part) explains the interpretation of the lexeme in terms of causality. Consider the following examples:

(82)   RESULTATIVE construction – [SUBJ V OBJ RESP]
  a. **He licks the plate clean** and looks up at us. (COCA, written)
  b. **These people drive me crazy**. (COCA, written)
  c. **My mother shook my father awake**. (COCA, written)

In all of these examples, the form [SUBJ V OBJ RESP] is associated with a particular resultative (or 'cause to become') interpretation which together form the RESULTATIVE construction (see Boas, 2003). For instance, in the sentence in (82c), we understand that 'my mother' is the reason for 'my father' to be awake as a result of her having shaken him. It is the semantics of this

---

[83] Naturally, although the metonymic framing is part of the construction's semantics, the exact category that the items in the X and Y positions actually refer to has to "be supplied by the hearer from accessible knowledge or context" (Dancygier and Sweetser, 2014: 154). The pragmatic roots of coercion will be discussed more fully in the next sections.

construction which provides (part of) the interpretation of *hammer* in (79) above. The particular resultative interpretation of the lexeme comes from the semantics of the construction in which it occurs. That is, the meaning of the lexeme accommodates to that of the construction (i.e. coercion). Its interpretation here is therefore not (solely) pragmatically motivated.

4.1.3 Creation of Ad Hoc Concepts or Mismatch Resolution: Respective Limits

CxG and RT contribute differently to the understanding of lexical semantics–pragmatics. The main challenge is to understand how to analyze sentences for which they provide contrasting analyses, such as those we just saw in the case of coercion. The aim of this section is to try and understand whether a more comprehensive understanding of this notion is possible. In order to do so, I will first discuss some of the weaknesses of CxG and RT. It will be shown that the respective limits of each theory actually represent the strength of the other.

The relevance-theoretic analysis, I want to argue, suffers from not distinguishing between coercion and other cases of meaning adjustment, as is done (although not explicitly) in CxG. For instance, it is argued that in all of the sentences in (83) and (84) the interpretation of the lexeme in italics involves the derivation of an ad hoc concept which is pragmatically inferred by the hearer in order to meet their expectations of relevance (i.e. the derivation of these ad hoc concepts is argued to be entirely pragmatically motivated by the search for relevance).

(83)   Either you become a *human being* or you leave the group. (Wilson and Carston, 2007: 242)

(84)   a. Federer is the new *Sampras*. (Wilson, 2003: 276)
        b. Handguns are the new *flick-knives*. (Wilson and Carston, 2007: 237)
        c. Ironing is the new *yoga*. (Wilson and Carston, 2007: 237)

This unitary approach can be easily explained by looking at the general scope of the theory. Within the relevance-theoretic framework, meaning is (almost) systematically discussed in relation to lexemes only. This is most probably due to one of the major aims of the theory, namely to explain the nature of lexical concepts (see Chapter 3). Comparatively little attention is given to morphemes, idioms or larger constructions, and in particular to how they interact with one another. It follows quite naturally from this perspective that the specific interpretations of (83) and (84) should receive the same analysis since in both cases the interpretation of the highlighted lexemes requires more than accessing their semantic content (see underdeterminacy thesis in Section 2.2.2).

From a constructionist point of view, however, different factors affect the interpretation of the sentences in (83) and (84). Both these factors are external to the lexemes used but are of a different nature. While for (83), construction-ists might agree that the interpretation of *human being* (in terms of an educated, well-behaved person) is derived pragmatically,[84] they would not agree that this is also the case for the lexemes identified in (84). In the sentences in (84), the lexemes *Sampras, flick-knives* and *yoga* are all understood as metonymically referring to a more generic category they stand for (respectively here, that of good tennis players, favorite weapons of choice and anti-stress activities). Constructionists readily recognize that this particular meaning is not part of the semantics of the lexemes themselves. Nevertheless, they do not fully attribute it to pragmatics either. Rather, they consider that this meaning (i.e. the reference to a larger, representative category) belongs to the X *is the new* Y construction in which these lexemes occur (see previous section). That is, this meaning is not entirely derived pragmatically, but it actually belongs to the particular construction in which the lexemes occur. In other words, the meaning is already linguistically (i.e. semantically) provided by the construction before being coerced onto the lexeme that occurs within it.

As will become clear in the following paragraphs, one of the challenges is to understand exactly how coercion operates, i.e. how the meaning of the con-struction becomes part of the meaning of the lexeme. First, however, it is important to underline that this view clearly contradicts the unitary treatment given in Relevance Theory, that is, solely in terms of pragmatics. And more specifically, it invites proponents of the relevance-theoretic tradition to recon-sider their analysis of sentences like those in (84), in particular by acknowledg-ing the construction status of (among other) argument structures, and the semantic origin of the reinterpretation of the lexemes that occur inside them. After all, these constructions have been given a lot of attention both within and outside CxG, from both theoretical and empirical perspectives (see Section 2.1.1 for references). Note that relevance theorists do not explicitly reject the possibility that larger, more abstract constructions might exist and be used. In fact, they most probably would agree there are such constructions. But there is a clear lack of identification of these patterns by relevance theorists, who prefer to play the 'all-pragmatics' card which, outside the pragmatics literature, many find unattractive. As I see it, it is essential to actually integrate larger constructions into a relevance-theoretic analysis and accept that not all meaning adjustment can be explained via pragmatics only. Such a move will strengthen the relevance-theoretic approach both at the descriptive and the theoretical levels and will thus enhance its explanatory potential.[85]

---

[84] In CxG, the interpretation of *human being* results from a conceptual mapping with the THING-FOR-PROPERTY-OF-THE-THING-metonymy, a cognitive process which is performed pragmatically (cf. Panther and Thornburg, 2003, 2007; see also Langacker, 2008: 40–42).

[85] Recently, such a move was made by Padilla Cruz (2022) when he points out that the interpret-ation of lexical items is not solely the result of pragmatic inferencing (i.e. of 'free' pragmatic

Perhaps the main difficulty for RT is to understand what type of semantics is encoded by those constructions and how exactly they contribute to the interpretation of the lexemes that occur within them. This will be discussed later in this chapter. More generally, however, bringing the constructional ideas on coercion within the relevance-theoretic approach seems quite feasible. However, some have argued precisely against it. For instance, Ziegeler (2007a, 2007b) strongly argues against adopting the constructionist perspective on coercion for natural languages and in favor of pragmatic accounts.[86] Interestingly, a critical analysis of her arguments provides a nice transition to discussing some limits of the CxG view on the matter and how they may be overcome. There are two main reasons why Ziegeler argues against the notion of coercion. First, she argues that postulating coercion by referring to the semantics of constructions is unnecessary given that the reinterpretation of the lexemes involved can be solely explained in terms of analogy, metonymy or metaphor (Ziegeler, 2007b). For instance, she discusses the following example:

(85)   She had a *beer.* (Ziegeler, 2007b: 1009)

She argues that the interpretation of the lexeme *beer* as 'a glass of beer' does not result from its being coerced by the INDEFINITE DETERMINATION construction (*a* NOUN) but rather is made possible by the CONTAINED FOR CONTAINER metonymy which pragmatically enables us to understand the lexeme. A couple of points are in order here, however. First, it is true that the example in (85) can also be explained in terms of this particular metonymy (and not only in terms of coercion, with the INDEFINITE DETERMINATION construction projecting its countable semantics onto the lexeme *beer*). Yet it is not clear why this necessarily provides a counter-argument to coercion by construction. There is no denying that this metonymic pattern has a role to play in the interpretation process (quite the contrary, see below), but it is exploited only because *beer* here occurs with the indefinite determiner, which is not expected given that it is a mass noun. Nevertheless, Ziegeler does not wish to call this a case of constructional coercion and insists that the interpretation process involved here is purely a matter of lexical pragmatics which involves metonymy.

In order to understand this perspective, it must be noted that Ziegeler finds more attractive accounts that "assume no *a priori* syntactic constructions" (Ziegeler, 2007b: 1024). The type of coercion presented in CxG, however, exists only because there are 'syntactic' constructions and, indeed, without such constructions, there is no (constructional) coercion. However, there is ample evidence that individuals do store and use these more schematic

---

enrichment) but that it is also mandated by the linguistic environment. Besides co-textual lexical triggers, he looks at evaluative morphemes in Spanish.
[86] Note that Ziegeler does not identify herself as a relevance theorist.

constructions, and this challenges Ziegeler's view.[87] Gonzálvez-García (2011) provides a detailed counter-argumentation to Ziegeler and very nicely shows that metonymy and metaphor alone cannot always explain cases of coercion. That is, the construction types discussed in CxG do contribute to the interpretation of the lexemes. Take the following example:

(86)   When a visitor passes through the village, young lamas stop picking up trash to mug for the camera. A gruff 'police monk' *barks* them to work. (Gonzálvez-García, 2011: 1317)

Gonzálvez-García recognizes that the use of the denominal verb *barks* in (86) requires a metaphorical mapping from the domain of dogs to that of human beings from which the 'police monk' can be understood as emitting particularly loud sounds. This part of the interpretation of *bark* is undoubtedly pragmatically derived. However, in this context, *bark* is primarily used to communicate the particular way in which the lamas are caused to go back to work by the monk. This caused-motion part of the interpretation cannot be explained in terms of metonymic or metaphorical mappings. It can, however, be explained in terms of the meaning of the CAUSED-MOTION construction (i.e. [SUBJ V OBJ OBL], see above) in which *bark* occurs. That is, part of the interpretation of the lexeme *bark* here is made readily available by the semantics of the (argument structure) construction in which it occurs. Constructions such as the CAUSED-MOTION construction therefore directly contribute to the interpretation of the lexemes found inside them (Gonzálvez-García, 2011: 1310). In other words, Gonzálvez-García convincingly shows that Ziegeler's view is flawed.

The recognition of the role played by metaphor and metonymy does not render superfluous the assumption that syntax in general and constructions in particular, understood as meaning-function correspondences, play an essential role in the phenomenon of slot-determined meaning in sentences involving coercion. (Gonzálvez-García, 2011: 1310)[88]

In spite of this observation, there is another, more fundamental, reason why Ziegeler is uneasy with the notion of coercion (and which, in fact, is much more consequential than that mentioned previously). When Ziegeler argues against coercion, she seems to be arguing against the view according to which constructions themselves automatically coerce their meanings onto the lexemes (Ziegeler, 2007b: 1005). In this case, coercion is a purely linguistic product whereby constructions act upon lexemes independently of the language user. However, Ziegeler (2007b: 999) strongly argues that it is the language user, not language itself, that can change the meaning of a particular word. In other

---

[87] The question of whether 'syntactic' constructions exist falls outside the scope of this chapter. I largely endorse the constructionist perspective. See Section 2.1 for specific references.

[88] For a similar observation, see Harder (2010: 247).

words, to use Lauwers and Willem's (2011: 1224) terminology, she favors the position of a 'language-user' coercion as opposed to a 'systemic' coercion. Note, however, that although she is most probably right to consider that coercion is not an automatic linguistic device (see below), she is wrong in assuming that this is the perspective adopted in CxG.

It is true that there are (many) unfortunate formulations that might have led Ziegeler to this particular conclusion. Goldberg (1995: 159), for instance, says that some meanings "are capable of being coerced *by particular constructions*" (original emphasis). In this case, she could indeed be understood to be suggesting that constructions themselves change the semantics of the lexemes that occur within them. Because of her firm cognitive (usage-based) orientation, however, it is unlikely that Goldberg or any of her followers think of coercion as a purely linguistic device. She explicitly attributes the creative potential of language, which involves cases of coercion, to speakers themselves and not to grammar: "grammars don't generate sentences, speakers do" (Goldberg, 2006: 22)[89]. It is mainly construction grammarians taking a strong formal approach to language who could be reproached for adopting a 'systemic' view of coercion. Lauwers and Willem (2011: 1225) argue that this is precisely what Michaelis (2004) does, for instance. Indeed, she refers to the "override principle" as a "coercion mechanism" whereby the semantics of the construction simply "wins out" over that of the lexeme (Michaelis, 2004: 25). In this case, the language user is only a witness to the linguistic mechanism. Once again, however, it is not clear whether Michaelis really conceives of coercion as such a strictly linguistic device. Consider the following quote:

Coercion effects are triggered when *the interpreter* must reconcile the meaning of a morphosyntactic construction with the meaning of a lexical filler. Coercion effects, rather than representing a special form of composition, are by-products of the ordinary significations of constructions. (Michaelis, 2004: 7; emphasis mine)

This strongly suggests that Michaelis also recognizes the role of the language user during the interpretation process which is triggered by the semantic mismatch.[90] Consider the following example:

(87)   ZAK BUSH: Talk me through your transition from professional surfer to writer.
        JAMIE BRISICK: I guess you could say I *back-doored* my way into writing.[91]

---

[89] A similar statement is made by Langacker (1987: 65), see Chapter 2.

[90] It is interesting to note that Ziegeler's (2007b) understanding of the various constructionist perspectives on coercion differs radically from mine. One the one hand, she reproaches Goldberg (1995) for being too systemic, and on the other, she appreciates Michaelis' (2004) more user-based approach. Yet it seems clear to me (as it does to Lauwers and Willem, 2011: 1225) that the more formal approach to constructions developed by Michaelis renders her view relatively more systemic than that defended by Goldberg.

[91] Zak Bush interviewing Jamie Brisick for the Outerknown Journey blog in 2017 (no longer available).

When arguing that there is coercion in (87), for instance, constructionists only refer to the semantic (and morphosyntactic) mismatch between the (poly)lexeme *back-door* and the WAY construction that, in context, the hearer has to resolve. The noun *back-door* is indeed not the prototypical 'manner of motion' verb that one expects to find in the WAY construction. Most of the time, the lexeme is reinterpreted in accordance with the semantics of the construction (see override principle above). In the sentence in (87), this observation is confirmed since the denominal verb *back-door* indeed includes the (metaphorical) 'manner of motion' sense that originally belongs to the WAY construction. Nevertheless, it is also clear to constructionists that the resolution process is carried out by speakers/hearers themselves in context and not by the language. As a consequence, there is no particular reason for relevance theorists not to adopt the constructional view on coercion and recognize the semantic origin of the interpretation.[92]

Now, in spite of the observations just made, Ziegeler (2007a: 105) rightly observes that constructionists "tend to pass over the role of the language user in the interpretive process." For instance, it is indeed not clear how the lexeme *back-door* inherits aspects of meaning from the WAY construction in (87). In a similar way, Yoon (2012: 7) says that the "the psychological process toward the resolution [is] not dealt with." That is, although they argue that the resolution process is performed by the language user, construction grammarians indeed fail to explain exactly how this process operates. And this is exactly where insights from Relevance Theory become very useful. While constructionists do not address in detail the role of language users, it will have become

---

[92] It could of course be argued that viewing coercion as a *language-user* or a *systemic* process might also depend on whether one takes the perspective of the speaker or the hearer. It is true, after all, that while speakers are (relatively) free to choose between different options to express the same thought (hence more user-dependent), the interpretation process carried out by hearers is directly guided by the linguistic items used by the speaker (hence more system-dependent). Unfortunately, the reality of how coercion operates seems more complex. First, speakers are not entirely free to create novel expressions as they please and are in their own way also subject to the system pressure. In CxG, it has been shown that creating novel sentences also largely depends on a number of crucial properties of the linguistic system, which they refer to in terms of *productivity, coverage, competition* and *statistical preemption* (see Chapter 2). Second, it is also clear in RT that, like hearers, speakers are constrained by the 'principle of relevance' (i.e. they need to provide the hearer with a *relevant* interpretation), and therefore they need to choose linguistic items that will guarantee the relevance of the intended interpretation (cf. Sperber and Wilson, 1995: 157). This has been discussed by Park and Clark (2022) in terms of a relevance-focused production heuristics. From this perspective, speakers are therefore not so free after all. In this book, focus is placed on the interpretation process from the perspective of the hearer. For more information on how speakers are constrained by the linguistic system, the reader is invited to look at the references mentioned in Chapter 2. In the rest of this chapter, it will be shown that although constrained by the linguistic items used by the speaker, the particular interpretation process referred to as 'coercion' is not performed by the linguistic system directly (and is not, therefore, systemic) but remains primarily a pragmatic process carried out by hearers themselves.

clear from the previous chapters that relevance theorists can. This is precisely when a cross-theoretical understanding of coercion becomes possible and even beneficial to both theories. Where constructionists are able to identify the source of the reinterpretation process (i.e. the semantic mismatch between a lexeme and a construction), relevance theorists can explain the strategy used to resolve the incompatibility. In particular, this strategy is the relevance-theoretic comprehension procedure mentioned in Chapter 2. What exactly does this procedure entail? Consider again the sentence in (87), for instance. If RT were to adopt the insights from CxG, the argument would go along the following lines: in accordance with their expectations of relevance, on the basis of their knowledge of the two constructions (the noun *back-door* and the WAY construction), as well as taking into account extra-linguistic information, the hearer will look for an interpretation that provides them with sufficient cognitive effects to justify the amount of effort put into the resolution process. From this perspective, it is relatively clear that the resolution process is more complex than just copy-pasting (to put it simply) the meaning of the construction onto that of the lexeme. Rather, the hearer has to inferentially work out exactly what interpretation was intended by the speaker when creatively putting together seemingly incompatible constructions, i.e. looking for the particular way in which the speaker is observing the principle of relevance.

This analysis receives support from experimental data (Yoon, 2012; Busso, Perek and Lenci, 2021). For instance, Yoon (2012) conducted a series of experiments in order to find evidence for the possibility that coercion is not a binary distinction (that is, coercion either takes place or does not), but that there is instead a cline of semantic (in)compatibility between constructions and lexemes. These experiments particularly involved looking at the hearer's processing effort (by measuring processing time) during the resolution process.[93] Some of her results corroborate relevance-theoretic predictions (in terms of a balance between cognitive effects and effort) as to the resolution process. She shows that the less semantically compatible a lexeme is with a construction, the more processing effort the resolution process requires (i.e. more processing time). Yoon (2012: 261) obviously sees these results as evidence that there is indeed a continuum of coercion events (more or less compatible combinations require more or less processing effort). Yet this is first and foremost evidence that coercion is not a purely linguistic device but that language users are particularly involved in the resolution process, i.e. that the meaning of the construction does not simply 'win out' over that of the lexeme, in order to derive a *relevant* interpretation (see also Yoon, 2012: 310). If the meaning of the construction simply won out over that of the lexeme, then different coercion events should result in the same cognitive process regardless

---

[93] She uses acceptability judgment tasks (Yoon, 2012: 57).

of the incompatibility. Yoon convincingly shows, however, that "coercion is not a binary concept" (Yoon, 2012: 158). Rather, coercion involves inferential pragmatic processes which require hearers to take into account extra-linguistic factors. Here, RT can help determine exactly how this process is carried out.

4.1.4   Coercion and Context-Sensitivity: Further Evidence

It could be argued that many of the examples I used in the previous section contradict the perspective I am trying to present here (in purely inferential terms) and suggest that perhaps coercion does not involve the same type of inferential process as that involved, for instance, during the process of *lexically regulated saturation* discussed in the previous chapter. Indeed, many of the examples I have used so far include only one sentence and their interpretation seems rather clear. This could be taken as evidence that the larger (extra-linguistic) context may not have as much of a role to play in the interpretation of coerced lexemes. In this section, I will provide examples that challenge and contradict this argument and I will show that the extra-linguistic context also plays a major role in the interpretation of coerced lexemes. This discussion will show the need to combine the constructionist and the relevance-theoretic approaches and stress the inferential roots of coercion. It is worth noting that the cognitive linguist Peter Harder also discusses the process of coercion in inferential terms:

> I have suggested the term "syntagmatic implicature" as a cover term for all accommo-dation- and coercion-type adjustments, in order to stress the continuity between the utterance-external pragmatic mechanism and the utterance-internal content-syntactic mechanism. So what appears to be purely *syntactic* "coercion", is really an utterance-internal manifestation of interactive, functional pressure to adapt to the context in which the coded meaning belongs. (Harder, 2010: 247)[94]

The use of the term *implicature* here explicitly refers to the primarily inferential nature of the resolution process involved. (Although I find the relevance-theoretic term *explicature* more appropriate in this context (see Chapter 2), I share Harder's view on coercion.) The aim of this section is to provide further evidence for the (linguistic and extra-linguistic) context-sensitivity of coercion as well as to show that it is necessary to combine insights from both CxG and RT to understand how exactly coercion operates.[95]

Examples of various types can be used to highlight the context-sensitivity of coercion. In the first part of this section, I want to focus on examples that cannot

---

[94] Note that Harder is not a construction grammarian (he more generally considers himself a cognitive linguist), so this quote does not challenge the previous arguments.

[95] Mazzarella (2014) provides an interesting discussion on the reasons why inference is necessary to pragmatics (see also Carston, 2007).

be easily interpreted out of context, i.e. cases where the resolution process can only take place given a specific context. Consider the following example:

(88)   ??Farmer Joe *grew* those vines onto his roof. (Goldberg, 1995: 169)

In this sentence, the verb *grow* occurs in the CAUSED-MOTION construction, the particular semantics of which needs to be coerced onto the lexeme given the semantic mismatch between the two constructions. Yet Goldberg (1995: 169) considers example (88) to be unconventional (and perhaps unacceptable) since the verb *grow* does not naturally take a directional prepositional phrase given the absence of motion in a typical scene of growing (and watering) plants. Nevertheless, Yoon (2012) convincingly shows that, given a specific context, this utterance and in particular the mismatch between the verb *grow* and the CAUSED-MOTION construction can be resolved by the hearer. It is the case, for instance, "if the situation is that Joe used wires and bars to support the vines so that they can reach the roof" (Yoon, 2012: 5). In this case, the sentence in (88) is judged as more acceptable by speakers of English. Yoon takes this as evidence that coercion is highly context-dependent since the context here clearly affects the resolution process. She explicitly argues that this process consists in the integration of both the "linguistic elements in the expressions and extra linguistic context" (Yoon, 2012: 37). A similar example is discussed by Boas (2011):

(89)   ??Ed hammered the metal *safe*. (Boas, 2011: 1271; emphasis mine)

(90)   The door of Ed's old Dodge had a piece of metal sticking out. When getting out of the car, Ed had cut himself on the metal and had to go to the hospital to get stitches. The next day, **Ed hammered the metal** *safe*. (Boas, 2011: 1271; emphasis mine)

These sentences are meant to illustrate a particular use of the RESULTATIVE construction (see above). Boas (2011: 1271) argues that in (89) the use of *safe* in the resultative matrix of *hammer* is generally not acceptable in English. That is, outside a specific context, it is difficult to coerce *safe* here into a resultative phrase. Yet, in the relevant context, coercion is possible. In (90), the same combination is preceded by a specific context which makes sense of the use of *safe*. In this case, the same sentence as in (89) is now judged as an acceptable sentence of English.[96] That is, provided the right context, coercion is possible.[97]

---

[96] Boas (2011) conducted a judgment task to check the acceptability of (90). Amongst 40 native speakers of English (undergraduate students), "23 informants found (90) acceptable, 9 judged it marginally acceptable, and 8 found the example unacceptable" (Boas, 2011: 1297).

[97] This example once more shows that construction grammarians are fully aware of the context-sensitive nature of coercion. Boas admits, however, that CxG does not yet "provide satisfactory mechanisms capable of dealing with contextual background information" (Boas, 2011: 1275).

There is another set of examples that can be used to show the highly context-dependent, inferential roots of coercion. If coercion only involved the linguistic environment, then the same sentence should receive exactly the same interpretation by different individuals (given that they access exactly the same linguistic environment). This hypothesis is not borne out, however. Consider the following sentence:

(91)   Strong is the new skinny. (*New York Post*; August 15, 2013)[98]

This title of a *New York Post* article illustrates the use of the X *is the new* Y construction in which the lexemes *strong* and *skinny* occur. I believe that the interpretation of the two lexemes is relatively clear. Out of context, the first interpretation that comes to mind is that looking strong (and muscular) is the new physical characteristic that makes an individual particularly attractive (instead of being skinny). In the context of this article, this interpretation is only partly correct, however. It is true that part of the interpretation concerns the attractiveness of muscular features. It is said that "the aesthetic is changing ... long and lean muscles are the new attractive." Yet what the linguistic environment of the sentence in (91) does not make clear is that this actually concerns women only. That is, in this article, looking strong is said to be the new attractive feature of women and nothing is said about men. Therefore, understanding the use of *strong* and *skinny* in this particular article is already quite context-sensitive and does not only depend on the use of the X *is the new* Y construction. The context-sensitivity of the interpretation of (91) goes even further than this, however. After the release of the article, the 'strong is the new skinny' phrase became quite controversial and new interpretations started to emerge to soften the misogynist blow that followed its publication. In particular, it has been suggested instead that *strong* should be understood not as the main feature of a woman's attractiveness but as an indicator of her health. That is, *strong* and *skinny* here are given an interpretation which requires the metonymic derivation of a different category than that mentioned previously. This interpretation is arrived at by taking into account different contextual factors, such as the fact that emphasis on sports activities and health-related issues are also mentioned in the article. This is further evidence that cases of coercion such as illustrated in (91) are never just constrained by the linguistic environment but also depend on the extra-linguistic context. Here is another list of examples:

(92)   a. Just in case you're not all *Biebered* out already, here's the full studio version of "Mistletoe". (Audring and Booij, 2016: 623)

Although he refers to particular processes of analogy, he does not explain exactly how context (and inference) can contribute to coercion, however.

[98] https://nypost.com/2013/08/15/strong-is-the-new-skinny/ (last accessed: May 31, 2023).

b. We hope this is the last time we hear any Bieber news, we don't know about you but we're completely *Biebered* out! (ZAlebs, May 14, 2013)[99]

c. Selena Gomez Rehab: Was She 'Exhausted', 'Drunk' Or *Biebered* Out? (INQUISITR, February 8, 2014)[100]

The sentences in (92) all illustrate the use of Justin Bieber's last name in the construction '*be* (intensifier) V-*ed out*' (see Hugou, 2013; Jackendoff, 2013: 89; Audring and Booij, 2016: 623). This construction is used when the speaker wants to communicate the particular way in which the subject is exhausted from experiencing (to excess) the action denoted by the verb (Jackendoff, 2013: 89). Examples of this construction include the following:

(93)   a. I thought I **was all loved out**. But my heart's filled right up again. I love you, Jessie. (COCA, written)

b. He**'s all knitted out**. [after knitting for three days solid] (Jackendoff, 2013: 89)

c. If you**'re** not **all festivaled out** this summer head for The Moors Festival. (Audring and Booij, 2016: 624)

In the sentence in (93a), the speaker expresses their feeling of having loved too much to be able to love again. In (93b), the subject referent is described as having had enough of knitting. Similarly in (93c), the denominal verb *festivaled* is used to communicate the particular way in which an individual might have been to too many festivals during the summer to enjoy yet another one. Although these examples receive different interpretations depending on which verb is used by the speaker, they have in common a general feeling of weariness with regards to a specific situation. In CxG, it is argued that this meaning is attached to the form *be* (intensifier) V-*ed out*. It is this very construction which explains the particular use and interpretation of *Bieber* in the examples in (92) above. All of these examples somehow refer to the subject referent being weary of Justin Bieber and this particular interpretation is coerced from the construction in which it occurs. (There is indeed both a semantic and morphosyntactic mismatch between the nominal item *Bieber* and the position it occupies in that construction.)

Now, if coercion indeed involved the linguistic environment only, then the sentences in (92) should all receive the same interpretation without any further sensitivity to extra-linguistic context (since they all involve the use of the same lexeme in the same construction). Yet they do not. Given the nature of Justin Bieber's popularity (as a singer), we could perhaps expect an interpretation according to which one is tired of listening to his songs. This is the interpretation that is found in (92a). Here, the speaker who announces Justin Bieber's

---

[99] www.zalebs.com/whats-hot/money-heist-at-biebers-jhb-concert/ (last accessed: May 31, 2023).
[100] www.inquisitr.com/1125991/selena-gomez-rehab-was-she-exhausted-drunk-or-biebered-out/ (last accessed: May 31, 2023).

latest tune "Mistletoe" acknowledges that her audience might be tired of having to listen to him. It is worth noting that it is only the second clause (*here's the full studio version of "Mistletoe"*) that actually makes it clear this is the meaning intended by the speaker. Example (92a) already shows the context-sensitive nature of the interpretation of *Bieber* in the *be* (intensifier) V-*ed out* construction. This context-sensitivity is substantiated by examples such as in (92b) and (92c). Those examples are used to convey different meanings from that found in (92a). In the case of (92b), the speaker is not weary of *listening* to Justin Bieber but is rather weary of hearing stories about him in the news. (Whether or not the speaker still enjoys listening to Justin Bieber is not mentioned here.) Although the same combination as in (92a) is used (i.e. the same lexeme and the same construction), a different interpretation is derived. This interpretation is arrived at on the basis of the contextual evidence one has access to. First, of course, there is the previous linguistic context ("we hope this is the last time we hear any Bieber news") without which this interpretation might not have been available to the hearer. But also, this interpretation in particular follows from being used in *ZAlebs*, an online tabloid about celebrities. Once more, contextual information is crucial to the interpretation of the lexeme. The clause *we don't know about you but we're completely Biebered out!* alone does not suffice to arrive at the specific interpretation intended by the speaker. The same observation is true for the sentence in (92c). This example also comes from an online tabloid, yet here the interpretation of *Bieber* radically differs from that in (92b). In order to understand in what way *Bieber* is being used, one needs to know who Selena Gomez and Justin Bieber are, that they have been in a relationship but recently split, after which Selena Gomez went into rehab. Here, *Bieber* is used to express Selena's collapse after her relationship with the singer. It is only on the basis of all this information (and also knowing the type of information discussed in the particular tabloid) that one is able to recover this particular interpretation.

What I hope is clear from the examples in (92) is that the integration of a lexeme within a particular construction, and the resolution process that follows from it, is not a linguistic, context-insensitive mechanism but that extra-linguistic contextual information is crucial to the interpretation process. In (92a) to (92c), the same lexeme occurs in exactly the same construction, yet in their respective contexts different interpretations are derived depending on which facets of the singer are in focus. This constitutes evidence that coercion primarily involves inferential processes that depend on extra-linguistic information in order to be carried out and does not simply consist in the integration of the lexeme within a particular construction. Of course, cases of coercion differ from other adjustment processes (such as '*free*' *pragmatic enrichment*) since the construction involved is itself meaningful and therefore greatly contributes to the interpretation. But even this meaning, as we saw in the examples in (92), is adjusted depending on the context.

This observation serves as a transition to the last type of example I will discuss to highlight the primarily inferential roots of coercion. It seems that if one assumes that coercion depends solely on the linguistic environment and not on the extra-linguistic context, then one espouses, as it were, the *systemic* view of coercion discussed above. In this case, the meaning of the construction indeed simply wins out over that of the lexeme. Yet, it will have now become clear that the interpretation of the lexeme depends as much on extra-linguistic information as it does on the semantics of the construction. The semantics of the construction therefore do not simply 'win out'. In fact, the context-sensitivity of coercion goes even deeper. Yoon (2012) indeed very elegantly shows that the resolution process may actually involve adapting the semantics of the construction to that of the lexeme. This is the case for the sentence in (94), for instance, which instantiates the Ditransitive construction (Subj V Obj1 Obj2, see Chapter 2).

(94)   David broke Jen the bread 6 hours ago. (Yoon, 2012: 178)

The Ditransitive construction is usually said to convey the notion of transfer. (A typical example of the Ditransitive construction is the sentence *John gave Mary the book.*) Yet in (94), the verb *break* does not easily receive a transfer interpretation. Rather, Yoon finds that her participants consider Jen a beneficiary (and not a recipient) only if the action involves breaking the bread into pieces (Yoon, 2012: 279). Here, the notion of 'transfer' originally part of the meaning of the construction is dropped during the interpretation process (Yoon, 2012: 280).[101] For this reason, Yoon makes the following observation:

Some semantic *properties of the verb and construction are suppressed while the others become more salient.* This interaction challenges the one-way direction of coercion proposed by Override Principle (Michaelis, 2005) that people try to coerce the verb meaning into the constructional meaning. (Yoon, 2012: 279; emphasis mine)

This observation necessarily pushes us to think of coercion in terms of inferential processes. Example (94) shows that even the meaning of the construction can be affected by the context and has no primacy over the lexeme. What is the main defining factor during the interpretation process is the *relevance* of the intended meaning, which is evaluated in context. Therefore, as Yoon rightly points out, the override principle should be understood not as a strict rule but

---

[101] This interpretation relates to none of the six senses of the Ditransitive construction that Goldberg (1995: 38) identifies.

instead as a strong tendency (see also Busso, 2020).[102] This observation once again supports the view that hearers do not simply try to force the constructional semantics onto the lexeme, but rather they contextually work out the speaker's intended interpretation.

4.1.5   Coercion: Semantically Constrained Pragmatic Effects

In the first part of this chapter, the aim was to compare the perspectives in CxG and RT on *coercion* in order to try and develop a more comprehensive understanding of this concept. In the previous sections, I showed that it is possible and even beneficial (to both theories) to combine both approaches. Indeed, while CxG can explain the origin of the reinterpretation process of (for instance) the lexemes *behave* and *carrier pigeon* in the sentences in (66) and (67), repeated here in (95) and (96), it was shown that RT can explain the interpretation process itself.

(95)   You can't talk your way out of something you *behaved* your way into. You have to *behave* your way out of it. (Twitter, @DougConant, 9 jan. 2016)

(96)   They *carrier pigeoned* me an invite this morning. (Twitter, @KyleShoreBBCAN, 3 jul. 2014)

The reinterpretation process originates, according to constructionists, in the semantic (and morphosyntactic) mismatch between the different lexemes and the larger construction in which they occur: the WAY construction in (95) and the DITRANSITIVE construction in (96). And Relevance Theory helps us to understand that the hearer will solve this mismatch by working out the speaker's intended interpretation on the basis of their knowledge of the different constructions (i.e. the lexemes and the argument structure constructions), extra-linguistic information and, most importantly, on the basis of their expectation of relevance (i.e. enough effects to justify the processing effort). And depending on the semantic incompatibility between the lexeme and the construction, this process will take more or less effort. This new perspective therefore sheds equal (or almost equal) light on the semantics of the constructions involved as well as on the role of the language user during the interpretation process.

In the next part of this chapter, I will look at the notion of procedural meaning discussed in RT and identify how it relates to coercion. Before doing so, there are a number of preliminary conclusions that I wish to draw. The first conclusion directly concerns RT. Regardless of the exact nature of the resolution process, the notion of *coercion* primarily rests on the observation that many

---

[102] Ziegeler (2007b: 994) suggests that this tendency might find an explanation in the more abstract and entrenched nature of the semantics of schematic constructions, which is less flexible than lexical meaning. This will be discussed more fully in the second part of this chapter.

lexemes actually inherit part of their interpretation from the larger constructions in which they occur. Although this observation is self-evident to most
constructionists, this is not necessarily the case in RT. To be more precise, there
is a tendency in RT not to pay attention to the larger structures in which lexemes
are found and to account for the (relatively) creative uses of lexemes solely in
terms of pragmatics. Yet it has been shown that the interpretation of a lexeme
also largely depends on the semantics of the construction in which it occurs.
Figure 4.1 lists a few of the constructions that have been discussed so far; they
are placed on the continuum of lexical fixedness introduced in Chapter 2.

As mentioned several times already, it is essential for relevance theorists
involved in lexical semantics–pragmatics not to focus on lexemes only (which
in Figure 4.1 can be found in the fixed part of the constructional continuum),
but also to take into consideration all the different types of constructions in
which they can occur (which can be found in the more schematic part of the
continuum). First, this makes for finer analyses. Constructions are indeed
strong indicators both of the intended interpretation and of the speaker's
intentions since they provide rich clues which the hearer will use in order to
recover the speaker's intended meaning. At a more theoretical level, the
integration of the constructionist perspective will enhance the position of RT
as an explanatory theory. Indeed, as mentioned above, the all-pragmatics
strategy adopted in RT tends to put off many who would otherwise find in
RT many interesting answers.

Another major conclusion that needs to be drawn from the previous sections
concerns CxG more directly. Although it is true that RT needs to take into
account more systematically the larger types of constructions identified above,
CxG also needs to give more room to pragmatics in its definition of coercion.
First of all, it needs to be stated more explicitly that the resolution process is not
a linguistic mechanism and that coercing the semantics of the construction onto
that of the lexeme is carried out by individuals themselves and not by constructions. As a result, coercion effects emerge from pragmatic processes which

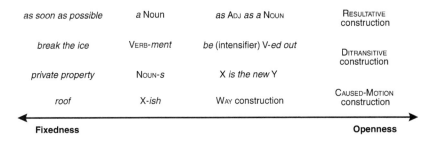

Figure 4.1 Lexicon–syntax continuum in CxG (2)

involve not only the lexeme and the construction but more largely the extra-linguistic context in which they occur. (A number of examples have been discussed in the previous section to illustrate this point.) In other words, coercion entails an inferential process which is primarily carried out in accordance with one's expectations of relevance. The distinctive feature of this process is simply that it is greatly constrained by the semantics of the construction used, which provides an indication of where relevance is to be found. This observation constitutes the last point that will be addressed in this section.

It was argued in the previous chapter that the interpretation of a lexeme largely consists in a systematic process of meaning construction. This process was referred to in terms of *lexically regulated saturation* and is meant to capture the observation that, regardless of the complexity of their semantics, the content of lexical items is systematically reconstructed inferentially in accordance with one's expectations of relevance (see Section 3.4). I want to argue that cases of coercion differ very little from this process of lexically regulated saturation and only constitute a special case: cases of coercion differ from other cases of meaning construction in the sense that the interpretation process is not only constrained by the search for a relevant interpretation but is also constrained by the semantics of the construction in which it occurs. But essentially, the same process of lexically regulated saturation is involved. Upon hearing the particular lexeme being used, the hearer will try to construct a relevant interpretation in accordance with their expectations of relevance and on the basis of the (activated parts of the) lexeme's semantic potential. The only difference is that, in addition, the hearer also has to take into account the semantics of the construction in which the lexeme occurs and which provides rich clues as to where relevance is to be found. I therefore completely agree with Michaelis (2004) when she states that "coercion effects, *rather than representing a special form of composition*, are by-products of the ordinary significations of constructions" (Michaelis, 2004: 7; emphasis mine). This is exactly the view defended here: cases of coercion are not as exceptional as they may seem. The use of a lexeme in those particular constructions is of course particularly innovative and gives rise to interesting interpretations. The interpretation process behind it, however, is not special. It is the same process (of lexically regulated saturation) which enables the interpretation of those lexemes. Constructions simply act as an additional (in this case, semantic) constraint for the derivation of a relevant interpretation, hence why I describe coercion in the title of this section as "semantically constrained pragmatic *effects*."

The view adopted here thus leaves open the possibility that the process of lexically regulated saturation (which is broader than coercion) operates every time a lexeme is embedded in a construction. This ties in well with the results in Yoon's (2012: 303) paper. She shows that there is indeed a cline of coercion events and that there is no simple opposition between semantic compatibility and semantic incompatibility. As soon as a lexeme is used in a particular construction, and regardless of the compatibility between the two, the construction acts as a constraint on the interpretation of the lexeme. I argued previously that the lexemes *fly* and *push* in the sentences in (32) and (75b), repeated here in (97) and (98), readily occur in the CAUSED-MOTION construction since their semantics already include the notion of motion. It follows from the perspective adopted here, however, that these examples involve exactly the same process as other cases of coercion: the lexeme is interpreted (via lexically regulated saturation) in accordance with both expectations of relevance and knowledge of the CAUSED-MOTION construction, which acts as an additional constraint on the derivation of the intended interpretation.

(97)   Our son was just three months old when we first *flew* him across the Atlantic. (COCA, written)

(98)   The lieutenant *pushed* the box across the table. (BNC, written)

That is, I want to argue that even in the case of examples like these, which not all constructionists might view as involving coercion, the same process of meaning construction as in other coercion-type examples is involved.[103]

4.2   Procedural Meaning and Lexical Pragmatics

Throughout the previous sections, the terms *constrain/constraint* were used to describe the particular way in which the semantics of a construction affects the interpretation of the lexemes it selects. Yet this terminology is not often used in CxG. (This is to be expected since these terms suggest an asymmetric semantic relation between the different types of construction involved, a perspective which is at odds with the CxG view, see Section 2.1.1.) The use of these terms, however, was a careful and deliberate choice. The idea that some constructions might encode constraints on utterance interpretation has been widely discussed in the framework of RT. This phenomenon is captured under the notion of *procedural encoding* which was introduced by Diane Blakemore (see Chapter 2, Section 2.2.3.2). In the rest of this chapter, I will discuss the notion of procedural meaning and pin down exactly how it relates to the view of coercion presented in the previous sections. The challenge involved stems from

---

[103] Note, of course, that although the underlying cognitive process is in principle the same, I still consider that the notion of coercion is useful as a separate concept to single out (more obvious) mismatch cases where the interpretation of a lexeme crucially depends on the semantics of the construction in which it occurs. After all, from the perspective of cognitive *relevance*, cases of semantic mismatch necessarily require more effort and naturally beg for a high(er) number of cognitive effects (to achieve *relevance*), the nature of which might be worth looking into (see Wilson and Carston (2019) for a recent discussion).

the fact that in RT the notion of procedural encoding applies to lexical units whereas in CxG, when the term is used, it occurs at a more schematic level. As mentioned at the beginning of this chapter, I will argue that it is (semi-) schematic constructions that have a procedural (rather than conceptual) type of semantics, which further supports the view that coercion effects are the result of a semantically constrained pragmatic process.

4.2.1   Procedures in RT

In order to understand the relation between the notion of procedural meaning and the view on coercion developed in the previous section, it is important to understand exactly what procedures are in the first place. The aim of this section is to reintroduce this notion and to make explicit the way in which procedures differ from concepts. In Sections 4.2.2 and 4.2.3, the aim will be to pin down exactly what type of constructions can encode procedures as well as to identify specifically what procedures actually consist of. Once more, insights from both RT and CxG will prove very useful.

Of all the notions introduced in RT since the publication of *Relevance* (Sperber and Wilson, [1986] 1995), that of procedural meaning perhaps best captures what the theory is all about: the optimization of relevance. It is quite largely assumed in RT that human communication is primarily an inferential process which the linguistic system simply renders more efficient. Sperber and Wilson (1995: 172) specifically argue that "languages are indispensable not for communication, but for information processing; this is their essential function." For relevance theorists, it follows logically from this view that language might not only give us access to specific mental representations (i.e. concepts) but also provide us with the tools to compute these mental representations (i.e. procedures):

Linguistic decoding provides input to the inferential phase of comprehension; inferential comprehension involves the construction and manipulation of conceptual representations. An utterance can thus be expected to encode two basic types of information: representational and computational, or conceptual and procedural – that is, information about the representations to be manipulated, and information about how to manipulate them. (Wilson and Sperber, 1993: 97)

From this perspective, procedural information is essentially information which enables speakers and hearers to manipulate conceptual information and which directly contributes to the optimization of relevance. Exactly what these procedures consist of will be discussed in section 4.2.3. So far, suffice it to say that constructions that have procedural meaning are usually described as encoding a constraint on inferential processes which guides the hearer towards relevance (Escandell-Vidal, Leonetti and Ahern, 2011: xxi). In RT, the typical example of constructions that encode procedural meaning are discourse connectives (e.g.

so, after all, therefore, etc.). This is due to the fact that Diane Blakemore, who introduced the notion of procedural meaning in RT, focused on discourse markers (Blakemore, 1987). Consider, for instance, the following examples:

(99)   a. He is a linguist. He is intelligent.
       b. He is a linguist, *so* he is intelligent.
       c. He is a linguist, *but* he is intelligent.

In (99a), the discourse relation between the two sentences *He is a linguist* and *He is intelligent* is left implicit and has to be inferred by the hearer. Most often, speakers of English will infer the particular causal relation whereby the intelligence of the subject referent is considered a direct consequence of his being a linguist.[104] If the speaker considers that the hearer might not be able to retrieve exactly this relation, however, she may decide to use a particular discourse marker which will guide him in this direction. This is the case in (99b), where *so* is used precisely to achieve that effect. Alternatively, the speaker may also entertain the (unbelievable) assumption that linguists are not intelligent and therefore use a marker which will signal a contrast between the two propositions expressed. The use of *but* in (99c) enables the hearer to make this particular inference. What is important for our discussion is that the discourse markers used by the speaker contribute to neither of the two propositions they connect but only guide the hearer to recover the discourse relation intended by the speaker and help him to draw the right inferences. In this case, it is said that the discourse marker encodes procedural meaning in the sense that it provides the hearer not with a particular mental representation but with a semantic constraint that enables him to manipulate other representations (here, the two propositions communicated by each clause) and thereby facilitates the optimization of relevance.

In the case of discourse markers, the procedure they encode constrains the type of *implicatures* that the hearer will derive (here, the implicated premises *linguists are intelligent* or *linguists are not intelligent*). It is clear in RT, however, that inference does not only occur at the level of implicatures but also permits the derivation of *explicatures* (i.e. enriched logical forms) as well as *higher-level explicatures* (which include the speaker's beliefs and attitudes with regard to a proposition).[105] Therefore, one might also expect some procedural expressions to constrain the derivation of explicatures and higher-level explicatures. This is precisely what is captured by Figure 4.2.

---

[104] Note that this assumption is not (only) based on the personal hope that society naturally thinks of linguists as intelligent people. Rather, this assumption (also) finds root in the empirical observation that, in the case of implicit discourse relations, by default, a causal relation seems to be assumed between the propositions expressed in the two consecutive clauses (see Murray, 1995, 1997; Sanders, 2005; Hoek and Zufferey, 2015).

[105] See Chapter 2, Section 2.2.2.

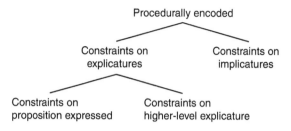

Figure 4.2 Procedural meaning: constraints on interpretation (adapted from Wilson and Sperber, 1993: 3)

In the relevance-theoretic literature, typical examples of expressions that constrain the derivation of explicatures (i.e. the proposition expressed) are pronouns and demonstratives, which are said to constrain the recovery of a specific referent (Wilson and Sperber, 1993; Scott, 2011, 2013, 2016). At the level of higher-level explicatures, different types of constructions have been discussed, such as sentence types (Clark, 1991) or prosodic patterns (e.g. Imai, 1998; Clark, 2007, 2012, 2013b; House, 2009). In both cases, the constructions involved are argued not to provide the hearer with a specific concept but rather to guide them during the inferential phase to recover the speaker's attitude with regard to the proposition expressed. Other types of procedural constraints on higher-level explicatures are discussed in Andersen and Fretheim (2000), such as the use of the pragmatic marker *like* in English (e.g. *Cos I need some friends around just to* like, *protect me*, Andersen, 2000: 30).

In comparison, the notion of procedural encoding is relatively absent in the constructionist literature. A noticeable exception can be found in the work of Elizabeth Traugott, who uses the term in her work on grammaticalization (Traugott and Dasher, 2002; Traugott and Trousdale, 2013; Traugott, 2014). Her understanding of procedural meaning, however, differs slightly from that in RT. This will be discussed more fully in Section 4.2.3. The term *procedural* is also briefly used by Bergs and Diewald (2009: 8) to describe the meaning of the French connective *parce que* ('because'). More generally, however, the terms *procedures* and *procedural* tend not to be used within CxG.[106] Rather, when the meaning of a construction affects not the proposition directly but an inferential process, different terms are used, such as 'discourse function', 'pragmatic function' or 'discourse-pragmatic function'. (These terms cover a number of phenomena such as illocutionary force, metalinguistic comments, speaker attitudes, scalar models and discourse parameters. See Kay (2004),

---

[106] More recently, the term also occurred in a volume by Coussé, Andersson and Oloffsson (2018a) on grammaticalization and CxG.

Nikiforidou (2009) and Cappelle (2017) for overviews.) This is the case, for instance, in the discussion of the *let alone* construction discussed in Chapter 2. Consider the following examples:

(100)   They couldn't write a complete sentence, *let alone* an entire essay. (COCA, spoken)

(101)   It's difficult to get people to stop at red lights, *let alone* a flashing yellow light. (COCA, spoken)

This construction, as mentioned previously, is used, first to contrast the two conjuncts, and to provide "constraints on the distribution of informativeness and relevance across the two propositions" (Cappelle, Dugas and Tobin, 2015: 73). In particular, the construction is used to ascribe more *relevance* to the second conjunct so as to reject the first conjunct "more forcefully" (p. 73). It is my understanding that, in RT, this particular type of meaning would be discussed in procedural terms. Both Fillmore, Kay and O'Connor (1988) and Cappelle, Dugas and Tobin (2015) say that this meaning contributes to the *pragmatics* of the construction. Yet, as mentioned in Chapter 2, it is not clear exactly what can count as the 'pragmatics of a construction'. Alternatively, the term *discourse function* is sometimes used in discussions about the meaning of a construction. Koops (2007), for instance, uses that term to describe the meaning of the INFERENTIAL construction (*It is . . . that . . .*), such as in the following examples (from Koops, 2007):

(102)   a. I cannot pay you back today.
        b. *It's* just *that* all the banks are closed.

(103)   I look under the hood and I see all the stuff under there and I say, boy, my chances of doing – how shall I say it? Everything's electronic. *It's* not *that* I'm against at least trying, *it's* just *that* there's so much, you know. You can't tune it yourself. You can't do anything.

In these two examples, the construction is used by the speaker "as a pragmatic instruction to its audience to regard its clause as an interpretation of its local context, that is, to be about, rather than of, its context" (Delahunty, 1995: 359). In other words, the construction is used by the speaker to introduce the proposition embedded in the *that*-clause as providing contextual information about the discourse context (i.e. an implicated premise) in order to reduce (or relocate) the range of possible inferences. This type of instruction in RT would be described in procedural terms. Yet Koops uses the term *discourse function* (Koops, 2007: 208).

In the next sections, one of the aims will be to show that the term *procedural meaning* used in the relevance-theoretic literature is preferable to the different notions used in CxG. From a purely terminological perspective, it is unclear why and how the different terms *pragmatic*, *discourse* or even *discourse-pragmatic function* are used in CxG (see Leclercq, 2020). They seem to be used relatively interchangeably. For the sake of terminological consistency and precision, however, only one term should be used.[107] The choice to employ the term *procedural meaning* here is not arbitrary, however. It is largely motivated by the observation that the term is used in RT in relation to a wider range of expressions and phenomena than the constructionist terms. (This observation can arguably be said to follow from the various degrees of attention given to pragmatics in the two frameworks.) As mentioned in Chapter 3, there is a tendency in CxG (as in cognitive linguistics more generally) to associate inferential processes (and the notion of pragmatics) with the derivation of *implicatures* only (or mostly). It is interesting to note that, as one might expect, the notions of discourse/pragmatic functions in CxG have also been largely applied to constructions that provide constraints on the derivation of implicatures. This is the case, for instance, for both the *let alone* construction and the INFERENTIAL construction discussed above. It is clear in RT, however, that inferential processes do not only occur at the level of implicatures but also affect the derivation of explicatures and higher-level explicatures. The notion of *procedural meaning* therefore applies to a much wider range of expressions than the constructionist terms and, more importantly, it is not associated with the derivation of implicatures only. The aim of adopting the relevance-theoretic terminology is therefore twofold. First, as we will see in the next sections, it is meant to account for a much wider range of constructions than the terms used in CxG actually do. More importantly, the aim is also to abandon the idea that inference is solely linked to implicatures.

In Section 4.2.2, I will try and pin down the type of constructions that encode procedural meaning. In Section 4.2.3, the aim will be to identify what procedures actually consist of. It will soon become clear that although I adopt the relevance-theoretic term, insights from CxG will also prove very useful to address these two questions. Eventually, it will be shown that there is a direct link between the notion of procedural meaning and that of coercion discussed at the beginning of this chapter.

4.2.2   Constructions with Procedural Meaning

In spite of the differences that can be found between RT and CxG, it is interesting to note that the linguistic units analyzed either in terms of procedural meaning or as having pragmatic/discourse functions are always

---

[107] This is particularly true since the notion of discourse/pragmatic properties is sometimes used to refer not to the type of meaning associated with a construction but rather to its contextual appropriateness (i.e. features about the situation, register, genre, discourse focus, politeness strategy, etc.). This is how Stephan Gries and Martin Hilpert seem to be using the term *discourse-pragmatic characteristics* in Hoffmann and Trousdale's (2013a) *The Oxford handbook of Construction Grammar*.

grammatical constructions (i.e. constructions that serve a grammatical function). The latest theoretical discussions on procedural meaning in RT confirm this observation (e.g. Escandell-Vidal, Leonetti and Ahern, 2011; Carston, 2016b; Wilson, 2016; Escandell-Vidal, 2017). In her investigation on the development of procedural meaning in RT, for instance, Carston (2016b: 155) explicitly points out that the difference between conceptual and procedural meaning is broadly consistent with the long-standing division "between the substantive lexicon (open-class words such as nouns, verbs and adjectives) and the functional lexicon (closed-class words like determiners, pronouns and connectives)."[108] The same is true for CxG, where the notion of pragmatic function is used a lot, for instance, in relation to information structure constructions (cf. Hilpert, 2019: ch. 5).

The aim of this section is to determine what types of constructions can (and do) encode procedural meaning. To begin, it is worth noting that the idea that there is a correspondence between grammatical constructions and procedural encoding is a view that receives support in both RT and CxG. In RT, Steve Nicolle has done considerable work to show the relationship between aspects of grammaticalization and the development of procedural content (see Nicolle, 1997b, 1998b, 2011, 2015). According to Nicolle, "grammaticalization begins with the addition of procedural information to the meaning of a construction" (Nicolle, 2011: 407). There is therefore a clear correspondence for him between grammatical constructions and procedural encoding (and between lexical constructions and concepts). It is interesting to note that it is precisely in research on grammaticalization that the term procedural encoding is also used in CxG. As mentioned earlier, Elizabeth Traugott and her co-authors also argue that the conceptual/procedural distinction coincides with the lexical/grammatical distinction (Traugott and Dasher, 2002; Traugott and Trousdale, 2013; Traugott 2014). Traugott and Trousdale specifically point out, for instance, that "the formal dimensions with which procedural meaning is usually linked are traditionally known as grammatical elements" (2013: 12)[109] Summing up, in both frameworks procedural meaning, i.e. information about how to manipulate conceptual information, is associated with grammatical constructions.

In the next section, the aim will be to identify exactly what procedural encoding consists of (as opposed to conceptual encoding). Before doing so, a number of questions concerning the correspondence between grammatical constructions and procedural encoding still need to be answered. The first question concerns the way in which the distinction between lexical and grammatical constructions is established in RT and CxG. In RT, for instance, there is

---

[108] See also Escandell-Vidal and Leonetti (2000), Leonetti and Escandell-Vidal (2004) and Escandell-Vidal (2017).
[109] See Section 4.2.3 for a discussion of grammaticalization processes.

an ongoing debate about what type of constructions encode procedural meaning. As Carston (2016b: 155) points out, it is usually assumed that this distinction broadly corresponds to that between the denotation of open-class words (e.g. noun, verbs, adjectives, adverbs) and closed-class words (e.g. auxiliaries, conjunctions, determiners). The categorical distinction is not always as clearcut as RT theoreticians might think, however.[110] One of the core tenets of CxG is that there is no such dichotomy between lexical items on the one hand and grammatical elements on the other. Rather, the *construct-i-con* (i.e. the mental repository of *constructions*) consists of a continuum of constructions from (more) lexical ones to (more) grammatical ones (see Figures 2.1 and 4.1). They are not categorically distinguished but rather form a cline from more lexically fixed to more schematic patterns. For that reason, it might be unclear in CxG exactly how the conceptual/procedural distinction aligns with the lexical/grammatical cline (see Coussé, Andersson and Olofsson (2018b: 8) for a similar observation). Therefore, although the two frameworks establish a similar link between 'grammatical constructions' and 'procedural meaning', they have a different understanding of what counts as a grammatical unit of the language. As a natural consequence, this also means that the two frameworks have different expectations of where procedural meaning is to be found.

Traugott and Trousdale (2013: 12), who work on the basis of the constructional continuum, argue that, in line with the general CxG tenet, the conceptual/procedural distinction is itself also gradual.[111] From this perspective, constructions encode different types of meaning that range from more conceptual to more procedural, depending on where they are found in the continuum. Figure 4.3 is an attempt to represent the correspondence between these two gradients.

In this approach, not all constructions are either conceptual or procedural. Instead, the more grammatical a construction, the more procedural its content (and the more lexical, the more conceptual). This is the reason why Traugott and Trousdale (2013: 13) argue that between fully contentful (e.g. *red*) and fully procedural (e.g. plural -*s*) constructions, there are a number of 'intermediate' constructions that have both conceptual and procedural properties (e.g. the WAY construction). At first sight, this view appears to face a challenge, however. Indeed, it is largely assumed in RT that the distinction between concepts and procedures is not gradual but instead that they form two discrete categories. Nicolle (1998b) specifically argues that "there is no information type intermediate between conceptual and procedural information" (Nicolle, 1998b: 6). Yet in Figure 4.3, the 'intermediate' constructions encode precisely such an

---

[110] See Aarts (2007: 34–79) for an insightful discussion on grammatical gradience.

[111] Note that Traugott and Dasher (2002: 10) specifically indicate that they prefer using the term *contentful* to *conceptual*. (The term *contentful* is also used in Traugott and Trousdale, 2013.) This will be discussed more fully in the next section.

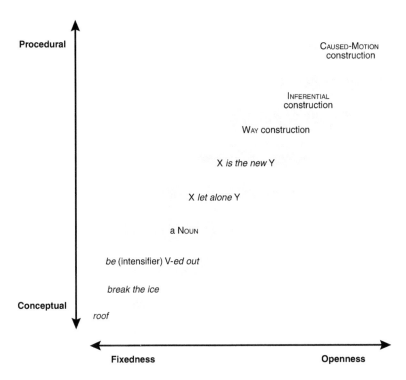

Figure 4.3 Constructions: correlation between formal and semantic gradients

intermediate type of information, neither fully conceptual nor fully procedural. This is not, however, what Traugott and Trousdale mean by *intermediate*. Constructions that are intermediate with regard to the conceptual–procedural distinction are simply understood as encoding both conceptual and procedural information and form "'hybrid' constructions" (Traugott and Trousdale, 2013: 26). That is, the distinction between purely conceptual and purely procedural types of information is maintained. It is simply assumed that many constructions encode both types of information.

The gradient approach turns out not to be incompatible with the relevance-theoretic view: here as well, it is argued that words can encode either a concept, a procedure, or both types of information. In RT, typical examples of expressions that encode both conceptual and procedural information are pronouns (see, for instance, Scott, 2011, 2016).[112] The main difference between RT and

---

[112] Pronouns are procedural in the sense that they act as instructions for the recovery of a specific referent; they are conceptual by specifying the referential category (i.e. gender, number, etc.).

CxG, however, has to do with the form that grammatical constructions take and, therefore, the type of construction that is assumed to encode procedural information. The relevance-theoretic approach is relatively lexeme-centered, and most of the attention is therefore given to grammatical *words*. The attention on the level of the lexeme most probably originates in the basic theoretical stance, which takes "a broadly Chomskyan approach to language and ... Fodorian assumptions about modularity" (Clark, 2013a: 95). From this perspective, there are, on the one hand, the syntactic rules which belong to the linguistic system and, on the other hand, the words of the lexicon which can be used within these structures. The type of grammatical units that relevance theorists have paid most attention to are grammatical words (e.g. pronouns, discourse markers, mood particles, etc.).[113] In CxG, however, there is no strict divide between elements of the lexicon and 'syntax'. Rather, our linguistic knowledge is composed of a variety of (more or less complex) constructions, i.e. form–meaning pairs, all of which equally contribute to our mental grammar (called the *construct-i-con*). A direct consequence of this approach is that the notion of grammatical constructions in CxG differs from that in other approaches. In CxG, as is clear in Figure 4.3, 'grammatical' constructions are not discussed at the atomic (lexical) level but often involve longer, phrasal or clausal, more schematic structures. As mentioned in Chapter 2, for instance, the *let alone* construction is often referred to as the X *let alone* Y construction, which puts emphasis on its mainly schematic nature as well as on the clausal level. In other words, while grammatical meaning is situated at the level of the lexicon in RT, it pertains to the schematic (word, phrasal or clausal) level in CxG.[114] Schematicity is indeed identified by constructionists (and in the literature on grammaticalization more generally) as a central feature of grammatical constructions (see Croft, 2001: 16; Langacker, 2008: 22; Trousdale, 2008a: 59, 2008b: 304, 2010: 51, 2012: 168; Traugott, 2008: 34, 2015: 61; Coussé, Andersson and Olofsson, 2018b, inter alia). Trousdale (2008a) specifically argues, for instance, that "as constructions grammaticalize, they become more schematic; as they lexicalize, they become more idiom-like" (Trousdale, 2008a: 59).[115] In this case, units of the language that encode procedural information are not atomic, fully specific constructions (i.e. not

---

[113] As mentioned previously, very recently they have started to look at morphemes as well (e.g. Padilla Cruz, 2022; Carston, 2022).

[114] It is worth noting, for instance, that Ruiz de Mendoza and Gómez-González (2014) and Erviti (2017) generally treat discourse markers, which are central to the discussion on procedural meaning in RT, as partially schematic constructions: X *so* Y construction, X *but* Y construction, etc.

[115] Although grammaticalization processes systematically entail constructional schematization, there is a real debate in CxG whether all cases of schematization necessarily relate to the development of grammatical meaning (see Noël, 2007; Traugott and Trousdale, 2013). For reasons that will become clear in the rest of this chapter, however, I will assume that a construction's schematicity and grammatical meaning are interrelated (see also Trousdale, 2012: 193).

words), but constructions that are formally more schematic.[116] In the remainder of this chapter, I will work on the basis of the constructionist assumption that grammatical constructions (with which a procedural meaning is associated) necessarily involve a level of schematicity. After all, in CxG it is precisely (semi-)schematic constructions that enable the syntagmatic combination of lexical items into larger phrasal or clausal units. It seems intuitively logical that procedural information be encoded by this type of construction, which precisely enables speakers of a language to manipulate the type of linguistic units that carry conceptual information: lexemes. In this sense, grammatical constructions serve both as syntactic and semantic glue.

The perspective on grammatical constructions adopted here meshes well with the approach to coercion outlined in Section 4.1.5. All of the coercive constructions that were discussed in Section 4.1 are (semi-)schematic constructions (e.g. the INDEFINITE DETERMINATION construction, the *be* (intensifier) V-*ed out* construction, the WAY construction or the CAUSED-MOTION construction, etc.). In CxG, it is generally assumed that "any construction that selects for a specific lexical class or phrasal daughter is a potential coercion trigger" (Michaelis, 2011: 1384). That (semi-)schematic constructions should have a coercive potential makes a lot of sense when we assume, as I do here, that these types of construction encode procedural rather than conceptual information.[117] That is, once we assume that these constructions encode specific constraints on how to interpret the concepts that occur within them, then it follows logically that hearers will interpret the lexemes in accordance with the semantics of the construction in which they occur. As it happens, the only time I came across the notion of *coercion* in RT is precisely in discussions about procedural meaning. Escandell-Vidal and Leonetti (2011: 88) argue that units which carry conceptual meaning are coercible and only units that carry procedural meaning have a coercive force. This link is interesting since it provides further support to some of the arguments presented in the previous sections, some of which will be taken up again here.

First of all, treating schematic/grammatical constructions in procedural terms justifies the view that coercion results from a semantically constrained pragmatic process. This process is semantically constrained since the procedural information associated with the schematic construction precisely provides a constraint which is meant to guide the hearer towards a particular interpretation during the inferential phase of comprehension. It is, however, a pragmatic process in the sense that in spite of the semantic constraint provided by the

---

[116] Accordingly, morphological constructions (e.g. VERB-*ment* in 'govern*ment*' and 'invest*ment*', NOUN-*al* in 'nation*al*' and 'natur*al*', *im*-ADJ in '*im*possible' and '*im*polite') also qualify as grammatical constructions given their partially schematic nature (see Booij and Audring, 2017; Booij, 2018).

[117] What exactly constitutes the content of this procedure will be discussed in the next section.

construction, it is the hearer himself who inferentially derives the speaker's intended interpretation (see Section 4.1.4). In that sense, I share the view adopted by Escandell-Vidal and Leonetti (2011) when they argue that they view coercion "not as a semantic operation, but as a pragmatic process guided and constrained by linguistic meaning" (Escandell-Vidal and Leonetti, 2011: 95). This is what procedures do: they only constrain the inferential phase of comprehension. In the previous chapter, I argued that the interpretation of a lexeme can be understood in terms of lexically regulated saturation. That is, the interpretation of a lexeme consists of an inferential process whereby individuals systematically reconstruct the meaning of a lexeme in accordance with their expectations of relevance and on the basis of the (more or less rich) conceptual information made accessible by the lexeme. The notions of procedural meaning and coercion are thus directly related to lexically regulated saturation:

- *Lexically regulated saturation* (lexical level).
  Hearers inferentially reconstruct the meaning of the lexical constructions that are used by speakers.
  - *Procedural meaning* (schematic level).
    In so doing, hearers are directly guided by the procedural meaning of the grammatical/schematic constructions in which lexical constructions occur.
  - *Coercion* (mismatch lexical/schematic levels).
    In some cases, there is incompatibility between the semantic (and morpho-syntactic) properties of a lexical construction and the position it occupies in a grammatical construction. These cases lead to coerced interpretations, whereby the lexical construction is interpreted in accordance with the meaning of the grammatical construction. (The procedural information associated with grammatical constructions has stronger coercive force than conceptual information (see below), hence the override principle.)

The representation in Figure 4.4 is an attempt to show more explicitly the interaction between the three notions discussed here. *Lexically regulated saturation* is central to the interpretation of a lexeme. The procedural semantics of grammatical constructions facilitate this inferential process by guiding the hearer in a particular direction. In some cases, a mismatch between the conceptual semantics of the lexeme and the procedural semantics of the grammatical construction will result in coercion effects; the lexeme is interpreted in accordance with the meaning of the grammatical construction.

There are two consequences that follow from the model outlined here. First, one of the main roles of grammatical constructions is simply to facilitate the inferential processes involved when interpreting an utterance (such as that of *lexically regulated saturation*), which hearers systematically have to perform regardless of which constructions are used by the speaker. As a result, the use of a particular grammatical construction directly affects the optimization of

Interpreting a lexeme involves:

CONTEXT-SENSITIVE INFERENTIAL PROCESSES

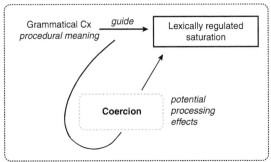

Figure 4.4 'Lexically regulated saturation' and utterance comprehension (1)

relevance since it helps the hearer recover the intended interpretation. In guiding the hearer in a particular direction, grammatical constructions reduce the search space and the amount of cognitive effort involved in the interpretation process. In this sense, I completely agree with the view defended by Nicolle (2011):

> Procedural information reduces processing effort by *constraining inferential processes that an addressee would have to perform in any case*; thus, the process of grammatical-ization can be viewed as being motivated by the principle of relevance, according to which an optimally relevant interpretation is one which achieves adequate cognitive effects for minimal processing effort. (Nicolle, 2011: 407; emphasis mine)

In other words, one of the motivations behind processes of grammaticalization (and, by the same token, the acquisition and use of grammatical constructions) simply comes from the pressure to optimize *relevance*. Grammatical constructions increase the overall relevance of an interpretation by reducing the amount of effort put into the interpretation process. Secondly, this perspective also reinforces the view defended earlier that the interpretation process of a coerced lexeme differs very little (if at all) from that of non-coerced lexemes. That is, whether coercion is involved or not, understanding a lexeme primarily consists in an inferential process (namely, lexically regulated saturation), which is systematically guided by the meaning of the grammatical constructions in which lexemes are used. Cases of coercion are more special in the sense that the meaning of the lexeme somehow clashes with that of the grammatical construction, but both cases of coerced and non-coerced lexemes involve the same process of interpretation. A similar line of reasoning motivates Traugott and Trousdale's claim that probably "coercion is not needed as a concept separate from metonymy and best-fit interpretations" (2013: 233). Unlike Traugott and Trousdale, however, I believe the term *coercion* is still useful. Indeed, although the actual process of interpretation is the same, the interpretation of a coerced lexeme is affected by the meaning of the grammatical construction in which it occurs to a much greater extent than that of non-coerced lexemes. Cases of coercion therefore involve an additional linguistic requirement that non-coerced lexemes do not have (since they already meet this requirement), hence the necessity to keep a distinct term so as to identify cases of coercion more clearly.

The notion of coercion is also useful as a distinct concept since it enables us to account for another observation. In CxG, the notion of coercion is often described in relation to the override principle introduced by Michaelis (2004). This principle states that in case of a semantic (and morphosyntactic) mismatch between a lexeme and the schematic/grammatical construction in which it occurs, the meaning of the lexeme will conform to that of the grammatical construction. It was shown in Section 4.1.3 that this principle may come across as an overgeneralization, since coercion can then be understood as the result of a semantic process operated by the linguistic system itself, disconnected from any considerations of pragmatic factors. Instead, it is preferable to think of the override principle as the observed *tendency* that in such situations language users indeed generally adapt the meaning of the lexeme in accordance with the meaning of the grammatical construction. This being said, the point remains essentially the same: it is usually the meaning of the lexeme which is adjusted and not that of the grammatical construction (see Section 4.1.4). Yet it is unclear exactly what motivates this relatively unilateral tendency. When one assumes (as construction grammarians often do) that the type of information that grammatical constructions encode is conceptual), then it should also be possible for them to be adjusted in context somehow, but they usually are not. (As mentioned above (footnote 102 in Section 4.1.5), this might be due to the more abstract and entrenched nature of the semantics of grammatical constructions which makes them less prone to change, but this is not necessarily obvious.) This problem is much less of a challenge, however, when one assumes (as I do here) that the grammatical constructions in which the lexemes occur encode not conceptual but procedural information. From this perspective, it is precisely the function of these constructions to constrain the inferential phase of comprehension and to guide the hearer towards the intended interpretation. It therefore follows from this that hearers will adjust the meaning of the lexemes that occur within grammatical constructions, and not the other way around. Escandell-Vidal argues that "a procedural instruction must be satisfied at any cost. Procedural meaning always prevails" (2017: 92).[118]

---

[118] It will be shown in the next section that procedural information does not "always prevail."

Indeed, it seems intuitively logical that individuals should adjust the meaning of the item which falls under a constraint rather than the constraint itself, even more so since the function of these constraints is to facilitate the use of conceptual information. The procedural semantics of grammatical constructions can therefore account for Michaelis' override principle. This is why the notion of coercion is needed as a separate concept. Although the interpretation of a coerced lexeme is pragmatically derived, in the same way that the interpretation of a non-coerced lexeme is, it is much more contingent on the procedural semantics of the grammatical construction in which it occurs than in cases of non-coerced lexemes.

The aim of this chapter is to identify some of the ways the linguistic environment in which lexemes occur directly affects their interpretation. This is why the notion of coercion was discussed in the first part. It was shown that many (partially) schematic constructions directly contribute to the interpretation of a lexeme, the meaning of which is usually adjusted in order to fit that of the construction in which it occurs. One of the main conclusions, however, is that it is not the constructions themselves which coerce their own semantics onto the lexemes, but rather that the resolution mechanism is primarily a pragmatic process which is carried out by the hearer in accordance with their expectations of relevance, and that the meaning construction process resembles that of non-coerced lexemes. This view is particularly interesting taking into account the fact that the schematic/grammatical constructions involved in cases of coercion in my view do not encode conceptual but procedural information. By definition, procedural information acts as a semantic constraint on pragmatic inferences. Therefore, it is logical that coercion effects should be viewed as resulting from a semantically constrained pragmatic process. The major challenge now is to understand exactly what procedural information consists of. This is the aim of the next section.

4.2.3   On the Nature of Procedural Encoding

It is necessary to define what procedural information consists of in order to understand exactly how grammatical constructions constrain the inferential processes involved during the interpretation of an utterance in general and of lexemes in particular. As mentioned in the previous section, the notion of procedural encoding is relatively absent in the framework of CxG. In RT, the notion still gives rise to much debate. In this section, the aim is to provide a critical discussion of the different views adopted in the literature. Eventually it will be suggested that procedural information might best be described in terms of meta-conceptual representations which function as expectation-like constraints.

4.2.3.1 Procedural Meaning in CxG   In CxG, the notion of procedural encoding has been used mostly by Elizabeth Traugott and Graeme Trousdale in their work on grammaticalization and grammatical meaning. Elsewhere in the constructionist literature, the term is generally not used and meaning is discussed solely in conceptual terms. It must be noted that, for those who do establish a distinction in CxG, the idea that some constructions essentially encode a more procedural type of information comes directly from the work carried out in RT. Traugott and Dasher (2002: 10), for instance, explicitly refer to RT and to Diane Blakemore's work. As a result, the expectation is that Traugott and Dasher essentially adopt the relevance-theoretic perspective on what exactly constitutes procedural content.[119] However, the integration of relevance-theoretic insights is mainly terminologically. Indeed, they assume that the nature of procedural information is also primarily conceptual and therefore prefer to make the distinction between *contentful* and *procedural* types of meaning (i.e. two types of conceptual information) rather than between conceptual and procedural (i.e. non-conceptual) types of meaning. They argue that "both procedural and non-procedural language-specific meanings are representations of more abstract Conceptual Structures" (2002: 10, fn. 10). In this case, however, it is less clear (than in RT) how procedural meanings differ from contentful ones. (This will be discussed more fully below.) Traugott and Dasher's view somewhat naturally follows from a long tradition in CxG which avoids differentiating between more lexical and more grammatical units of the language. All units of the language are argued to be meaningful, and this meaning is necessarily conceptual. The meaning of argument-structure constructions, for instance, is usually discussed in such conceptual terms.[120] A direct consequence of this view is that the procedural nature of grammatical expressions simply consists in conceptual representations of a more abstract (or schematic) nature.[121] This is what Langacker (2008) argues when he considers that "highly schematic meanings" are "characteristic of 'grammatical' elements" (Langacker, 2008: 178). This is also very explicit in Trousdale (2008b):

Langacker (1987, 1991a) has repeatedly suggested that the meaning of grammatical elements is usually quite schematic, but given the gradient nature of schematicity, it would not be unwarranted to assume that some grammatical elements are more

---

[119] Note that this is the case even though relevance theorists do not fully agree on what procedural encoding means (see below).

[120] Concerning argument-structure constructions, Goldberg (1995: 39) argues in favor of a "scene encoding hypothesis," according to which these types of constructions "designate scenes essential to human experience." Similarly, Langacker (2008: 33) refers to *conceptual archetypes*.

[121] In the case of the grammatical category NOUN, for instance, Langacker (1987: 189) argues that its "semantic pole instantiates the schema [THING]."

schematic than others, and that the process by which grammatical elements become more schematic is known more generally in linguistic theory as grammaticalization. (Trousdale, 2008b: 317)

It is unclear whether grammaticalization can be reduced to a semantically higher level of schematicity, however. It is generally assumed that lexical and grammatical elements of the language serve different functions in discourse. It is therefore reasonable to assume that the shift from lexical to grammatical meaning also involves a change in the actual nature of the encoded content, for otherwise it is not clear what the distinction between lexical (contentful conceptual) and grammatical (procedural conceptual) constructions is actually trying to capture. Later in this chapter, it will be argued that of course some form of conceptual abstraction is involved in the process of grammaticalization and in the development of procedural encoding. There are different reasons why grammaticalization cannot be reduced to conceptual abstraction alone, however. First of all, it is unclear at what point a meaning is schematic enough to be considered grammatical and not lexical anymore. One must not forget that processes of schematization/ abstraction are also involved at the lexical level. The different senses of a lexeme are abstracted away from actual usage, and it was shown previously (Chapter 2) that some senses in a conceptual network might be schematic relative to other senses. It follows that the level of schematicity at which the grammatical threshold should occur has to be quite high, at which point one might actually question its relevance. More importantly, it has been quite extensively shown that grammaticalization does not only involve semantic bleaching (i.e. loss of lexical/contentful conceptual properties), but it also primarily consists in semantic change. In particular, Elizabeth Traugott has shown that the shift from lexical to grammatical meaning often involves the conventionalization of implicatures (which she refers to as *invited inferences*) as well as a process of subjectification (e.g. Traugott and König, 1991; Traugott, 1995, 2003, 2010; Traugott and Dasher, 2002; Hopper and Traugott, 2003; Traugott and Trousdale, 2013). Langacker also recognizes the major role of subjectification in the process of grammaticalization:

My central claim is that *subjectification* represents a common type of semantic change, and that it often figures in the process of *grammaticization,* whereby "grammatical" elements evolve from "lexical" sources. (Langacker, 1990: 16)

Although Traugott and Langacker define *subjectification* differently (cf. Langacker, 1999: 149; Traugott, 1999: 187; Athanasiadou, Canakis and Cornillie, 2006: 4), the point remains that grammaticalization is often not solely the product of conceptual schematization (or semantic bleaching) but also involves a shift in the semantic value of the grammaticalizing item.[122] Regardless of how one defines subjectification, however, the main challenge is still there: the encoded content of grammatical constructions in CxG (and cognitive linguistics more generally) is still assumed to be primarily conceptual and, therefore, of the same nature as that of lexical constructions. As mentioned earlier, I agree with relevance theorists that there must be a difference in the actual nature of the encoded content. If (more) grammatical constructions also encode conceptual information, then it is unclear how they can still be argued to contribute to the understanding of an utterance in a way that is different from that of (more) lexical items. It could of course be argued that it is precisely the point of CxG to consider that there is no such distinction and that (more) lexical and (more) grammatical elements make a similar contribution to the interpretation process. Perhaps the process of subjectification mentioned above suffices to distinguish between lexical and grammatical items. Yet it is not clear that this is the view that all constructionists (want to) espouse. Indeed, in spite of rejecting a clear-cut distinction between lexical and grammatical constructions, they still often assume that more lexical and more grammatical items serve a different function in discourse. This is exactly what motivates the distinction between contentful and procedural encoding in Traugott's work in the first place, for instance. In the rest of this chapter, it is my aim to argue that the semantics of (more) lexical and (more) grammatical constructions actually differ in nature.

The relevance-theoretic approach to procedural encoding will be presented shortly. Before doing so, it is important to make a couple of observations concerning the constructionist view on the information encoded by 'grammatical' constructions. When arguing that there is a continuum of constructions from more lexical to more grammatical ones, constructionists simply assume that there is no strict distinction between words of the lexicon on the one hand and abstract syntactic rules on the other. Rather, it is argued that individuals store a network of more or less complex and more or less schematic constructions, all of which are associated with a specific function/meaning. In CxG, constructions are defined as the conventional combination of a form and a meaning, and that is why, for instance, both the lexeme *roof* and the DITRANSITIVE pattern equally qualify as constructions (see Chapter 2). Unfortunately, there is one possible pitfall with this approach. One must not forget that although the form–meaning correspondence is indeed characteristic of both lexical and grammatical constructions, this is as far as the similarity goes between the different types of constructions. That is, even though *everything is a construction* in CxG, lexical and grammatical

---

[122] The notion of subjectification will be addressed more fully later in this chapter. In particular, the notion of subjectivity discussed by Traugott will prove particularly useful in defining the notion of procedural encoding in meta-conceptual terms.

constructions remain located on opposite ends of the constructional continuum. As Diessel (2019: 107) puts it, "one must not overlook the differences between lexemes and constructions."[123] On the formal side, grammatical constructions are in general more schematic than lexical ones. This distinction seems to have particular consequences that one cannot ignore. Pulvermüller, Cappelle and Shtyrov (2013) provide solid experimental evidence, for instance, that the physical brain treats lexical and grammatical constructions differently and that distinct neurophysiological processes are involved when using the different types of constructions (see also Divjak et al., 2022). This strongly suggests that the form of a construction is encoded differently by the brain depending on whether it is more lexical or more grammatical. As a consequence, it is reasonable to assume that, similarly, the semantics of these different constructions may itself also be of a different nature and encoded differently. This does not challenge the view that both are form–meaning pairs but, rather, the assumption that they should capture the same type of meaning.

It is worth noting more generally that research in grammaticalization has for a long time focused on the formal distinctions between lexical and grammatical units. Interest in the semantic implications of this process is comparatively more recent. Harder and Boye (2011) point out that (see also Boye and Harder, 2012)

typical definitions are circular – for instance, grammatical expressions are defined as expressions that have grammatical meaning, but grammatical meaning is then defined ostensively in terms of examples of expressions that most linguists would intuitively agree are grammatical. (p. 60)

As the different contributions in Narrog and Heine (2011) illustrate, research on the semantics of grammatical expressions has given rise to a number of different perspectives, with varying degrees of (in)compatibility across views. It will have become clear in this chapter that I wish to pursue the idea put forward in RT, and in particular defended by Nicolle (2011), that grammatical items encode a procedural type of meaning. Now, the aim is to identify exactly what such a procedural content consists of. This will enable me to explain more specifically how more grammatical constructions (i.e. schematic constructions, be they atomic or complex) directly contribute to the interpretation of lexical items and account for cases of coercion.

---

[123] It is interesting to note that Diessel (2019: 107–108) in fact argues that unlike lexical meaning, constructional meanings "do not directly tap into encyclopedic knowledge but ... provide processing instructions for the interpretation of lexical items." This is exactly the view developed in Relevance Theory (cf. Section 4.2.3.2), which provides further support for the integration of the two approaches.

4.2.3.2 Procedural Meaning in RT   In spite of the pervasive attention to procedural meaning in RT since Blakemore's seminal papers and books, the notion remains relatively ill-defined. Relevance theorists disagree on its scope of application and in what contexts it can or should be used. For instance, although she argues the task may not be easy given the variety of expressions which are assumed to encode procedural information, Carston (2016b: 155) readily recognizes that RT needs a proper definition of procedural encoding. There is some common understanding of what counts as procedural encoding. First of all, it is relatively common in RT to describe procedural information in terms of either semantic *constraints* or *instructions*. These two terms have been used by Blakemore herself:

Such expressions impose *constraints* on the context in which the utterances containing them must be interpreted. (1990: 363; emphasis mine)

[They] encode *instructions* for processing propositional representations. (1992: 152, emphasis mine)

In both cases, however, it is left to the reader's appreciation to understand what the terminology used is actually meant to capture. Indeed, as far as semantics is concerned, it is not obvious what a semantic constraint or instruction consists of, and even less so how they might be acquired and cognitively processed. Curcó (2011) quite rightly points out that "in the literature on procedural meaning very little is asserted about how exactly such meaning is embodied" (Curcó, 2011: 35).[124] As a result, it is not clear what the relevance-theoretic approach to procedural meaning consists of. Indeed, there seem to be as many views of what constitutes procedural meaning as there are papers published on the topic. The dominant view is as follows: at the heart of the distinction between conceptual and procedural encoding lies the assumption that some pieces of information directly contribute to our mental representations (i.e. concepts) while others enable us to compute, or manipulate, these representations (i.e. procedures). The idea that procedural encoding is of a computational format is very strong in RT. Diane Blakemore argues that procedural items "map directly onto computations themselves – that is, onto mental processes" (Blakemore, 1987: 144). Similarly, Wilson also argues that "the function of procedural expressions is to activate or trigger domain-specific cognitive procedures which may be exploited in inferential communication" (Wilson, 2011: 12). According to Escandell-Vidal (2017), "a linguistic procedure can be modelled as an algorithm to be read by processing systems" (Escandell-Vidal, 2017: 92). In this case, the term *procedural encoding* is used in a quite literal

---

[124] A similar observation has been made by Bezuidenhout (2004: 106), who Wilson argues "is right to point out that the nature of the procedural information encoded by lexical items has been insufficiently addressed in relevance theory" (Wilson, 2016: 10).

sense since it corresponds to a cognitive procedure. Unfortunately, it is once again not clear what it means for the semantics of a linguistic item – and in particular here that of grammatical constructions – to consist of a mental computation/process. As will become clear in the rest of this section, this view has resulted in a lot of discussion within RT (see, for instance, Bezuidenhout, 2004; Curcó, 2011).[125]

Another way in which these cognitive procedures have been described is in terms of computational rules: "a procedural item triggers the application of a specific rule represented in its entry" (Curcó, 2011: 35). From this perspective, using a procedural expression triggers the activation of a specific rule which one naturally has to apply to the appropriate conceptual information available in the context of use. Curcó (2011) notes that:

Given certain conceptual representations as input, the activation of a procedure instructs the hearer to manipulate them in a specific way. The process whereby the rule is executed produces as output conceptual representations too. (p. 36)

So, for instance, the use of the pronoun *she* requires the identification of a particular female referent whom, once found, will constitute the new conceptual representation. Similarly, the use of the discourse marker *therefore* (e.g. *He is an Englishman; he is,* therefore, *brave*) requires the hearer to represent the second conjunct (*he is brave*) as being naturally entailed by the information provided in the first conjunct (*He is an Englishman*), thus enabling the recovery of a particular implicated premise or conclusion (*Englishmen are brave*). The difficulty, however, remains to understand exactly, as mentioned above, how

---

[125] Note that it has been suggested (Gundel, 2011: 224; Escandell-Vidal, Leonetti and Ahern, 2011: xx) that the difference in RT between conceptual and procedural information might actually correspond to the distinction established between declarative and procedural memory in neuroscience (cf. Cohen and Squire, 1980; Eichenbaum, 2002; Squire, 2004, inter alia). In short, declarative memory contains all the stored information that one gradually acquires or learns (e.g. the color of one's dog, the name of one's neighbor, etc.), while procedural memory retains processing skills for how to perform a specific task (e.g. tying your shoes, riding a bike, etc.). I will not go into the detail of this discussion here, but it is not clear whether the parallel can be so easily drawn between the two, however. It is simply worth pointing out that there are quite a number of questions that this view naturally raises, from trying to understand exactly what it means for a linguistic item to give access to such a type of procedural memory, as well as pinning down the extent to which it can actually capture specific nuances between similar but distinct grammatical expressions (such as *so* and *therefore*, for instance). More specifically, it is important to note that procedural memory has been generally identified as sustaining the whole of linguistic performance, i.e. as generally providing support for language use (see Bybee, 1998; Paradis, 2009). This is particularly true on the formal side of language, whereby procedural memory particularly enables the use (and combination) of both lexical and grammatical expressions (cf. Paradis, 2009: 14) and accounts for the generativity of language (though see Divjak et al., 2022 for recent discussion). It is therefore unlikely that procedural memory is only related to the subtype of semantic encoding that RT describes as procedural information. In spite of the terminological similarity, procedural encoding as used in RT must be given a definition of its own.

such rules are actually embodied. In the different suggestions that have been made (see Bezuidenhout, 2004; Curcó, 2011; Wilson, 2016), these rules are generally assumed to be "either purely dispositional or formulated in a sub-personal 'machine language' distinct from the language of thought" (Wilson, 2016: 11). In other words, these rules have their very own format, the exact nature of which is not accessible to us. Curcó (2011) has explicitly argued against the approach defended by Bezuidenhout (2004) in terms of causal dispositions[126] and suggests that the rules encoded by procedural expressions might actually be of a conceptual type.[127] Only the use of those rules would require distinct abilities (e.g. of a dispositional nature) which enable us to access them and perform the required action. Curcó herself points out, however, that the perspective she puts forward is but one possibility among many others (Curcó, 2011: 44). Whichever format these rules might take, a rule-based approach to procedural meaning simply fails to win unanimous support in RT. For instance, Wharton (2009: 65) has expressed strong doubts about this idea. He argues that although the notion of rule encoding might apply easily to some procedural items (e.g. discourse connectives), it does not easily extend to all the different types of expressions that have been described in procedural terms (e.g. pronouns, mood indicators). He admits that procedural expressions primarily serve to indicate "the general direction in which the intended meaning is to be sought" (Wharton, 2009: 63), but this need not be in the format of a rule or instruction.[128]

The conclusion so far is that it is not obvious even to relevance theorists themselves exactly what constitutes the content of procedural expressions and that there is little consensus among those who address the question. There is only agreement that procedural information is used to "indicate, guide, constrain, or direct the inferential phase of comprehension" (Carston, 2002a: 162).

In the rest of this section, it is my aim to try and define the procedural meaning of grammatical constructions, be they atomic or complex, many of which directly affect the interpretation of lexical items. I have expressed strong doubts that the function of grammatical constructions consists of the same

---

[126] Dispositions are not representations (i.e. concepts) but are embodied "as ways in which the system acts on representations" (Bezuidenhout, 2004: 109), i.e. as potential action triggers.

[127] In earlier work, Groefsema (1992: 220) also suggests that these rules are encoded as concepts. The notion of *pragmatic features* in Moeschler (2016) also seems to go in that direction.

[128] In addition, one must not forget that for many relevance theorists, concepts consist of three entries, one of which (the logical entry) gives access to deductive rules that are used to compute the logical forms in which a concept occurs (cf. Chapter 2). I have argued against this view in the previous chapter. Nevertheless, for those who maintain that concepts give access to such rules, it becomes essential to spell out exactly in what sense the rules encoded by procedural expressions differ from those encoded by concepts. This is particularly true since it has been argued that many expressions actually encode both conceptual and procedural information. It is unclear exactly how the content of these expressions might then be acquired and how the different types of rules they simultaneously give access to can possibly be computed.

conceptual type of information as lexical items, as is assumed in CxG. At the same time, the more computational model presented in RT also fails to be entirely convincing. I assume that, like concepts, procedural encoding remains of a relatively representational format, in the sense that it consists of some information available to us rather than a cognitive process located in a sub-personal system. The challenge for this view is that representations are usually assumed to be conceptual. This might be why, as mentioned above, Traugott argues that procedures also consist of conceptual structures. It is exactly what motivates Bezuidenhout (2004) to argue that procedures are therefore not representational but dispositional. It could be argued that maintaining a representational format for procedural encoding thus contradicts my previous claim that unlike lexical items, grammatical expressions most probably do not encode concepts but a different type of information. This need not be so, however. As mentioned above, I want to suggest that the content of grammatical constructions might best be understood in terms of meta-conceptual knowledge which provides background information on which to compute lexical concepts. This view will be outlined in the rest of this section.[129]

4.2.3.3 Procedural Meaning: New Hypothesis   The hypothesis is inspired by the following observation: the common denominator in relevance-theoretic approaches is that procedural encoding provides specific constraints on inferential processes.[130] They are commonly used to reduce the search space during inferential processes and, therefore, to optimize relevance. Unfortunately, to argue that some expressions encode particular constraints on interpretation is rather uninformative in a framework like RT. Indeed, the ostensive-inferential approach to communication adopted in RT (see Chapter 2) rests on the assumption that language provides support for the inferential processes that enable the recovery of a speaker's intentions and is therefore largely used to indicate where relevance is to be found.[131] From this perspective, even expressions that encode concepts can be thought of as constraints on inferential processes. Sperber and Wilson's (1995: 168) analysis of the sentences in (104) and (105) supports this view.

(104)   George has a big cat.

(105)   George has a tiger.

---

[129] Note that the main focus of this book remains lexical semantics–pragmatics. Therefore, the hypothesis briefly formulated in the rest of this section constitutes more a suggestion for further research than a definite claim and full-fledged proposal.

[130] After all, the notion of procedural encoding was introduced to RT in a book called "Semantic *constraints* on relevance" (Blakemore, 1987; emphasis mine).

[131] Wilson and Sperber (1993: 102) argue that "linguistic decoding feeds inferential comprehension."

They argue that, in the case that George possesses a tiger, the sentence in (105) is more relevant than the one in (104) since it obviously enables the faster recovery of the speaker's intended interpretation (i.e. that George owns a tiger and not a domestic cat). Here, choosing the conceptual expression *tiger* instead of *big cat* therefore directly affects the inferential process involved during the comprehension phase. So it appears that conceptual items also put constraints on the inferential phase of comprehension. This is particularly true, for instance, since the use of (105) also makes accessible specific assumptions which enable the derivation of a number of implicatures with regard to the situation. These examples are meant to illustrate that in order to keep the notion of procedural meaning distinct from conceptual encoding, it is necessary to specify exactly in what sense procedural expressions act as constraints on inferential processes (i.e. how they do so differently compared to items that encode concepts).

One of the earliest descriptions of procedural information which appears most appealing is that in Wilson and Sperber (1993) when they argue that constructions that encode procedural information provide "information about how to manipulate [conceptual representations]" (Wilson and Sperber, 1993: 97). That is, these expressions are used to put concepts together and form larger representations. This description is particularly interesting since it corresponds very closely to most of the descriptions that are generally given of the semantics of grammatical constructions (which I argue encode procedural information, see previous section). For instance, von Fintel (1995: 184) argues that the semantics of grammatical expressions constitute "a sort of functional glue tying together lexical concepts." Similarly, Langacker (2011) argues that:

Despite the absence of a definite boundary, lexicon and grammar serve different primary functions. Lexical items have a descriptive function: their conceptual content serves to specify some portion of the objective situation. *The role of grammar is to abet and supplement their description. Grammatical constructions sanction and symbolize the integration of lexical content to form more complex conceptions.* . . . This supplementary function corresponds to what Boye and Harder (2009; see also Harder and Boye, 2011) identify as the basic feature distinguishing grammar from lexicon, namely the "coding of secondary information status." (p. 82; emphasis mine)

These two quotes illustrate the general tendency to think of grammatical function in terms of the mental organization (and manipulation) of particular conceptual representations into larger, more complex conceptions. It is this particular view which inspires me to argue that the procedural content associated with grammatical constructions consists of meta-conceptual information. Indeed, it implies that the grammatical/procedural function primarily provides an indication of how the embedded lexical concepts are to be employed. Yet in order to achieve this type of conceptual arrangement, it is necessary to adopt a specific perspective on these concepts. That is, acquiring the meaning of grammatical constructions cannot simply consist in abstracting away from lexical concepts (since in spite of their more abstract nature, the function of grammatical concepts is essentially of the same type as those of lexical concepts), but rather has to involve some form of mental stepping back from them. It is in that sense that grammatical constructions seem to be conventionally associated with meta-concepts: they provide access not to mental representations but to "mental representations of mental representations" (Sperber, 2000b: 3).[132] In other words, the information provided by grammatical constructions does not simply complement that of lexical constructions but rather directly serves to compute lexical concepts.

An approach in meta-conceptual terms is in line with some of the findings discussed in the literature on the function of grammatical constructions (be they atomic or complex). For instance, as opposed to basic representations, meta-representations are often described as constituting representations of a higher (or second) order (cf. Sperber, 2000c). Grammatical constructions have been discussed in such terms as well. For instance, the cognitive psycholinguist Michael Tomasello, advocate of the usage-based approach adopted in CxG, refers to grammatical constructions as second-order symbols: "these may be seen as basically second-order symbols because they indicate how the first-order symbols are to be construed" (Tomasello, 1992: 6). This view also receives support from research in neuroscience where grammatical constructions are also argued to provide "second-order constraints" (Bergen and Wheeler, 2010: 156).[133] Bergen and Wheeler argue that they use the term *second order* in the following sense:

We use the term "second-order" here because in this function, grammar serves not to directly propose content to be mentally simulated, but rather operates over this content. (p. 156)

It is exactly in this sense that I understand the notion of meta-concepts. Support for the view advocated here also comes from research on theory of mind (ToM) abilities, introduced in Chapter 2. It has been observed that the acquisition of ToM abilities involves incremental stages, where more advanced ToM abilities gradually develop throughout childhood (see Zufferey, 2010: 30–35). In particular, it is often argued that a critical stage in their acquisition precisely

---

[132] Note that the notion of meta-representations is also discussed in RT, but mostly in relation to meta-represented thoughts or propositions such as in the case of irony or meta-linguistic negation (see Allott (2017) for a detailed overview), and usually not in relation to grammatical/procedural meaning.

[133] It has also been suggested in developmental biology that "the development of second-order cognition is a necessary prerequisite for the formation of fully grammatical language" (Langer, 1996: 269) and that this is most probably what makes human language different from other animal communication systems (such as that used by chimpanzees, for instance).

concerns the ability to use meta-representations (e.g. (false) beliefs and attitudes), at around three or four years of age,[134] at which point ToM abilities are often assumed to be fully developed. It is worth making a couple of observations here. First of all, research in the field of language acquisition shows that adultlike grammatical knowledge develops and starts to be productive at about the same age (Tomasello, 2003; Clark, 2009).[135] This therefore constitutes an interesting observation for the hypothesis presented here whereby grammatical meaning consists of meta-representations. The link between grammatical constructions and meta-representations also receives support from clinical linguistics. Some individuals show abnormal developments of ToM abilities such as, for instance, individuals with autism spectrum disorder (ASD). It has been observed that one of the skills affected by ASD is theory of mind. In particular, most ASD subjects lack meta-representational abilities (cf. Baron-Cohen, Leslie and Frith, 1985; Baron-Cohen, 1989, 1995; Zufferey, 2015: 164). It appears that a majority of ASD individuals also suffer from language impairment and particularly lack grammatical skills (see, for instance, Eigsti, Bennetto and Dadlani, 2007; Zufferey, 2010; Eigsti et al., 2011; Wittke et al., 2017, and references cited therein). This further suggests that meta-representational abilities and grammatical function are related.[136] Finally, as mentioned earlier, the assumption that grammatical constructions (atomic or complex) give access to meta-conceptual information is also consistent with the observation that their development typically involves a process of subjectification. Traugott (1995: 31) uses the term *subjectification* to refer to the

process whereby "meanings become increasingly based in the speaker's subjective belief state/attitude toward the proposition", in other words, towards what the speaker is talking about. (Traugott, 1989: 35)

This perspective once more seems to go hand in hand with the meta-conceptual hypothesis presented in this section. Indeed, the attitude expressed towards a specific proposition naturally imposes a particular representation (the attitude) onto another representation (the proposition) and therefore consists of a meta-representation. Ronald Langacker also uses the notion of subjectivity in relation to grammatical constructions but, as mentioned earlier, does so differently from Traugott. According to him, grammatical constructions are more

---

[134] Exactly at what age children manage to use meta-representations remains a bit of a debate. For a critical discussion of this issue, see Zufferey (2010: 33–34).

[135] Naturally, children acquire a number of word-combination patterns (such as formulaic phrases, pivot schemas and item-based constructions) at earlier stages, but these bear "no communicative significance" (Tomasello, 2003: 115) and most often only act as "usage-based syntactic operations" (p. 307).

[136] It also reinforces the view that acquiring grammatical constructions (or failing to do so) does not only involve a process of abstraction/generalization (contra Johnson, Boyd and Goldberg, 2012).

subjective than lexical constructions in the sense that their conceptual construal does not explicitly represent the subject of conceptualization as constituting its content but is rather located "offstage," "inhering in the very process of conception without being its target" (Langacker, 1999: 149). That is, the conceptual material provided by grammatical constructions provides tools for conceptualization (which Talmy (2018: 4) refers to as a "conceptual structure"), which is once more consistent with the meta-conceptual view adopted here.

When the procedural semantics of grammatical constructions are described in meta-conceptual terms, one can more easily explain in what sense grammatical constructions act as constraints on interpretation processes. Grammatical constructions precisely serve to provide information about the concepts that occur within their open slots, thus directly providing an indication to the hearer of where relevance is to be found. The types of grammatical constructions discussed in the section on coercion provide information about the types of lexical concepts that typically occur in a given slot, and hence directly affect the recovery of the explicature (i.e. the proposition expressed). As mentioned previously, however, procedures also constrain the recovery of higher-level explicatures and implicatures. Grammatical constructions that constrain the recovery of higher-level explicatures provide information about the type of attitude or speech act intended by the speaker (e.g. sentence types; Clark, 1991). Grammatical constructions that constrain the recovery of implicatures provide information about the type of links between different propositions (e.g. discourse connectives; Blakemore, 1987, 2002).

The aim of this section was to spell out more explicitly what constitutes the semantics of (atomic or complex) grammatical constructions in order to pin down more specifically the way in which they constrain the interpretation of the lexemes that are used within them and to better understand the notion of coercion discussed in the previous section. It was shown that neither of the two views adopted in CxG and RT is fully convincing. Nevertheless, given their respective arguments and on the basis of additional evidence, it has been suggested that procedural/grammatical content might consist of meta-conceptual representations, i.e. information about the (lexical) concepts that are embedded within these structures.[137] When described in meta-conceptual terms, procedural information is understood as providing information of a secondary status, the role of which is to provide a structure against which the concepts that fall within its scope can be mentally construed. This view is fully compatible with and, in fact, helps to explain the perspective on coercion

---

[137] Exactly how these meta-concepts are embodied has not been spelled out. This constitutes a topic for further research and will not be explored here. An interesting hypothesis, following Curcó (2011: 44), might be to consider that procedural/meta-conceptual information simply involves a kind of mental bracketing (i.e. encapsulation) different from conceptual content.

adopted in Section 4.1.5. First of all, as mentioned above, it can account for the relative unidirectionality (captured by the override principle) of the resolution process. Indeed, in this case the function of the lexical item and that of the grammatical construction with which there is a mismatch do not have exactly the same status and contribute in different ways to the interpretation process. It seems intuitively more logical that concepts should conform to the way in which they are meta-represented rather than the other way around. This is particularly true since the meta-conceptual information provided by grammatical constructions supposedly provides a more rigid structure against which the process of meaning construction operates (since they are based on higher-level cognitive abilities and therefore less amenable to change). It is interesting to note that in RT, *rigidity* is considered to be the main property of procedural information (cf. Escandell-Vidal and Leonetti, 2011). This view can therefore explain the natural tendency captured by the override principle (and left relatively unexplained in CxG). At the same time, by virtue of remaining in the format of an information (rather than a cognitive process), the view adopted here still makes it possible for the procedural information associated with grammatical constructions to change. That is, in spite of being more rigid than lexical concepts (i.e. less easily prone to contextual modulation), procedural encoding is not as change-proof as it is often assumed to be in RT. It has been shown in Section 4.1.4 that in some cases, it is precisely the meaning of the construction which is adjusted in accordance with the meaning of the lexical concept. This directly follows from their being acquired and learned in context on the basis of the conceptual elements which occur in them, i.e. from their usage-based origin. As a result, the lexemes used and the context in which a (more) grammatical construction occurs might sometimes have greater coercive force than the grammatical construction itself, which therefore directly affects the meta-representation associated with it. In CxG, it is taken for granted that the function of grammatical constructions can change given that language is assumed to emerge from usage and to be "constantly changing" (Bybee, 2013: 49.)[138] Finally, and perhaps most importantly, defining the function of grammatical constructions in terms of meta-conceptual representations further supports the view that coercion effects are the result of a semantically constrained pragmatic process. Indeed, as mentioned several times already, coercion is semantically constrained given that the meta-conceptual information associated with the grammatical constructions provides

[138] It must be noted that, from a usage-based approach, 'regular' cases of coercion (where it is the meaning of the lexeme which adapts to that of the grammatical construction) must also affect the function of the grammatical construction used. That is, although in this case coercion mostly has an impact on the meaning of the lexeme, its eventual interpretation most certainly also deviates (even slightly) from the meta-conceptual information stored by the grammatical construction and therefore leaves a trace in its representation (and thus contributes to its possible change). Bybee (2010: 186) has explicitly defended this perspective.

a structure against which to understand the lexical concepts that occur within them. At the same time, this meta-conceptual information does not itself constitute the content of these concepts (or the proposition to which they contribute) but simply acts as additional background information on the basis of which the pragmatic process of *lexically regulated saturation* (see previous chapter) can be carried out by the hearer (independently of whether there is a mismatch between the concept encoded by the lexeme and the meta-conceptual information associated with the grammatical construction, see Section 4.1.4).

4.3   Lexemes and Idioms

The aim of this chapter is to identify and explain the ways in which the interpretation of a lexeme is affected by its linguistic environment. A central assumption is that interpreting a lexical construct systematically involves the inferential process of lexically regulated saturation. In Sections 4.1 and 4.2, it was shown that this process is directly constrained by the procedural semantics of the grammatical constructions in which lexemes occur, which sometimes leads to coercion effects. In this section, it will be shown that interpreting a lexeme also largely depends on the hearer's ability to recognize the use of larger (fixed) sequences to which the lexical item may belong, namely idioms. It is widely acknowledged in linguistics that on top of knowing specific lexical units, speakers of a given language also store a number of rather fixed lexical sequences, often referred to as idioms or idiomatic expressions, which are associated with a specific interpretation. The term *idiom* can be found in both CxG and RT, which provides an interesting basis for comparison. The challenge is twofold, however. First, CxG and RT have opposite understandings of what idiomaticity consists of and they do not pay an equal amount of attention to idioms. Second, they focus on different facets of idiomatic expressions. In CxG, the main goal is to identify their formal and semantic properties; in RT, it is the interpretation process of idioms that constitutes the main focus of attention. This section aims to integrate the two perspectives and to provide a cross-theoretical understanding of the interaction between lexical constructions, idioms and the process of lexically regulated saturation.

Although in RT some research addresses the underlying cognitive strategies used by hearers to interpret idioms (e.g. Vega Moreno, 2001, 2003, 2005; Eizaga Rebollar, 2009), these papers stand out as exceptions since the contribution of idiomatic expressions is otherwise never discussed in the relevance-theoretic literature.[139] This is to be expected given that RT adopts a Chomskyan view of

---

[139] The terms *idiom*, *idiomatic* and *idiomaticity* figure in none of Sperber and Wilson (1995), Carston (2002a), Wilson and Sperber (2012) or Clark (2013a), all of which I consider to be reference books in RT.

language, where idioms are considered to be "a relatively marginal phenomenon" (Jackendoff, 2002: 167).[140] In the papers that do address idioms, the term is used in a rather technical sense to refer to (relatively) lexically fixed sequences that usually receive figurative interpretations. This includes patterns such as in (106) to (108).

(106)   *to kick the bucket* – [to die]
   a. They're waiting for me to *kick the bucket* cause then they'll get more money. (COCA, written)
   b. I will work hard to make a niche for myself and wait until one of the old doctors *kicks the bucket*. (COCA, written)

(107)   *to spill the beans* – [to reveal secret information]
   a. Jones tried to get him to *spill the beans* about his true allegiances, but he's not talking. (COCA, written)
   b. But since Bill and Monica have *spilled the beans*, you might want to recast your votes. (COCA, written)

(108)   *to be barking up the wrong tree* – [to be wrong]
   a. If you're looking for good nutrition in a hot dog, you*'re barking up the wrong tree*. (COCA, written)
   b. Most of them agreed with us that TV news "stars" *are barking up the wrong tree* when they focus on their "great" good looks, rather than on the news and the reportorial task at hand. (NOW)

In CxG, idioms of this type have been referred to as *core idioms* (Wulff, 2008: 2). They are so called because constructionists assume that typical features of idiomaticity (i.e. non-compositionality and formal fixedness) are actually shared by a much larger range of constructions than those discussed here. This actually follows from a strict application of the central CxG idea that "any construction can be conceived of as idiomatic" (Wulff, 2008: 18), since most are either formally or semantically unpredictable. Wulff (2008) makes the following observation:

Construction grammar is indeed all about idioms – not in the sense that its scope is restricted to the analysis of phrases like *kick the bucket* or *red herring*, but in the sense that construction grammar defines idiomaticity as a property that is inherent in all linguistic items regardless of their size and degree of schematization. (p. 18)

For this reason, the terms *idiom* and *idiomatic* are extremely frequent in CxG research.[141] From an external standpoint, such a perspective naturally challenges the necessity of keeping the notion of idiom as a separate concept. It is my understanding that construction grammarians might argue this is precisely the point of CxG, and that idioms do not constitute a distinct category of

---

[140] Note that Jackendoff is critical of this view.
[141] CxG was after all developed on the observation that features of idiomaticity pervade linguistic knowledge (Fillmore, Kay and O'Connor, 1988).

constructions (see Wulff, 2013). There are reasons to believe that the notion of idiom is still useful as a distinct concept, even in a theory like CxG. First, there is a general consensus that the term *idiom* does not refer to atomic constructions (i.e. the word-level) but necessarily entails formal complexity (Wulff, 2013: 287). Second, it is also (tacitly) assumed that idiomatic phrases involve a certain level of lexical specification; they are not fully schematic (Wulff, 2013: 287). This is exactly how Goldberg (2006: 5) uses the term. She applies the notion only to fixed (e.g. *going great guns, give the Devil his due*) and semi-fixed (e.g. *jog* < someone's > *memory, send* < someone > *to the cleaners*) constructions. This view is also explicitly spelled out in Wulff (2013):

First, constructions differ in terms of their complexity: morphemes and words are simple constructions, whereas idioms and grammatical frames are increasingly complex. Second, constructions differ in their degree of schematization or lexical specification: words are fully lexically specified, whereas grammatical frames are maximally unspecified with regard to the lexical material that can be inserted. Idioms occupy the space in between these two extremes, with some like *shoot the breeze* being fully lexically filled and others like *pull X's leg* being only partially specified. (p. 278)

The term *idiom* here refers to any construction that is formally complex and lexically (semi-)fixed (see also Croft and Sutton, 2017: 2–3). This view offers an interesting trade-off between what may come across as two extreme views. On the one hand, it enables us to keep the notion of idiom distinct from that of construction, i.e. not all constructions are idioms. On the other hand, it also enables one to extend the scope of the concept to constructions other than those identified in (106) to (108). From this perspective, all of the following constructions can also be viewed as idiomatic phrases: *global warming, wide awake, all of a sudden, from now on, answer the door, fall in love, cost a fortune, catch a bus, run a business, pay* < someone > *a visit, drive* < someone > *crazy*, etc. Some of these constructions show little (formal or semantic) irregularity and might simply be referred to as collocations rather than as idioms.[142] Yet, although these lexical patterns are semantically more transparent than core idioms, they too are acquired and stored by speakers of English as individual constructions. It is for that reason that the term *idiom* (or *idiomatic phrase*) is used for any substantial pattern that ranges "from collocations to [core] idioms" (Wulff, 2013: 287). A direct consequence of this view is that idioms do not constitute marginal cases but rather pervade language: "there are thousands of them – probably as many as there are adjectives" (Jackendoff, 2002: 167). Goldberg (2019: 53) also argues that "the use of lexically specified constructions is a hallmark of native-like speech."

---

[142] See Schmid (2014: 254–259) for a detailed overview of the terminology used.

The idea that speakers of English store such a wide variety of idiomatic phrases (i.e. more or less fixed lexical sequences) has long since become a central tenet of CxG. This is not the case in RT, however. Apart from the core idioms, few linguistic units other than lexemes have been given much attention in RT. This naturally follows from the Chomskyan view of language on which the theory was developed. At the same time, the focus on the lexical level in RT is not motivated by a fundamental objection to the existence of larger lexical patterns. That is, in spite of their largely Chomskyan approach, it is my understanding that many relevance theorists would share the assumption that such patterns exist.[143] It is crucial to understand that the identification of such sequences is not meant to diminish the role played by pragmatics during the interpretation of an utterance (see below). Rather, the aim is only to show that the meaning of a lexical construct in an utterance may also be determined by idiomatic phrases in which it is embedded. Consider the verb *open*, for instance. Carston (2002a: 65) lists a number of examples (e.g. *open the window, one's mouth, a book, a briefcase, the curtains, a wound*) to show that the lexical item can be used to express a variety of (slightly) different meanings in different contexts and argues that each interpretation is arrived at via pragmatic inference in accordance with the principle of relevance, i.e. the hearer systematically has to derive an ad hoc concept OPEN*. While I admit that the interpretation of *open* typically depends on the process of lexically regulated saturation, there are cases where the interpretation of the verb is determined by the idiomatic phrase in which it occurs. Considers the following examples:

(109)   *open the bidding* – [make the first offer]
    a. I *open the bidding* at five thousand dollars. (COCA, written)
    b. He was glad he had *opened the bidding* low. (COCA, written)

(110)   *open one's mouth* – [say something]
    a. Don't *open your mouth* before the dealer does. (COCA, written)
    b. Every time he *opens his mouth*, he gets more popular than the rest of them. (COCA, spoken)

(111)   *open the door to something* – [make something possible]
    a. If we deny anyone's humanity, we *open the door to* unimaginable horror. (COCA, written)
    b. But what actually *opened the door to* Globalization was the economic collapse of 1973-the depression that never was. (COCA, written)

---

[143] There might be relevance theorists who will prefer to ignore idiomatic phrases given the complexity of understanding the underlying cognitive principles that make their use possible. (It is due to a lack of a "strong guiding principle" that Carston (2002a: 219) rejects a polysemous approach to meaning.) But I doubt that all relevance theorists are willing to do so.

In these examples, the verb *open* receives different interpretations. It might be tempting to argue that those interpretations are pragmatically derived in accordance with the hearer's expectations of relevance. I believe, however, that the patterns I identified in (109) to (111) are actually stored as individual constructions by English speakers,[144] and therefore that the particular meaning retrieved is not (solely) the product of pragmatic processes. That is, the hypothesis is that interpreting a lexeme also largely depends on the hearer's ability to recognize the idiomatic phrases in which lexemes are embedded (and which provide their own conceptual information). Here are some further examples:

(112)   *answer the door*
        a. That morning, my doorbell rings. So I jump up and I go *answer the door*, and I look out and I see a bunch of officers. (COCA, spoken)
        b. Funny phrase, *"answer the door."* Excuse me, door, what exactly was your question? (COCA, written)

(113)   *paralyzed with fear*
        a. Some women, like Moyer, also become *paralyzed with fear* and concern for the baby's safety. (COCA, written)
        b. And I remember just sitting there. And I was *paralyzed with fear.* I didn't know what to do. (COCA, spoken)

(114)   *shining example of*
        a. This couple was a *shining example of* two people who have been married for 63 years, and have together, constructed a story of positive reflections and lifelong commitment. (COCA, written)
        b. You know, the BBC stands as a *shining example of* what can be done by radio broadcasting. (COCA, spoken)

In these examples, the lexemes *answer, paralyzed* and *shining* are not interpreted literally but receive a more specific interpretation. In (112), the verb *answer* is used in the sense of opening the (front) door for someone. In the examples in (113), *paralyzed* does not refer to a medical diagnosis but simply indicates one's inability to perform an action. In (114), the adjective *shining* is used to refer to a particularly good example. If one focuses on the lexical level only, then it could be argued that these interpretations require the pragmatic derivation of the ad hoc concepts ANSWER*, PARALYZED* and SHINING*. However, I want to argue, in accordance with CxG, that the patterns identified in (112) to (114) actually constitute idiomatic phrases that speakers of English store individually from the lexemes themselves, and that the particular interpretations just mentioned are made directly accessible by these patterns. In other words, the resulting interpretations are not solely the result of pragmatic inferencing.

---

[144] Entries for each of them can be found in dictionaries such as, for example, the Cambridge Dictionary.

There is no reason why relevance theorists would reject this view. It is not in contradiction with any of the core RT assumptions. The only rightful objection that relevance theorists might raise is that, although it provides a more accurate view of the type of constructions that contribute to the interpretation process, this account does not explain exactly in what way these idiomatic phrases enter the interpretation process. In other words, it is one thing to posit the existence of such constructions, but another to explain how the hearer manages to interpret utterances that contain them. CxG does not provide an answer to this question. In the rest of this section, it is my aim to show that RT can help shed some light on this issue.

One possibility consists in arguing that the meaning encoded by this type of idiomatic construction is directly accessed and systematically prevails over that of the lexemes found inside them. This is most probably due to the exact same intellectual shortcut that leads many to falsely believe that coercion in CxG is viewed as a systemic mechanism, namely that the hearer understands the utterance "because they know the construction." This I want to refer to as the *grammarian's fallacy*. Such a view can be found in previous research. The corpus linguist John Sinclair, for instance, argues that this is one of the implications of what he calls the *idiom principle* (Sinclair, 1991: 110–115). However, the interpretation process involved must be more complex: understanding utterances that contain idiomatic phrases certainly involves elaborate cognitive processes that go beyond simple recognition of those patterns. Consider, for instance, the construction *"open the door to < something >"* discussed previously. This construction is typically used by a speaker to express a meaning along the lines of 'making something possible'. The two examples in (115) are typical instantiations of this idiomatic phrase. In this case, it could be tempting to argue that the hearer's interpretation of the sentence simply follows from their knowing the *"open the door to < something >"* construction. Examples such as in (116) challenge this perspective, however.

(115)   a. There was adamant opposition to anything that might *open the door to* government encroachment into school governance, admission, curriculum, or operations. (COCA, written)
        b. Such a definition challenges Catholic doctrine on gender role "complementarity" and *opens the door to* acknowledging different sexual orientations. (COCA, written)

(116)   I could think of no more reasons to delay. I took a deep breath and *opened the door to* the exam room where the police were waiting. (COCA, written)

In this case, although the formal make-up of the sentence in (116) corresponds exactly to that of the construction found in the two previous examples, it is not interpreted in accordance with the description given above. This necessarily calls into question the interpretation process of these sequences, and in particular the ways in which one actually recognizes a sequence as being an

instantiation of a particular construction (thus leading to one particular interpretation) or not. It is precisely my aim now to sketch a brief proposal of how
utterances containing these patterns might be interpreted.

By and large, the view adopted here is that interpreting an utterance which
contains a sequence of words that might be identified as an instantiation of
a specific idiomatic phrase involves a similar type of process as that involved in
the case of homonymy (i.e. ambiguity): there are two conflicting interpretations
available but one is contextually (dis-)preferred. Applied to the analysis of
sentences like (115) to (116), the idea is that hearers' recovery of the speaker's
intended interpretation therefore systematically involves a relative conflict
between a regular syntactic parsing of these sentences and the recovery of the
function associated with the pattern "*open the door to* < something >". How
one is to decide whether or not a particular sequence of words is best analyzed
as an instantiation of an idiomatic phrase is then determined in context in
accordance with the principle of relevance. Together with the linguistic environment, the extra-linguistic context in which this sequence occurs makes one
interpretation more relevant to an individual than another. As a result, one may
not even test the meaning of the idiomatic construction for relevance if its
function is contextually obstructed, such as in example (116). This means that
we need not postulate the primacy of the idiomatic phrase's meaning, let alone
the need to cancel this meaning if it is deemed irrelevant.[145] The approach
adopted here makes syntactic parsing an equal candidate during the search for
relevance and, therefore, the overall interpretation process is viewed as being
much more context-sensitive than previously assumed.

This view is entirely consistent with the *relevance-guided comprehension
procedure* adopted in RT discussed earlier. Whether or not a particular string of
words is recognized as an instantiation of a particular construction really
depends on whether, during the search for relevance, its meaning is easily
accessed and satisfies one's expectations of relevance. In RT, Vega Moreno
(2001, 2003, 2005), who analyzes core idioms from a relevance-theoretic
approach, provides a detailed and well-documented argument that supports
this analysis. Her approach is captured very well in the following quote:

This paper argues in favour of an account of idioms which is not committed to the
existence of different processing modes in language understanding. It pursues the view
that speakers do not aim at literalness (Bobrow and Bell, 1973) or at figurativeness
(Gibbs, 1994) but at optimal relevance (Sperber and Wilson, 1995). The comprehension
of idioms is achieved through just the same processing mechanisms as the comprehension of non-idiom strings. That is, in understanding an idiom, as in understanding any
other instance of language, the hearer is guided by the relevance-theoretic

[145] In other words, like RT rejects the "encoded-first" hypothesis, I hereby reject the "idiom-first"
hypothesis (i.e. the idea that the meaning encoded by the idiomatic phrases is always tested
before the meaning of the individual words that compose the idiom).

comprehension procedure. Since utterance processing is not optional, both the concepts underlying the individual constituents in the string and the concept underlying the idiom as a holistic unit are activated as the idiom is heard. Precisely which of this activated information is accessed follows from considerations of relevance. (Vega Moreno, 2001: 100)

A consequence of this perspective is that although there might be contexts in which the meaning of the idiomatic phrase is tested first then rejected (thus giving rise to garden-path effects; see Slattery et al., 2013), there must also be contexts in which it is not even tested and only the interpretation obtained via regular syntactic parsing is considered (as seems to be the case in example (116)). This view is consistent with most of the work carried out in cognitive science on the processing of sentences containing idioms (see Jurafsky, 1992, 1993, 1996; Tabossi, Fanari and Wolf, 2009; Beck, 2020, and references cited therein). The overview provided by Jurafsky (1993: 3) convincingly shows that the processing of this type of sentence is indeed both *parallel* and *context-sensitive*.

Essentially, the main assumption here is that upon hearing (or reading) sentences like (115) to (116), one cannot entirely escape the process of lexically regulated saturation introduced in the previous chapter (which applies to atomic lexical items). That is, whether or not a particular utterance contains a more lexically fixed/idiomatic pattern, the early stages of the inferential process (which makes possible the recovery of the speaker's intended interpretation) will typically involve reconstructing the meaning of lexical items in accordance with one's expectations of relevance. Depending on a number of factors, such as contextual accessibility and relevance, recognizing one of the more idiomatic phrases will have an impact on the interpretation process and may redirect the hearer's cognitive resources to new inferential paths to reconstruct the meaning of the idiom. In this case, the process of lexically regulated saturation is simply suspended, and the hearer relocates their cognitive resources in such a way as to optimize the relevance of the interpretation (by managing the amount of cognitive effort required to obtain sufficient cognitive effects). There will be contexts, of course, where the meaning of these (idiomatic) constructions will be so salient that it might be tested for relevance almost immediately during the inferential phase of comprehension (thus giving the impression that the interpretation process is therefore 'short-circuited', as Cappelle and Depraetere (2016) argue). The main assumption here, however, is that the meaning of these idiomatic phrases will not systematically be tested first for relevance and only canceled in inappropriate contexts.

A direct consequence of this view is that lexically regulated saturation therefore lies at the heart of the interpretation process of a lexeme, in the sense that it is systematically performed during the inferential phase of comprehension. This is, of course, not to say that lexical processing necessarily precedes idiom processing (as mentioned above, these are seen as running in parallel). Rather, the claim is that, in the early stages of the comprehension phase, idiom processing does not *ipso facto* block lexical processing. These processes involve context-sensitive cognitive procedures that require the hearer to determine in context which construction (i.e. the lexeme or the idiomatic phrase) is being used in order to recover the speaker's intended interpretation. As a result, early stages of the comprehension process systematically involve lexically regulated saturation, which may simply be suspended (i.e. in the sense of interrupted) if processing the meaning of the idiom seems more relevant to the hearer. The representation in Figure 4.5 is an attempt to visualize the (relatively) central role of lexically regulated saturation during the interpretation phase of an utterance.

The left part of Figure 4.5 captures the approach introduced in Section 4.2.2: lexical constructions are systematically interpreted via the inferential process of lexically regulated saturation, which is guided by the procedural meaning of the grammatical constructions in which they occur and as a result of which coercion effects sometimes emerge. In addition, the right part of this figure is meant to capture the observation made in this section according to which the interpretation of an utterance also often involves parallel processing of lexical constructions and the larger idiomatic patterns in which they occur, an inferential process which may lead to the suspension of lexically regulated saturation during the search for relevance in favor of idiom processing. Once more, therefore, I hope to have shown how complementary Construction Grammar and Relevance Theory are when it comes to providing cognitively accurate descriptions of language use. Reconstructing the meaning of an utterance is neither fully the result of pragmatic inference (RT), nor simply the recovery of

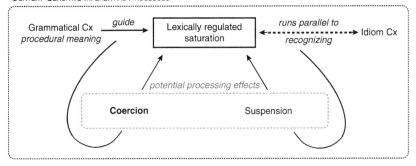

Figure 4.5 'Lexically regulated saturation' and utterance comprehension (2)

a construction's encoded meaning (CxG), but is a complex interaction of these two aspects.

4.4   Conclusion

This chapter started off with the simple observation that a negative conse-quence falls out of the respective aims of CxG and RT: CxG tends to over-emphasize the role played by an individual's linguistic knowledge whereas RT tends to minimize it in favor of inferential processes. I have shown that these two aspects contribute equally to the (construction and) interpretation of an utterance in general, and lexemes in particular. In the case of lexemes, the process of lexically regulated saturation discussed in the previous chapter is meant to capture this very observation. The discussion of this process remained relatively lexeme-centered, however, and the central aim of this chapter was precisely to investigate the role played by the linguistic and extra-linguistic context in which lexemes are used and identify exactly how it affects the interpretation of lexical constructions (i.e. how it affects the process of lexically regulated saturation). In order to do so, a number of notions were discussed. In Sections 4.1 and 4.2, I focused on the concepts of coercion and procedural meaning. In Section 4.3, I looked at 'idiomatic' constructions.

It is a central assumption in CxG that in addition to specific lexemes, language users know a large variety of more schematic constructions in which lexemes are used and which have their own function (e.g. the DITRANSITIVE construction, the CAUSED-MOTION construction, the WAY con-struction, etc.). Therefore, understanding a lexeme also crucially depends on the semantics of the construction in which it occurs. Of course, one could naturally expect the meaning of the lexeme to be compatible with that of the construction. This is not always the case, however. There is often a semantic (and morphosyntactic) mismatch between the lexeme and the particular slot of the construction in which it is used. CxG argues that in such a case the meaning of the lexeme (almost) systematically conforms to the semantics of the larger construction. These have been referred to as cases of coercion, since the meaning of the construction is coerced onto that of the lexeme. The notion of coercion proves particularly interesting since it shows that not all cases of lexical adjustments are therefore necessarily pragmatically (i.e. non-linguistically) motivated, as is often argued in RT. Rather, the interpretation of a lexeme is also a function of the semantics of the constructions in which it can be used and is, therefore, slightly more language-driven than is assumed in RT. The challenge is to understand exactly how the meaning of the construction is coerced onto that of the lexeme. CxG does not offer any explanation, however. By virtue of being a usage-based theory, most constructionists agree it is the language user that coerces the meaning of the construction onto the lexeme (and not the construction itself), but none explain exactly how this process is actually carried out. This is when insights from RT become essential. Cases of coercion are best described as the result of an inferential process whereby the hearer constructs a relevant interpretation on the basis of their linguistic knowledge as well as taking into account the speaker's intention and extra-linguistic factors. In particular, I have argued that the process involved during coercion is exactly the same process as in non-coerced cases: lexically regulated saturation. The difference is that in the case of coercion, this process is constrained by the semantics of the construction in which lexemes are found to a greater extent than in the case of non-coerced lexemes (hence the need to keep coercion as a distinct concept).

In RT, the idea that some linguistic items might provide particular constraints during the interpretation process is usually discussed under the notion of procedural meaning. Items that have a procedural function do not contribute to the proposition expressed directly but simply affect the inferential process involved during its recovery. Given the particular perspective on coercion adopted here (in terms of semantic constraints), it therefore seemed interesting to identify to what extent the two notions actually overlap. It has been shown that there is a relation. First, both frameworks identify coercion and procedural meaning as associated with grammatical constructions. Unfortunately, CxG and RT have a different understanding of what counts as a grammatical unit of the language. Nevertheless, it has been argued that procedurality is particularly characteristic of the more schematic constructions identified in CxG (precisely those that are involved in the process of coercion). To treat these grammatical constructions in procedural terms provides further support for the view that coercion involves a semantically constrained pragmatic process since it is precisely the function of procedural expressions to act as constraints on inferential processes. The main challenge of course is to understand exactly what procedural encoding consists of and how it actually constrains the interpretation process. It was shown that the respective views developed in CxG and RT fail to be entirely convincing. For this reason, building on various arguments, a tentative hypothesis was put forward. I argued that the procedural content of grammatical constructions might best be described in meta-conceptual terms. In this case, the information associated with a grammatical construction is viewed as having a secondary status in that it is primarily used as background information to manipulate the concepts which occur within its scope.

In the third part of this chapter, it was shown that the interpretation of a lexeme also largely depends on whether it is embedded in a larger, idiomatic phrase. This naturally requires us to define what counts as idiomatic, and I argued that the term *idiomatic phrase* can be used to refer to any fixed lexical sequences that one stores as an individual construction (e.g. *global warming*, *answer the door*, *spill the beans*). These constructions make available a specific interpretation for the lexemes that are found inside them which directly influ-ences the process of lexically regulated saturation. The challenge is to know exactly in what way the meaning of these patterns enters the interpretation process. I argue that the meaning of idioms does not have priority over the meaning of the individual lexical items found inside them, but rather that interpreting a sentence that contains idiomatic phrases involves a complex, parallel process largely determined by considerations of relevance. In other words, early stages of the interpretation process involve lexically regulated saturation, which only gets suspended when the meaning of the idiom is contextually more relevant.

Generally, I hope to have shown that the interpretation of a lexeme system-atically involves the pragmatic process of lexically regulated saturation. In the meantime, although pragmatic in nature, this process remains largely con-strained linguistically by many schematic constructions in which lexemes occur (sometimes giving rise to coercion effects) or by the more idiomatic phrases in which they are embedded. There is a real equilibrium, therefore, between the contribution made by a speaker's linguistic knowledge and infer-ential pragmatic processes to the interpretation of a lexical item. Bringing together insights from CxG and RT thus once more proves beneficial to the understanding of lexical semantics–pragmatics. Although they share the intu-ition that the interpretation of a lexeme can largely be influenced by the semantics of the larger structures in which it occurs, it was shown that neither theory fully explains the role played by these constructions and the cognitive mechanisms that enable the integration of the different levels of meaning in context. Critical evaluation of the different arguments led to a new proposal regarding the complex nature of the interaction between lexically regulated saturation, procedural meaning, coercion and idioms.

5   Conclusion

The aim of this book was to provide a new perspective on the semantics–pragmatics interface by combining insights from Construction Grammar and Relevance Theory. The main driving force behind this work was the commitment to obtaining cognitively accurate descriptions of language use. As mentioned in the introduction, such a commitment to cognitive plausibility and descriptive accuracy led to the development of the two frameworks. Given their respective domains of interest, however, they sometimes make different predictions and provide opposite analyses of the same linguistic phenomena. In Construction Grammar, more room is given to knowledge than in Relevance Theory, in which greater emphasis is placed on inferential processes. As a consequence, this naturally questions their capacity to achieve descriptive accuracy. The main challenge of this book was therefore twofold. Primarily, this contribution to the field can be viewed as an attempt to identify where descriptive accuracy actually lies. More generally, though, the aim was also to identify the extent to which the integration of the two frameworks generates further and better insights into the underlying mechanisms of verbal communication. It was not the aim of this book simply to act as a judge as to which framework is better at achieving descriptive accuracy, and therefore to draw up a list of concessions that the other theory has to make. Rather, my aim has been to enhance the explanatory power of each framework through their combination; the new model presented consists of more than just the sum of the two different approaches.

Needless to say, this integration first requires a thorough examination of the two theories and their respective strengths and weaknesses. This is why I introduced each of the frameworks individually in detail in Chapter 2.

In Chapter 3, the main focus was on lexical semantics–pragmatics. In this case, it was shown that CxG and RT have radically different understandings of the degree to which semantics and pragmatics actually contribute to the interpretation of a lexeme. First, it became apparent that a critical analysis of the notion of 'concept' was necessary. Both frameworks use this term, but in radically different ways. Moreover, it was shown that in RT the standard (i.e. referential atomic) view is incompatible with some of the central tenets of the theory. I argued that the best alternative is to define concepts in terms of (a rich body of) encyclopedic knowledge. The main challenge from this perspective is to explain exactly how this type of conceptual information enters the interpretation process of a lexeme. I have shown that viewing the interpretation of a lexeme as depending on both very rich semantics and strong pragmatic principles is possible and, in fact, actually accounts for the various observations made in the literature on lexical processing. This view was articulated around the notion of *lexically regulated saturation* (a term borrowed from Depraetere, 2010, 2014), which captures the complex relation between semantics and pragmatics: in spite of the very rich semantics that a lexical item makes accessible, its actual function is systematically reconstructed in context in accordance with the principle of relevance. This naturally requires adopting a particular view on what counts as semantic content and pragmatic inferencing. The suggested analysis makes for a more powerful analysis than either of CxG or RT alone can.

In Chapter 4, the aim was to understand more specifically how the direct linguistic environment in which a lexeme occurs can affect the interpretation process of lexically regulated saturation. In RT, little attention is given to larger linguistic structures. By contrast, constructionists prefer to identify the larger structures in which lexical constructions are embedded. In the first part of the chapter, I focused on more grammatical (i.e. schematic) types of constructions. In CxG, the term *coercion* is typically used when a lexical item inherits part of its content from the grammatical construction in which it is used. The only problem with this notion is that CxG fails to explain in detail how the lexeme inherits the meaning associated with the grammatical construction. It was shown that RT can help to describe the exact nature of coercion. First, I argued that coercion is itself also primarily a pragmatic process carried out by the language user. More precisely, I argued that the actual nature of the interpretation process behind coercion is the same as in non-coerced cases, namely that of lexically regulated saturation, and that the function of the constructions in which lexemes occur is simply to act as an additional constraint on the recovery of the intended interpretation. The next step was to spell out exactly what the role of the constructions involved in the process of coercion is. It was shown that coercive constructions are formally (semi-) schematic (i.e. grammatical) and have a procedural function. This view in turn required defining what counts as procedural meaning. It was shown that there is as yet no clear and uncontroversial definition of this notion. I compared various approaches to procedural meaning (and grammatical encoding more generally) and put forward the tentative claim that the procedural nature of schematic constructions follows from their encoding meta-conceptual information, i.e. information about the type of concept which is expected to occur in a given position of a construction. This actually resulted in adjusting the strong views adopted in both CxG and RT with regard to the nature of coercion and procedural encoding (that the meaning of the grammatical constructions usually, though not systematically, wins over that of the lexemes found in them). In the final part of that chapter, I focused on more idiomatic (i.e. lexically fixed) constructions. It was shown that the interpretation of a lexeme is also often determined by larger sequences in which it occurs. The main challenge was to understand how these constructions enter into the interpretation process and how they affect the process of lexically regulated saturation usually performed for the individual words that occur in these patterns. In accordance with the approach developed in RT, I argued that interpreting utterances that contain idiomatic constructions also primarily involves pragmatic processes that are guided by the principle of relevance. That is, interpreting a sentence containing an idiomatic construction consists in a context-sensitive reconstruction of the most relevant interpretation, the function of the construction being a strong candidate but not the only possibility. When the hearer reconstructs the meaning of the idiomatic patterns, there are felt to be contextual effects whereby lexically regulated saturation is 'suspended'. What the chapter therefore shows is that the pragmatic process of lexically regulated saturation is central to the interpretation of lexical constructions. This process is guided by the procedural semantics of the grammatical constructions in which lexemes occur, which can lead to coercion effects. Also, lexically regulated saturation may be suspended when the hearer recognizes the use of an idiomatic construction in which the lexeme is embedded. In each case, this involves an intricate interaction between one's rich linguistic knowledge and relevance-guided pragmatic processes. This approach was then represented as in Figure 5.1.

Once more, this book was therefore meant to be an illustration that combining insights from the two theories helps to increase the overall explanatory

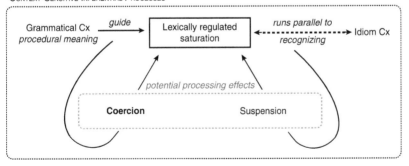

Figure 5.1 'Lexically regulated saturation' and utterance comprehension (2)

power of each framework. Of course, this book contains a mainly theoretical investigation, and critics might rightly argue that the resulting model still needs to be put to the test. However, in a chapter in Depraetere et al.'s recent book, *Models of Modals*, I actually used this theoretical apparatus to look at modal verbs in English (Leclercq, 2023), and the discussion reveals that greater precision can be obtained when combining CxG and RT as I have done in this book. While emphasizing the inferential nature of the interpretation of modal verbs (in terms of lexically regulated saturation), I showed that a vast network of modal constructions in fact intervenes in the process. For instance, speakers of English also know a great number of modal 'idioms', such as those in (117) and (118), which may short-circuit lexically regulated saturation.

(117)   S<small>UBJ</small> *must surely* VP
          She *must surely* be the most beautiful in the world. (Cappelle, Depraetere and Lesuisse, 2019: 231)

(118)   *I can't tell you how* ...
          Sweet loyal Jack. *I can't tell you how* good it is to see you. (Leclercq, 2022: 239)

The 'S<small>UBJ</small> *must surely* VP' construction typically triggers a strong epistemic interpretation of *must*, as is the case in (117). Likewise, the verb *can* in (118) is not simply used (if at all) to communicate the speaker's inability to be specific about all sorts of (metaphorical) quantities, but it actually puts emphasis on their extremely positive feelings with regard to the situation at hand, a function that is associated with the '*I can't tell you how* ... ' construction. So the interpretation of these verbs is not just a matter of lexically regulated saturation. At the same time, understanding sentences like these does not simply consist of the recovery of these constructions and their function but rather results from the context-sensitive reconstruction of the speaker's intended interpretation in accordance with one's expectation of relevance. That is, understanding sentences like (118), for instance, is more complex than simply recovering the function of the pattern '*I can't tell you how* ... ', which then only gets canceled in inappropriate contexts. Rather, understanding this sequence of words consists in a parallel, context-sensitive reconstruction of the speaker's intended interpretation via considerations of optimal relevance.

In addition, Leclercq (2023) shows that modal verbs can also be used in more schematic modal patterns from which they inherit their function (i.e. whose function can be viewed as being 'coerced' onto the modal verbs). This is the case of the sentences in (119) and (120), for instance.

(119)   S<small>UBJ</small> M<small>OD</small> *be* C<small>OMPL</small>
          It's so incredible what your mother did. She *must* be a saint. (COCA)

(120) *I don't think we* Mod VP
       I don't think we *may* consider Trump as a "coronabuster", on the contrary, but
       at least the cartoon is well rendered.[146]

The pattern in (119) is typically associated with an epistemic interpretation, which the verb *must* here receives. Also, comparing corpus data from different sources, Leclercq (2023) establishes that speakers of English most probably store the construction identified in (120), which typically conveys an invitation not to perform the action denoted by the VP. In this pattern, it is usually necessity verbs that are used (e.g. *I don't think we should change things now*, Cappelle, Depraetere and Lesuisse, 2019: 232; *And let me be clear on this. I don't think we need to have our boots on the ground*, Leclercq, 2023: 74), which means that the modal value is typically rather strong. The sentence in (120) inherits the general function of this construction, and the verb *may*, whose modal value is typically rather weak, seems to express a stronger kind of possibility meaning. Once again, this means that the interpretation process is not solely the result of lexically regulated saturation. At the same time, the resolution process involved, although undeniably being constrained by the semantics of both the modal verb and the construction in which it occurs, is again context-sensitive and only contextual relevance enables the hearer to derive the exact interpretation intended by the speaker. As mentioned in Chapter 4, the pragmatic (i.e. inferential) understanding of *may* in this sentence follows naturally from the procedural semantics encoded by the (grammatical) construction in which *may* occurs, the exact function of which precisely constrains the inferential process of lexically regulated saturation involved while interpreting the lexeme.

Modality is of course one domain of application, and further research is needed to show the benefits of combining CxG and RT. Still, beyond the various theory-internal developments suggested throughout this book, I hope to have shown that a better understanding of linguistic communication (and human cognition more generally) can be achieved when integrating insights from frameworks whose primary commitment is cognitive plausibility.

A number of further conclusions fall out from my investigation. On the question of whether it is possible to combine insights from CxG and RT, I hope to have convinced the reader that the answer is positive. More importantly, concerning the explanatory power of this integration, the various arguments developed show quite clearly that a deeper understanding of the semantics–pragmatics interface (in particular) and of verbal communication more generally is possible and that the respective approaches can indeed benefit from one another in order to achieve even more descriptive accuracy. It was shown that

---

[146] From: https://twitter.com/LatuffCartoons/status/1265597766186786816 (last accessed: May 31, 2023).

this sometimes requires articulating various aspects of language use in more complex ways than is sometimes the case in either framework. The aim of this book was not to provide a simple model, however, but one which makes more cognitively accurate predictions than CxG and RT manage to do on their own. Instead of reducing the domain of application of each framework, I believe this work therefore opens up a wide array of new research possibilities within (and across) these two already far-reaching theories. Here are some of the directions for future research.

Concerning the semantics–pragmatics interface, it might be important to carry out additional experimental work to test the hypothesis that the function of the (idiomatic) patterns does not necessarily have priority over that of the individual lexemes found inside them. The literature in psycholinguistics already seems to support this view, yet more evidence might be needed to further substantiate this claim. In addition, the discussion in Chapter 4 on the nature of grammatical constructions and procedural encoding also leaves open a number of questions. It was shown that providing a specific definition for what grammatical/procedural encoding consists of is necessary. I put forward the hypothesis that this type of meaning consists in a form of meta-conceptual encoding. This particular hypothesis also needs to be elaborated further and has to be tested experimentally. More generally, there are other areas of research that I think could benefit from integrating CxG and RT. For instance, I think it would be interesting to see how much the *principle of relevance* affects the gradual process of language acquisition and, therefore, the development of the construct-i-con. This observation applies equally well to the domain of language variation and change. In a similar spirit, it might also be interesting to investigate the extent to which combining CxG and RT can contribute to a better understanding of the cognitive strategies used by individuals with particular language impairments (e.g. dyslexia, aphasia, autism, Alzheimer's, etc.). Finally, in more applied approaches to language, this integration might also be fruitfully applied in the context of discourse analysis when looking at the various strategies that speakers use in order to direct their speech in a particular direction.

Bibliography

Aarts, Bas. 2007. *Syntactic gradience: The nature of grammatical indeterminacy.* Oxford: Oxford University Press.

Abbot-Smith, Kirsten and Michael Tomasello. 2006. Exemplar-learning and schematization in a usage based account of syntactic acquisition. *The Linguistic Review* 23: 275–290.

Aït-Kaci, Hassan. 1984. *A lattice-theoretic approach to computation based on a calculus of partially ordered type structures.* Ph.D. thesis, University of Pennsylvania.

Akmajian, Adrian and Frank W. Heny. 1975. *An introduction to the principles of transformational syntax.* Cambridge, MA: MIT Press.

Allen, Kachina, Francisco Pereira, Mathew Botvinick and Adele E. Goldberg. 2012. Distinguishing grammatical constructions with fMRI pattern analysis. *Brain and Language* 123: 174–182.

Allott, Nicholas. 2002. Relevance and rationality. *UCL Working Papers in Linguistics* 14: 69–82.

Allott, Nicholas. 2013. Relevance Theory. In Alessandro Capone, Franco Lo Piparo and Marco Carapezza (Eds.), *Perspectives on linguistic pragmatics*, 57–98. Berlin: Springer International Publishing.

Allott, Nicholas. 2017. Metarepresentation. In Anne Barron, Yueguo Gu and Gerard Steen (Eds.), *The Routledge handbook of pragmatics*, 295–309. Abingdon: Routledge.

Allott, Nicholas. 2020. Relevance theory [annotated bibliography]. In Mark Aronoff (Ed.), *Oxford bibliographies in linguistics. [Online Resource].* Oxford: Oxford University Press.

Allott, Nicholas and Mark Textor. 2012. Lexical pragmatic adjustment and the nature of ad hoc concepts. *International Review of Pragmatics* 4 (2): 185–208.

Allwood, Jens. 2003. Meaning potential and context: Some consequences for the analysis of variation in meaning. In Hubert Cuyckens, René Dirven and John R. Taylor (Eds.), *Cognitive approaches to lexical semantics*, 29–65. Berlin: Mouton de Gruyter.

Andersen, Gisle. 2000. The role of the pragmatic marker *like* in utterance interpretation. In Gisle Andersen and Thorstein Fretheim (Eds.), *Pragmatic markers and propositional attitude*, 17–38. Amsterdam: John Benjamins.

Andersen, Gisle and Thorstein Fretheim. 2000. *Pragmatic markers and propositional attitude.* Amsterdam: John Benjamins.

Arnon, Inbal and Neal Snider. 2010. More than words: Frequency effects for multi-word phrases. *Journal of Memory and Language* 62 (1): 67–82.

Assimakopoulos, Stavros. 2008. Intention, common ground and the availability of semantic content: A relevance-theoretic perspective. In Istvan Kecskes and Jacob Mey (Eds.), *Intention, common ground and the egocentric speaker-hearer*, 105–126. Berlin: Mouton de Gruyter.

Assimakopoulos, Stavros. 2012. On encoded lexical meaning: Philosophical and psychological perspectives. *Humana Mente Journal of Philosophical Studies* 23: 17–35.

Assimakopoulos, Stavros. 2022. Ostension and the communicative function of natural language. *Journal of Pragmatics* 191: 46–54.

Athanasiadou, Angeliki, Costas Canakis and Bert Cornillie. 2006. *Subjectification: Various paths to subjectivity*. Berlin: Mouton de Gruyter.

Audring, Jenny and Geert Booij. 2016. Cooperation and coercion. *Linguistics* 54: 617–637.

auf der Straße, Alexander. 2017. *Constructions in use*. Düsseldorf: Düsseldorf University Press.

Austin, John L. 1962. *How to do things with words*. Oxford: Clarendon Press.

Bach, Kent. 1994a. Semantic slack: What is said and more. In Savas L. Tsohatzidis (Ed.), *Foundations of speech act theory*, 267–291. New York: Routledge.

Bach, Kent. 1994b. Conversational impliciture. *Mind & Language* 9: 124–162.

Bardzokas, Valandis. 2023. Narrowed and broadened concepts: A contribution to current issues and future directions. *Journal of Pragmatics and Discourse Analysis* 2 (1): 1–15.

Baron-Cohen, Simon. 1989. The autistic child's theory of mind: A case of specific developmental delay. *Journal of Child Psychology and Psychiatry* 30: 285–297.

Baron-Cohen, Simon. 1994. How to build a baby that can read minds: Cognitive mechanisms in mindreading. *Current Psychology of Cognition* 13 (5): 513–552.

Baron-Cohen, Simon. 1995. *Mindblindness: An essay on autism and theory of mind*. Cambridge, MA: MIT Press.

Baron-Cohen, Simon, Alan M. Leslie and Uta Frith. 1985. Does the autistic child have a "theory of mind"? *Cognition* 21: 37–46.

Barsalou, Lawrence W. 1983. Ad hoc categories. *Memory and Cognition* 11: 211–227.

Barsalou, Lawrence W. 1985. Ideals, central tendency, and frequency of instantiation as determinants of graded structure in categories. *Journal of Experimental Psychology: Learning, Memory, and Cognition* 11: 629–654.

Barsalou, Lawrence W. 1987. The instability of graded structure: Implications for the nature of concepts. In Ulric Neisser (Ed.), *Concepts and conceptual development*, 101–140. New York: Cambridge University Press.

Barsalou, Lawrence W. 1989. Intra-concept similarity and its implications for inter-concept similarity. In Stella Vosniadou and Andrew Ortony (Eds.), *Similarity and analogical reasoning*, 76–121. New York: Cambridge University Press.

Barsalou, Lawrence W. 1990. On the indistinguishability of exemplar memory and abstraction in category representation. In Thomas K. Srull and Robert S. Wyer (Eds.), *Advances in social cognition, volume III: Content and process specificity in the effects of prior experiences*, 61–88. Hillsdale, NJ: Lawrence Erlbaum.

Barsalou, Lawrence W. 1992a. Frames, concepts, and conceptual fields. In Adrienne Lehrer and Eva F. Kittay (Eds.), *Frames, fields, and contrasts: New essays in semantic and lexical organization*, 21–74. Hillsdale, NJ: Lawrence Erlbaum.

Barsalou, Lawrence W. 1992b. *Cognitive psychology: An overview for cognitive scientists*. Hillsdale, NJ: Lawrence Erlbaum.

Barsalou, Lawrence W. 1993. Flexibility, structure, and linguistic vagary in concepts: Manifestations of a compositional system of perceptual symbols. In Alan F. Collins, Susan E. Gathercole, Martin A. Conway and Peter E. Morris (Eds.), *Theories of memory*, 29–101. Hove: Lawrence Erlbaum.

Barsalou, Lawrence W. 1999. Perceptual symbol systems. *Behavioral and Brain Sciences* 22: 577–609.

Barsalou, Lawrence W. 2000. Concepts: Structure. In Alan E. Kazdin (Ed.), *Encyclopedia of psychology*, vol. 2, 245–248. New York: Oxford University Press.

Barsalou, Lawrence W. 2012. The human conceptual system. In Michael J. Spivey, Ken McRae and Marc Joanisse (Eds.), *The Cambridge handbook of psycholinguistics*, 239–258. New York: Cambridge University Press.

Barsalou, Lawrence W. 2016. Situated conceptualization: Theory and applications. In Yann Coello and Martin H. Fischer (Eds.), *Foundations of embodied cognition (vol. 1): Perceptual and emotional embodiment*, 11–37. East Sussex, UK: Psychology Press.

Barsalou, Lawrence W., Wenchi Yeh, Barbara J. Luka, Karen L. Olseth, Kelly S. Mix and Ling-Ling Wu. 1993. Concepts and meaning. In Katherine Beals, Gina Cooke, David Kathman, Sotaro Kita, Karl-Eric McCullough and David Testen (Eds.), *Chicago Linguistics Society (29): Papers from the parasession on conceptual representations*, 23–61. Chicago, IL: Chicago Linguistics Society.

Bartsch, Renate. 1984. Norms, tolerance, lexical change, and context-dependent meaning. *Journal of Pragmatics* 8: 367–393.

Bates, Elizabeth and Judith C. Goodman. 1997. On the inseparability of grammar and the lexicon: Evidence from acquisition, aphasia, and real-time processing. *Language and Cognitive Processes* 12: 507–586.

Bates, Elizabeth and Judith C. Goodman. 1999. On the emergence of grammar from the lexicon. In Brian MacWhinney (Ed.), *The emergence of language*, 29–79. Mahwah, NJ: Lawrence Erlbaum.

Beck, Sara Donnell. 2020. *Native and non-native idiom processing: Same difference*. Ph.D. thesis, Universität Tübingen.

Behrens, Heike. 2009. Usage-based and emergentist approaches to language acquisition. *Linguistics* 47: 383–411.

Bencini, Giulia M.L. and Adele E. Goldberg. 2000. The contribution of argument structure constructions to sentence meaning. *Journal of Memory and Language* 43: 640–651.

Bencini, Giulia M.L. and Virginia V. Valian. 2008. Abstract sentence representations in 3-year-olds: Evidence from language production and comprehension. *Journal of Memory and Language* 59: 97–113.

Berbeira Gardón, José Luis. 1996. *Los Verbos Modales Ingleses: Estudio Semántico-Pragmático*. Cadiz: Cadiz University, Servicio de Publicaciones.

Berbeira Gardón, José Luis. 1998. Relevance and modality. *Revista Alicantina de Estudios Ingleses* 11: 3–22.

Berbeira Gardón, José Luis. 2006. On the semantics and pragmatics of *will*. In Marta Carretero, Laura Hidalgo Downing, Julia Lavid, Elena Martinez Caro, Joanne Neff, Soledad Perez de Ayala and Esther Sanchez-Pardo (Eds.), *A pleasure of life in words: A Festschrift for Angela Downing*, vol. 1, 445–465. Madrid: Universidad Complutense de Madrid.

Bergen, Benjamin. 2016. Embodiment, simulation and meaning. In Nick Riemer (Ed.), *Routledge handbook of semantics*, 142–157. London: Routledge.

Bergen, Benjamin and Kathryn Wheeler. 2010. Grammatical aspect and mental simulation. *Brain and Language* 112 (3): 150–158.

Bergs, Alexander. 2018. Learn the rules like a pro, so you can break them like an artist (Picasso): Linguistic aberrancy from a constructional perspective. *Zeitschrift für Anglistik und Amerikanistik* 66 (3): 277–293.

Bergs, Alexander and Gabriele Diewald. 2009. *Contexts and constructions*. Amsterdam: John Benjamins.

Berkeley, George. 1709. *An essay towards a new theory of vision*. Dublin: Pepyat.

Bezuidenhout, Anne. 2002. Truth-conditional pragmatics. *Philosophical Perspectives* 16: 105–134.

Bezuidenhout, Anne. 2004. Procedural meaning and the semantics/pragmatics interface. In Claudia Bianchi (Ed.), *The semantics/pragmatics distinction*, 101–131. Stanford, CA: CSLI Publications.

Blakemore, Diane. 1987. *Semantic constraints on relevance*. Oxford: Blackwell.

Blakemore, Diane. 1990. Constraints on interpretation. In *Proceedings of the 16th Annual Meeting of the Berkeley Linguistics Society*, 363–370. Berkeley, CA: Berkeley Linguistics Society.

Blakemore, Diane. 1992. *Understanding utterances*. Oxford: Blackwell.

Blakemore, Diane. 2002. *Relevance and linguistic meaning: The semantics and pragmatics of discourse markers*. Cambridge: Cambridge University Press.

Bloom, Paul. 1996. Intention, history, and artifact concepts. *Cognition* 60: 1–29.

Blumenthal-Dramé, Alice. 2012. *Entrenchment in usage-based theories: What corpus data do and do not reveal about the mind*. Berlin: Mouton de Gruyter.

Boas, Hans C. 2003. *A constructional approach to resultatives*. Stanford, CA: CSLI Publications.

Boas, Hans C. 2011. Coercion and leaking argument structures in Construction Grammar. *Linguistics* 49 (6): 1271–1303.

Boas, Hans C. 2013. Cognitive Construction Grammar. In Thomas Hoffmann and Graeme Trousdale (Eds.), *The Oxford Handbook of Construction Grammar*, 233–254. Oxford: Oxford University Press.

Boas, Hans C. 2021. Construction grammar and frame semantics. In Xu Wen and John R. Taylor (Eds.), *The Routledge handbook of cognitive linguistics*, 43–77. New York: Routledge.

Bobrow, Samuel A. and Susan M. Bell. 1973. On catching on to idiomatic expressions. *Memory and Cognition* 1: 343–346.

Booij, Geert. 2018. *The construction of words: Advances in construction morphology*. Berlin: Springer International Publishing.

Booij, Geert and Jenny Audring. 2017. Construction morphology and the parallel architecture of grammar. *Cognitive Science* 41: 277–302.

Borg, Emma. 2004. *Minimal semantics*. Oxford: Oxford University Press.

Borg, Emma. 2016. Exploding explicatures. *Mind & Language* 31: 335–355.

Boyd, Jeremy K. and Adele E. Goldberg. 2011. Learning what not to say: The role of statistical preemption and categorization in "a"-adjective production. *Language* 81 (1): 1–29.

Boyd, Jeremy K., Erin A. Gottschalk and Adele E. Goldberg. 2009. Linking rule acquisition in novel phrasal constructions. *Language Learning* 93: 418–429.

Boye, Kasper and Peter Harder. 2009. Evidentiality: Linguistic categories and grammaticalization. *Functions of Language* 16: 9–43.

Boye, Kasper and Peter Harder. 2012. A usage-based theory of grammatical status and grammaticalization. *Language* 88 (1): 1–44.

Brandom, Robert. 1998. *Making it explicit: Reasoning, representing, and discursive commitment.* Cambridge MA: Harvard University Press.

Brandom, Robert. 2000. *Articulating reasons: An introduction to inferentialism.* Cambridge, MA: Harvard University Press.

Burton-Roberts, Noel. 2005. Robyn Carston on semantics, pragmatics, and "encoding." *Journal of Linguistics* 41: 389–407.

Burton-Roberts, Noel. 2007. Varieties of semantics and encoding: Negation, narrowing/loosening and numericals. In Noel Burton-Roberts (Ed.), *Pragmatics*, 90–114. Basingstoke: Palgrave Macmillan.

Busso, Lucia. 2020. Constructional creativity in a Romance language: Valency coercion in Italian. *Belgian Journal of Linguistics* 34: 17–29.

Busso, Lucia, Florent Perek and Alessandro Lenci. 2021. Constructional associations trump lexical associations in processing valency coercion. *Cognitive Linguistics* 32 (2): 287–318.

Bybee, Joan L. 1998. The emergent lexicon. In M. Catherine Gruber, Derrick Higgins, Kenneth S. Olson and Tamra Wysocki (Eds.), *Papers from the thirty-fourth regional meeting of the Chicago Linguistic Society*, 421–435. Chicago, IL: Chicago Linguistics Society.

Bybee, Joan L. 2006. From usage to grammar: The mind's response to repetition. *Language* 82: 711–733.

Bybee, Joan L. 2010. *Language, usage and cognition.* Cambridge: Cambridge University Press.

Bybee, Joan L. 2013. Usage-based theory and exemplar representations. In Thomas Hoffmann and Graeme Trousdale (Eds.), *The Oxford handbook of Construction Grammar*, 49–69. Oxford: Oxford University Press.

Cappelen, Herman and Ernie Lepore. 2005. *Insensitive semantics: A defense of semantic minimalism and speech act pluralism.* Oxford: Blackwell.

Cappelle, Bert. 2006. Particle placement and the case for "allostructions." *Constructions Online* 1 (7): 1–28.

Cappelle, Bert. 2014. Conventional combinations in pockets of productivity: English resultatives and Dutch ditransitives expressing excess. In Ronny Boogaart, Timothy Colleman and Gijsbert Rutten (Eds.), *Extending the scope of Construction Grammar*, 251–282. Berlin: Mouton de Gruyter.

Cappelle, Bert. 2017. What's pragmatics doing outside constructions? In Ilse Depraetere and Raphael Salkie (Eds.), *Semantics and pragmatics: Drawing a line*, 115–151. Berlin: Springer International Publishing.

Cappelle, Bert. To appear. *Can Construction Grammar be proven wrong?* Cambridge: Cambridge University Press.

Cappelle, Bert and Ilse Depraetere. 2016. Short-circuited interpretations of modal verb constructions: Some evidence from *The Simpsons. Constructions and Frames* 8 (1): 7–39.

Cappelle, Bert, Ilse Depraetere and Mégane Lesuisse. 2019. The necessity modals *have to, must, need to* and *should*: Using n-grams to help identify common and distinct semantic and pragmatic aspects. *Constructions and Frames* 11 (2): 220–243.

Cappelle, Bert, Edwige Dugas and Vera Tobin. 2015. An afterthought on *let alone*. *Journal of Pragmatics* 80: 70–85.

Carruthers, Peter and Peter K. Smith. 1996. *Theories of theories of mind*. Cambridge: Cambridge University Press.

Carston, Robyn. 1988. Implicature, explicature and truth-theoretic semantics. In Ruth Kempson (Ed.), *Mental representations: The interface between language and reality*, 155–181. Cambridge: Cambridge University Press. (Reprinted in Steven Davis (Ed.) (1991), *Pragmatics: A reader*, 33–51. Oxford: Oxford University Press.)

Carston, Robyn. 1997a. Relevance-theoretic pragmatics and modularity. *UCL Working Papers in Linguistics* 9: 29–53.

Carston, Robyn. 1997b. Enrichment and loosening: Complementary processes in deriving the proposition expressed? *Linguistische Berichte* 8: 103–127.

Carston, Robyn. 1999. The semantics/pragmatics distinction: A view from Relevance Theory. In Ken P. Turner (Ed.), *The semantics/pragmatics interface from different points of view*, 85–125. Oxford: Elsevier.

Carston, Robyn. 2000. The relationship between generative grammar and (relevance-theoretic) pragmatics. *Language and Communication* 20: 87–103.

Carston, Robyn. 2002a. *Thoughts and utterances: The pragmatics of explicit communication*. Oxford: Blackwell.

Carston, Robyn. 2002b. Linguistic meaning, communicated meaning and cognitive pragmatics. *Mind & Language* 17: 127–148.

Carston, Robyn. 2004. Explicature and semantics. In Steven Davis and Brendan Gillon (Eds.), *Semantics: A reader*, 817–845. Oxford: Oxford University Press.

Carston, Robyn. 2006. Modularity. In Keith Brown (Ed.), *Encyclopedia of language and linguistics*, 215–217. Amsterdam: Elsevier.

Carston, Robyn. 2007. How many pragmatic systems are there? In Maria J. Frápolli (Ed.), *Saying, meaning and referring: Essays on François Recanati's philosophy of language*, 18–48. Basingstoke: Palgrave Macmillan.

Carston, Robyn. 2009. The explicit/implicit distinction in pragmatics and the limits of explicit communication. *International Review of Pragmatics* 1: 35–62.

Carston, Robyn. 2010. Explicit communication and 'free' pragmatic enrichment. In Belén Soria and Esther Romero (Eds.), *Explicit communication: Robyn Carston's pragmatics*, 217–285. Basingstoke: Palgrave Macmillan.

Carston, Robyn. 2012. Word meaning and concept expressed. *The Linguistic Review* 29: 607–623.

Carston, Robyn. 2013. Word meaning, what is said and explicature. In Carlo Penco and Filippo Domaneschi (Eds.), *What is said and what is not*, 175–203. Stanford, CA: CSLI Publications.

Carston, Robyn. 2016a. Linguistic conventions and the role of pragmatics. *Mind & Language* 31 (5): 612–624.

Carston, Robyn. 2016b. The heterogeneity of procedural meaning. *Lingua* 175: 154–166.

Carston, Robyn. 2019. Ad hoc concepts, polysemy and the lexicon. In Kate Scott, Billy Clark and Robyn Carston (Eds.), *Relevance, pragmatics and interpretation*, 150–162. Cambridge: Cambridge University Press.

Carston, Robyn. 2021. Polysemy: Pragmatics and sense conventions. *Mind & Language* 36 (1): 108–133.

Carston, Robyn. 2022. Syntactic structures and pragmatic meanings. *Synthese* 200 (6): 1–28.

Carston, Robyn and Alison Hall. 2012. Implicature and explicature. In Hans-Jörg Schmid (Ed.), *Cognitive pragmatics*, 47–84. Berlin: Mouton de Gruyter.

Chang, Franklin, Kathryn Bock, and Adele E. Goldberg. 2003. Do thematic roles leave traces in their places? *Cognition* 90 (1): 29–49.

Chomsky, Noam. 1965. *Aspects of the theory of syntax*. Cambridge, MA: MIT Press.

Chomsky, Noam. 2000. *New horizons in the study of language and mind*. Cambridge: Cambridge University Press.

Chomsky, Noam. 2003. Reply to Ludlow. In Louise M. Antony and Norbert Hornstein (Eds.), *Chomsky and his critics*, 287–295. Oxford: Blackwell.

Churchland, Patricia S. 1986. *Neurophilosophy: Toward a unified science of the mind-brain*. Cambridge, MA: MIT Press.

Clark, Billy. 1991. *Relevance Theory and the semantics of non-declaratives*. Ph.D. thesis, University College London.

Clark, Billy. 2007. Blazing a trail: Moving from natural to linguistic meaning in accounting for the tones of English. In Randi A. Nilsen, Nana A. A. Amfo and Kaja Borthen (Eds.), *Interpreting utterances: Pragmatics and its interfaces*. Essays in honour of Thorstein Fretheim, 69–81. Oslo: Novus.

Clark, Billy. 2012. The relevance of tones: Prosodic meanings in utterance interpretation and in relevance theory. *The Linguistic Review* 29 (4): 643–661.

Clark, Billy. 2013a. *Relevance Theory*. Cambridge: Cambridge University Press.

Clark, Billy. 2013b. Procedures and prosody: Understanding weak communication. In Frank Liedtke and Cornelia Schulze (Eds.), *Beyond the words: Content, context and inference*, 151–182. Berlin: Mouton de Gruyter.

Clark, Billy. 2017. Drawing things together: Concluding remarks. In Ilse Depraetere and Raphael Salkie (Eds.), *Semantics and pragmatics: Drawing a line*, 343–354. Berlin: Springer International Publishing.

Clark, Billy. 2018. Cognitive pragmatics: Relevance-theoretic methodology. In Andreas H. Jucker, Klaus P. Schneider and Wolfram Bublitz (Eds.), *Methods in pragmatics*, 185–216. Berlin: Mouton de Gruyter.

Clark, Eve V. 2009. *First language acquisition* (2nd ed.). Cambridge: Cambridge University Press.

Cohen, Neal J. and Larry R. Squire. 1980. Preserved learning and retention of pattern analyzing skill in amnesia: Dissociation of knowing how and knowing that. *Science* 210: 207–210.

Coussé, Evie, Peter Andersson and Joel Olofsson. 2018a. *Grammaticalization meets Construction Grammar*. Amsterdam: John Benjamins.

Coussé, Evie, Peter Andersson and Joel Olofsson. 2018b. Grammaticalization meets Construction Grammar: Opportunities, challenges and potential incompatibilities. In Evie Coussé, Peter Andersson and Joel Olofsson (Eds.), *Grammaticalization meets Construction Grammar*, 3–19. Amsterdam: John Benjamins.

Cowie, Fiona. 1998. Mad dog nativism. *British Journal for the Philosophy of Science* 49: 227–253.

Cowie, Fiona. 1999. *What's within? Nativism reconsidered*. Oxford: Oxford University Press.

Croft, William. 2001. *Radical construction grammar: Syntactic theory in typological perspective*. Oxford: Oxford University Press.

Croft, William. To appear. Philosophical reflections on the future of construction grammar. *Constructions and Frames*.

Croft, William and D. Alan Cruse. 2004. *Cognitive linguistics*. Cambridge: Cambridge University Press.

Croft, William and Logan Sutton. 2017. Construction grammar and lexicography. In Patrick Hanks and Gilles-Maurice de Schryver (Eds.), *International handbook of modern lexis and lexicography*. Berlin: Springer International Publishing.

Curcó, Carmen. 2011. On the status of procedural meaning in natural language. In Victoria Escandell-Vidal, Manuel Leonetti and Aoife Ahern (Eds.), *Procedural meaning: Problems and perspectives*, 33–54. Bingley: Emerald Group Publishing.

Dancygier, Barbara and Eve Sweetser. 2014. *Figurative language*. Cambridge: Cambridge University Press.

Davidson, Donald. 1967. Truth and meaning. *Synthese* 17: 304–323.

Davidson, Donald. 1984. Reality without reference. In Donald Davidson (Ed.), *Inquiries into truth and interpretation*, 215–225. Oxford: Oxford University Press.

Davies, Mark. 2004. *BYU-BNC*. (Based on the British National Corpus from Oxford University Press). Available online at www.english-corpora.org/bnc/.

Davies, Mark. 2008-. *The Corpus of Contemporary American English (COCA): 520 million words, 1990-present*. Available online at www.english-corpora.org/coca/.

Davies, Mark. 2016. *Corpus of News on the Web (NOW): 3+ billion words from 20 countries, updated every day*. Available online at www.english-corpora.org/now/.

Dehaene, Stanislas. 1997. *The number sense: How mathematical knowledge is embedded in our brains*. New York: Oxford University Press.

Delahunty, Gerald P. 1995. The inferential construction. *Pragmatics* 5: 341–364.

Depraetere, Ilse. 2010. Some observations on the meaning of modals. In Bert Cappelle and Naoaki Wada (Eds.), *Distinctions in English grammar, offered to Renaat Declerck*, 72–91. Tokyo: Kaitakusha.

Depraetere, Ilse. 2014. Modals and lexically-regulated saturation. *Journal of Pragmatics* 7: 160–177.

de Saussure, Ferdinand. 1916. *Cours de linguistique générale*. Paris: Payot.

de Swart, Henriëtte. 2000. Tense, aspect and coercion in a cross-linguistic perspective. In Miriam Butt and Tracy H. King (Eds.), *Proceedings of the Berkeley Formal Grammar conference*. Berkeley, CA: CSLI Publications.

de Swart, Henriëtte. 2011. Mismatches and coercion. In Claudia Maienborn, Klaus von Heusinger and Paul Portner (Eds.), *Semantics: An international handbook of natural language meaning*, 574–597. Berlin: De Gruyter.

Diessel, Holger. 2007. Frequency effects in language acquisition, language use, and diachronic change. *New Ideas in Psychology* 25: 108–127.

Diessel, Holger. 2013. Construction Grammar and first language acquisition. In Thomas Hoffmann and Graeme Trousdale (Eds.), *The Oxford handbook of Construction Grammar*, 347–363. Oxford: Oxford University Press.

Diessel, Holger. 2015. Usage-based construction grammar. In Ewa Dąbrowska and Dagmar Divjak (Eds.), *Handbook of cognitive linguistics*, 296–321. Berlin: De Gruyter Mouton.

Diessel, Holger. 2019. *The grammar network: How linguistic structure is shaped by language use.* Cambridge: Cambridge University Press.

Divjak, Dagmar, Petar Milin, Srdan Medimorec and Maciej Borowski. 2022. Behavioral signatures of memory resources for language: Looking beyond the lexicon/grammar divide. *Cognitive Science* 46 (11): e13206.

Eichenbaum, Howard. 2002. *The cognitive neuroscience of memory.* New York: Oxford University Press.

Eigsti, Inge-Marie, Loisa Bennetto and Mamta B. Dadlani. 2007. Beyond pragmatics: Morphosyntactic development in autism. *Journal of Autism and Developmental Disorders* 37: 1007–1023.

Eigsti, Inge-Marie, Ashley B. de Marchena, Jillian M. Schuh and Elizabeth Kelley. 2011. Language acquisition in autism spectrum disorders: A developmental review. *Research in Autism Spectrum Disorders* 5 (2): 681–691.

Eizaga Rebollar, Bárbara. 2009. Letting the cat out of the bag: On idiom use and representation. In Christina Alm-Arvius, Nils-Lennart Johannesson and David C. Minugh (Eds.), *Selected papers from the 2008 Stockholm metaphor festival. Stockholm Studies in English,* 139–153. Stockholm: Stockholm University.

Ellis, Nick. 2002. Frequency effects in language processing: A review with implications for theories of implicit and explicit language acquisition. *Studies in Second Language Acquisition* 24 (2): 143–188.

Elman, Jeffrey, Elizabeth Bates, Mark H. Johnson, Annette Karmiloff-Smith, Domenico Parisi and Kim Plunkett. 1996. *Re-thinking innateness: A connectionist perspective on development.* Cambridge, MA: MIT Press.

Erviti, Aneider I. 2017. An exploratory study of complementary contrastive discourse constructions in English. *Revista Española de Lingüística Aplicada/Spanish Journal of Applied Linguistics* 30 (1): 210–239.

Escandell-Vidal, Victoria. 2017. Notes for a restrictive theory of procedural meaning. In Rachel Giora and Michael Haugh (Eds.), *Doing pragmatics interculturally: Cognitive, philosophical, and sociopragmatic perspectives,* 79–95. Berlin: Walter de Gruyter.

Escandell-Vidal, Victoria. and Manuel Leonetti. 2000. Categorías funcionales y semántica procedimental. In Marcos M. Hernández, Dolores del Pino García Padrón, Dolores Corbella Díaz, Cristóbal José Corrales Zumbado, Francisco José Cortés Rodríguez, et al. (Eds.), *Cien años de investigación semántica: De Michel Bréal a la actualidad,* vol. I, 363–378. Madrid: Ediciones Clásicas.

Escandell-Vidal, Victoria and Manuel Leonetti. 2002. Coercion and the stage/individual distinction. In Javier Gutiérrez-Rexach (Ed.), *From words to discourse: Trends in Spanish semantics and pragmatics,* 159–179. Amsterdam: Elsevier.

Escandell-Vidal, Victoria and Manuel Leonetti. 2011. The rigidity of procedural meaning. In Victoria Escandell-Vidal, Manuel Leonetti and Aoife Ahern (Eds.), *Procedural meaning: Problems and perspectives,* 81–102. Bingley: Emerald Group Publishing.

Escandell-Vidal, Victoria, Manuel Leonetti and Aoife Ahern. 2011. Introduction: Procedural meaning. In Victoria Escandell-Vidal, Manuel Leonetti and Aoife Ahern (Eds.), *Procedural meaning: Problems and perspectives,* xvii–xlv. Bingley: Emerald Group Publishing.

Evans, Vyvyan. 2006. Lexical concepts, cognitive models and meaning-construction. *Cognitive Linguistics* 17 (4): 491–534.

Evans, Vyvyan. 2009. *How words mean: Lexical concepts, cognitive models and meaning construction*. Oxford: Oxford University Press.

Evans, Vyvyan and Melanie Green. 2006. *Cognitive linguistics: An introduction*. Edinburgh: Edinburgh University Press.

Evans, Vyvyan, Benjamin K. Bergen and Jörg Zinken. 2007. The cognitive linguistics enterprise: An overview. In Vyvyan Evans, Benjain K. Bergen and Jörg Zinken (Eds.), *The cognitive linguistics reader*, 1–60. London: Equinox Publishing.

Falkum, Ingrid L. 2011. *The semantics and pragmatics of polysemy: A relevance-theoretic account*. Ph.D. thesis, University College London.

Falkum, Ingrid L. 2015. The how and why of polysemy: A pragmatic account. *Lingua* 157: 83–99.

Fantl, Jeremy. 2017. Knowledge how. In Edward N. Zalta (Ed.), *The Stanford encyclopedia of philosophy* (Fall 2017 Ed.). https://plato.stanford.edu/archives/fall2017/entries/knowledge-how/ (last accessed: May 31, 2023).

Fauconnier, Gilles and Mark Turner. 2003. Polysemy and conceptual blending. In Brigitte Nerlich, Zazie Todd, Vimala Herman and David D. Clarke (Eds.), *Polysemy: Flexible patterns of meaning in mind and language*, 79–94. Berlin: Mouton de Gruyter.

Fillmore, Charles J. 1975. An alternative to checklist theories of meaning. In Cathy Cogen, Henry Thompson, Graham Thurgood, Kenneth Whistler and James Wright (Eds.), *Proceedings of the first annual meeting of the Berkeley Linguistics Society*, 123–131. Berkeley, CA: University of California at Berkeley.

Fillmore, Charles J. 1976. Frame semantics and the nature of language. In *Annals of the New York Academy of Sciences: Conference on the Origin and Development of Language and Speech* 280: 20–32.

Fillmore, Charles J. 1982. Frame semantics. In Linguistic Society of Korea (Ed.), *Linguistics in the morning calm*, 111–138. Seoul: Hanshin.

Fillmore, Charles J. 1985a. Syntactic intrusions and the notion of grammatical construction. In Mary Niepokuj, Mary VanClay, Vassiliki Nikiforidou and Deborah Feder (Eds.), *Proceedings of the Eleventh Annual Meeting of the Berkeley Linguistics Society*, 73–86. University of California, Berkeley: Berkeley Linguistics Society.

Fillmore, Charles J. 1985b. Frames and the semantics of understanding. *Quaderni di Semantica* 6: 222–253.

Fillmore, Charles J. 1988. The mechanisms of 'Construction Grammar'. In Shelley Axmaker, Annie Jaisser and Helen Singmaster (Eds.), *Proceedings of the Fourteenth Annual Meeting of the Berkeley Linguistics Society*, 35–55. University of California, Berkeley: Berkeley Linguistics Society.

Fillmore, Charles J. 1989. Grammatical construction theory and the familiar dichotomies. In Rainer Dietrich and Carl F. Graumann (Eds.), *Language processing in social context*, 17–38. North Holland: Elsevier.

Fillmore, Charles and Paul Kay. 1995. *Construction Grammar*. Stanford, CA: CSLI Publications.

Fillmore, Charles J., Paul Kay and Mary C. O'Connor. 1988. Regularity and idiomaticity in grammatical constructions: The case of *let alone*. *Language* 64: 501–538.

Finkbeiner, Rita. 2019a. Reflections on the role of pragmatics in Construction Grammar. *Constructions and Frames* 11 (2): 171–192.

Finkbeiner, Rita (Ed.). 2019b. On the role of pragmatics in Construction Grammar. Special issue of *Constructions and Frames* 11 (2).

von Fintel, Kay. 1995. The formal semantics of grammaticalization. *Proceedings of the North East Linguistics Society* 25 (2): 175–189.

Fodor, Janet D., Jerry A. Fodor and Merrill F. Garrett. 1975. The psychological unreality of semantic representations. *Linguistic Inquiry* 4: 515–531.

Fodor, Jerry A. 1975. *The language of thought.* Cambridge, MA: Harvard University Press.

Fodor, Jerry A. 1982. Cognitive science and the twin-earth problem. *Notre Dame Journal of Formal Logic* 23: 98–118.

Fodor, Jerry A. 1983. *Modularity of mind: An essay on faculty psychology.* Cambridge, MA: MIT Press.

Fodor, Jerry A. 1998. *Concepts: Where cognitive science went wrong.* New York: Oxford University Press.

Fodor, Jerry A. 2008. *LOT 2: The language of thought revisited.* Oxford: Oxford University Press.

Fodor, Jerry A. and Ernest Lepore. 2002. *The compositionality papers.* New York: Oxford University Press.

Fodor, Jerry A., Merrill F. Garrett, Edward C. T. Walker and Cornelia H. Parkes. 1980. Against definitions. *Cognition* 8: 263–367.

Frazier, Lyn and Keith Rayner. 1990. Taking on semantic commitments: Processing multiple meanings vs. multiple senses. *Journal of Memory and Language* 29: 181–200.

Fried, Mirjam. 2015. Construction Grammar. In Tibor Kiss and Artemis Alexiadou (Eds.), *Syntax – Theory and Analysis: An International Handbook*, vol. 2, 974–1003. Berlin: Mouton de Gruyter.

Fried, Mirjam and Jan-Ola Östman. 2004. Construction Grammar: A thumbnail sketch. In Mirjam Fried and Jan-Ola Östman (Eds.), *Construction Grammar in a cross-language perspective*, 11–86. Amsterdam: John Benjamins.

Frisson, Steven. 2009. Semantic underspecification in language processing. *Language and Linguistics Compass* 3: 111–127.

Frisson, Steven and Martin J. Pickering. 2001. Obtaining a figurative interpretation of a word: Support for underspecification. *Metaphor and Symbol* 16: 149–171.

Gärdenfors, Peter. 1999. Some tenets of cognitive semantics. In Jens S. Allwood and Peter Gärdenfors (Eds.), *Cognitive semantics: Meaning and cognition*, 19–36. Amsterdam: John Benjamins.

Geeraerts, Dirk. 2010. *Theories of lexical semantics.* Oxford: Oxford University Press.

Geeraerts, Dirk. 2016. Sense individuation. In Nick Riemer (Ed.), *The Routledge handbook of semantics*, 233–247. New York: Routledge.

Geeraerts, Dirk. 2017. Lexical semantics. In *Oxford research encyclopedia of linguistics.* Available at: doi.org/10.1093/acrefore/9780199384655.013.29.

Geeraerts, Dirk. 2021. Cognitive semantics. In Xu Wen and John R. Taylor (Eds.), *The Routledge Handbook of Cognitive Linguistics*, 19–29. New York: Routledge.

Geeraerts, Dirk and Hubert Cuyckens. 2007. *The Oxford handbook of cognitive linguistics.* Oxford: Oxford University Press.

Gibbs, Raymond W. 1994. *The poetics of mind.* Cambridge: Cambridge University Press.

Gibbs, Raymond W. and Gregory A. Bryant. 2008. Striving for optimal relevance when answering questions. *Cognition* 106 (1): 345–369.

Gibbs, Raymond W. and Markus Tendahl. 2011. Coupling of metaphoric cognition and communication: A reply to Deirdre Wilson. *Intercultural Pragmatics* 8 (4): 601–609.

Gigerenzer, Gerd, Peter M. Todd and the ABC Research Group. 1999. *Simple heuristics that make us smart*. Oxford: Oxford University Press.

Girotto, Vittorio, Markus Kemmelmeir, Dan Sperber and Jean-Baptiste van der Henst. 2001. Inept reasoners or pragmatic virtuosos? Relevance and the deontic selection task. *Cognition* 81: 69–76.

Givón, Talmy. 1995. *Functionalism and grammar*. Amsterdam: John Benjamins.

Glynn, Dylan. 2022. Emergent categories: Quantifying analogically derived similarity in usage. In Karolina Krawczak, Marcin Grygiel and Barbara Lewandowska-Tomaszczyk (Eds.), *Analogy and contrast in language*, 246–282. Amsterdam: John Benjamins.

Goldberg, Adele E. 1995. *Constructions: A construction grammar approach to argument structure*. Chicago, IL: University of Chicago Press.

Goldberg, Adele E. 2002a. Construction Grammar. In *Encyclopedia of Cognitive Science*. London: Macmillan Nature Publishing Group.

Goldberg, Adele E. 2002b. Surface generalizations: An alternative to alternations. *Cognitive Linguistics* 13 (4): 327–356.

Goldberg, Adele E. 2003. Constructions: A new theoretical approach to language. *Trends in Cognitive Science* 7 (5): 219–224.

Goldberg, Adele E. 2004. Pragmatics and argument structure. In Laurence R. Horn and Gregory L. Ward (Eds.), *The handbook of pragmatics*, 427–441. Oxford: Blackwell.

Goldberg, Adele E. 2006. *Constructions at work: The nature of generalization in language*. Oxford: Oxford University Press.

Goldberg, Adele E. 2011. Corpus evidence of the viability of statistical preemption. *Cognitive Linguistics* 22 (1): 131–154.

Goldberg, Adele E. 2013. Constructionist approaches. In Thomas Hoffmann and Graeme Trousdale (Eds.), *The Oxford Handbook of Construction Grammar*, 15–31. Oxford: Oxford University Press.

Goldberg, Adele E. 2019. *Explain me this: Creativity, competition and the partial productivity of constructions*. Princeton, NJ: Princeton University Press.

Goldberg, Adele E. and Giulia M. L. Bencini. 2005. Support from processing for a constructional approach to grammar. In Andrea E. Tyler, Mari Takada, Yiyoung Kim and Diana Marinova (Eds.), *Language in use: Cognitive and discourse perspectives on language and language learning*, 3–18. Washington, DC: Georgetown University Press.

Goldman, Alavin I. 2012. Theory of mind. In Eric Margolis, Richard Samuels and Stephen P. Stich (Eds.), *The Oxford handbook of philosophy of cognitive science*, 402–424. Oxford: Oxford University Press.

Gonzálvez-García, Francisco. 2011. Metaphor and metonymy do not render coercion superfluous: Evidence from the subjective-transitive construction. *Linguistics* 49 (6): 1305–1358.

Gonzálvez-García, Francisco. 2020. Maximizing the explanatory power of constructions in Cognitive Construction Grammar(s). *Belgian Journal of Linguistics* 34: 111–122.

Grady, Joseph E. 2007. Metaphor. In Dirk Geeraerts and Hubert Cuyckens (Eds.), *The Oxford handbook of cognitive linguistics*, 188–213. New York: Oxford University Press.

Grice, H. Paul. 1989. *Study in the way of words*. Cambridge, MA: Harvard University Press.

Gries, Stefan T. and Anatol Stefanowitsch. 2004. Extending collostructional analysis: A corpus-based perspective on 'alternations'. *International Journal of Corpus Linguistics* 9 (1): 97–129.

Groefsema, Marjolein. 1992. *Processing for relevance: A pragmatically based account of how we process natural language*. Ph.D. thesis, University College London.

Groefsema, Marjolein. 1995. *Can, may, must* and *should*: A relevance theoretic account. *Journal of Linguistics* 31: 53–79.

Groefsema, Marjolein. 2007. Concepts and word meaning in Relevance Theory. In Noël Burton-Roberts (Ed.), *Pragmatics*, 136–157. Basingstoke: Palgrave Macmillan.

Gundel, Jeanette K. 2011. Child language, theory of mind, and the role of procedural markers in identifying referents of nominal expressions. In Victoria Escandell-Vidal, Manuel Leonetti and Aoife Ahern (Eds.), *Procedural meaning: Problems and perspectives*, 205–234. Bradford: Emerald Group Publishing.

Haegeman, Liliane. 1989. *Be going to* and *will*: A pragmatic account. *Journal of Linguistics* 25: 291–317.

Haiman, John. 1980. Dictionaries and encyclopedias. *Lingua* 50: 329–357.

Hall, Alison. 2011. Ad hoc concepts: Atomic or decompositional. *UCL Working Papers in Linguistics* (23): 1–10.

Hall, Alison. 2017. Lexical pragmatics, explicature and ad hoc concepts. In Ilse Depraetere and Raphael Salkie (Eds.), *Semantics and pragmatics: Drawing a line*, 85–100. Berlin: Springer International Publishing.

Halliday, Michael A. K. 1973. *Explorations in the functions of language*. London: Edward Arnold.

Halliday, Michael A. K. 1994. *An introduction to functional grammar* (2nd ed.). London: Edward Arnold.

Hampe, Beate. 2005. *From perception to meaning: Image schemas in cognitive linguistics*. Berlin: Mouton de Gruyter.

Hampton, James A. 2016. Categories, prototypes and exemplars. In Nick Riemer (Ed.), *The Routledge handbook of semantics*, 125–141. New York: Routledge.

Hanna, Jeff and Friedemann Pulvermüller. 2014. Neurophysiological evidence for whole form retrieval of complex derived words: A mismatch negativity study. *Frontiers in Human Neuroscience* 8: 886.

Harder, Peter. 2010. *Meaning in mind and society: A functional contribution to the social turn in cognitive sociolinguistics*. Berlin: Walter de Gruyter.

Harder, Peter and Kasper Boye. 2011. Grammaticalization and functional linguistics. In Heiko Narrog and Bernd Heine (Eds.), *The Oxford handbook of grammaticalization*, 56–68. Oxford: Oxford University Press.

Hare, Mary L. and Adele E. Goldberg. 1999. Structural priming: Purely syntactic? In Martin Hahn and Scott C. Stones (Eds.), *Proceedings of the 21st annual meeting of the Cognitive Science Society*, 208–211. Mahwah, NJ: Lawrence Erlbaum.

Harris, Catherine L. 1998. Psycholinguistic studies of entrenchment. In Jean-Pierre Koenig (Ed.), *Conceptual structure, discourse and language*, 55–70. Stanford, CA: CSLI Publications.

Haugh, Michael. 2008. Intention in pragmatics. *Intercultural Pragmatics* 5: 99–110.

Haugh, Michael and Kasia M. Jaszczolt. 2012. Speaker intentions and intentionality. In Keith Allan and Kasia M. Jaszczolt (Eds.), *The Cambridge handbook of pragmatics*, 87–112. Cambridge: Cambridge University Press.

Hilpert, Martin. 2019. *Construction grammar and its application to English* (2nd ed.). Edinburgh: Edinburgh University Press.

Hobbs, Jerry R. and Paul Martin. 1987. Local pragmatics. In *Proceedings of the tenth international joint conference on artificial intelligence*, 520–523. Milan, Italy.

Hobbs, Jerry R., Donald E. Walker and Robert A. Amsler. 1982. Natural language access to structured text. In *COLING 82: Proceedings of the 9th conference on computational linguistics*, 127–132. Prague: Academia.

Hobbs, Jerry R., Mark E. Stickel, Douglas E. Appelt and Paul Martin. 1993. Interpretation as abduction. *Artificial Intelligence* 63 (1–2): 69–142.

Hoek, Jet and Sandrine Zufferey. 2015. Factors influencing the implicitation of discourse relations across languages. In Harry Bunt (Ed.), *Proceedings of the 11th joint ACL-ISO workshop on interoperable semantic annotation (ISA-11)*, 39–45. TiCC, Tilburg Center for Cognition and Communication.

Hoffmann, Thomas. 2018. Creativity and Construction Grammar: Cognitive and psychological issues. *Zeitschrift für Anglistik und Amerikanistik* 66 (3): 259–276.

Hoffmann, Thomas. 2022. *Construction Grammar: The structure of English*. Cambridge: Cambridge University Press.

Hoffmann, Thomas and Graeme Trousdale. 2013a. *The Oxford handbook of Construction Grammar*. Oxford: Oxford University Press.

Hoffmann, Thomas and Graeme Trousdale. 2013b. Construction Grammar: Introduction. In Thomas Hoffmann and Graeme Trousdale (Eds.), *The Oxford handbook of Construction Grammar*, 1–12. Oxford: Oxford University Press.

Hogeweg, Lotte and Agustín Vicente. 2020. On the nature of the lexicon: The status of rich lexical meanings. *Journal of Linguistics* 56: 865–891.

Hopper, Paul and Elizabeth C. Traugott. 2003. *Grammaticalization*. Cambridge: Cambridge University Press.

Horsey, Richard. 2006. *The content and acquisition of lexical concepts*. Ph.D. thesis, University College London.

House, Jill. 2009. Prosody and context selection: A procedural approach. In Dagmar Barth-Weingarten, Nicole Dehé and Anne Wichmann (Eds.), *Where prosody meets pragmatics*, 129–142. Bingley: Emerald.

Hugou, Vincent. 2013. The X*ed out* construction: Between productivity and creativity. *Quaderns de Filologia. Estudis lingüístics* 18: 83–95.

Hume, David. [1739]1978. *A treatise of human nature*. Oxford: Oxford University Press.

Ifantidou, Elly. 2001. *Evidentials and relevance*. Amsterdam: John Benjamins.

Imai, Kunihiko. 1998. Intonation and relevance. In Robyn Carston and Seiji Uchida (Eds.), *Relevance theory: Applications and implications*, 69–86. Amsterdam: John Benjamins.

Israel, Michael. 1996. The way constructions grow. In Adele E. Goldberg (Ed.), *Conceptual structure, discourse and language*, 217–230. Stanford, CA: CSLI Publications.

Jackendoff, Ray. 1990. *Semantic structures*. Cambridge, MA: MIT Press.

Jackendoff, Ray. 1997. *The architecture of the language faculty*. Cambridge, MA: MIT Press.

Jackendoff, Ray. 2002. *Foundations of language: Brain, meaning, grammar, evolution*. New York: Oxford University Press.

Jackendoff, Ray. 2013. Constructions in the parallel architecture. In Thomas Hoffmann and Graeme Trousdale (Eds.), *The Oxford handbook of Construction Grammar*, 70–92. Oxford: Oxford University Press.

Johnson, Mark. 1987. *The body in the mind: The bodily basis of meaning, imagination, and reason*. Chicago, IL: University of Chicago Press.

Johnson, Matt A. and Adele E. Goldberg. 2013. Evidence for automatic accessing of constructional meaning: Jabberwocky sentences prime associated verbs. *Language and Cognitive Processes* 28 (10): 1439–1452.

Johnson, Matt A., Jeremy K. Boyd and Adele E. Goldberg. 2012. Construction learning in children with autism. In Alia K. Biller, Esther Y. Chung and Amelia E. Kimball (Eds.), *Proceedings of the thirty-sixth annual Boston University conference on language development: Supplemental*, 1–15. Boston, MA: Boston University.

Jucker, Andreas H. 1997. The relevance of cleft constructions. *Multilingua* 16: 187–198.

Jurafsky, Daniel. 1992. *An on-line computational model of sentence interpretation: A theory of the representation and use of linguistic knowledge*. Ph.D. dissertation, University of California at Berkeley.

Jurafsky, Daniel. 1993. *A cognitive model of sentence interpretation: A construction grammar approach*. Technical Report TR-93-077. Berkeley, CA: International Computer Science Institute.

Jurafsky, Daniel. 1996. A probabilistic model of lexical and syntactic access and disambiguation. *Cognitive Science* 20: 137–194.

Kaschak, Michael P. and Arthur M. Glenberg. 2000. Constructing meaning: The role of affordances and grammatical constructions in sentence comprehension. *Journal of Memory and Language* 43 (3): 508–529.

Kay, Paul. 2004. Pragmatic aspects of grammatical constructions. In Lawrence R. Horn and Gregory Ward (Eds.), *Handbook of pragmatics*, 675–700. Oxford: Blackwell.

Kay, Paul and Charles J. Fillmore. 1999. Grammatical constructions and linguistic generalizations: The *What's* X *doing* Y? construction. *Language* 75: 1–33.

Kay, Paul and Laura A. Michaelis. 2012. Constructional meaning and compositionality. In Claudia Maienborn, Klaus von Heusinger and Paul Portner (Eds.), *Semantics: An international handbook of natural language meaning*, vol. 3, 2271–2296. Berlin: Mouton de Gruyter.

Kemmer, Suzanne and Michael Barlow. 2000. Introduction: A usage-based conception of language. In Michael Barlow and Suzanne Kemmer (Eds.), *Usage-based models of language use*, vii–xxviii. Stanford, CA: CSLI Publications.

Kisielewska-Krysiuk, Marta. 2008. The epistemic/non-epistemic distinction as exemplified by *must*: A relevance-theoretic perspective. In Ewa Mioduszewska and Agnieszka Piskorska (Eds.), *Relevance Round Table I*, 43–65. Warsaw: Warsaw University Press.

Klinge, Alex. 1993. The English modal auxiliaries: From lexical semantics to utterance interpretation. *Journal of Linguistics* 29: 315–357.

Koops, Christian. 2007. Constraints on inferential constructions. In Günter Radden, Klaus-Michael Köpcke, Thomas Berg and Peter Siemund (Eds.), *Aspects of meaning construction*, 207–224. Amsterdam: John Benjamins.

Kuzai, Einat. 2020. Pragmatic information in constructions: What do speakers generalize? *Belgian Journal of Linguistics* 34: 215–227.

Lakoff, George. 1987. *Women, fire, and dangerous things: What categories reveal about the mind*. Chicago, IL: University of Chicago Press.

Lakoff, George. 1988. Cognitive semantics. In Umberto Eco, Marco Santambrogio and Patrizia Violi (Eds.), *Meaning and mental representations*, 119–154. Bloomington, IN: Indiana University Press.

Lakoff, George. 1989. Some empirical results about the nature of concepts. *Mind & Language* 4: 103–129.

Lakoff, George. 1991. Cognitive versus Generative linguistics: How commitments influence results. *Language and Communication* 11 (1–2): 53–62.

Lakoff, George. 2014. Mapping the brain's metaphor circuitry: Is abstract thought metaphorical thought? *Frontiers in Human Neuroscience* 8: 958.

Lakoff, George and Mark Johnson. 1980. *Metaphors we live by*. Chicago, IL: University of Chicago Press.

La Mantia, Francesco. 2018. Where is meaning going? Semantic potentials and enactive grammars. *Acta Structuralica* 1: 89–113.

Langacker, Ronald W. 1987. *Foundations of cognitive grammar*. Vol. 1, *Theoretical prerequisites*. Stanford, CA: Stanford University Press.

Langacker, Ronald W. 1988. A usage-based model. In Brygida Rudzka-Ostyn (Ed.), *Topics in Cognitive Linguistics*, 127–161. Amsterdam: John Benjamins.

Langacker, Ronald W. 1990. Subjectification. *Cognitive Linguistics* 1: 5–38.

Langacker, Ronald W. 1991a. *Foundations of cognitive grammar*. Vol. 2, *Descriptive application*. Stanford, CA: Stanford University Press.

Langacker, Ronald W. 1991b. *Concept, image, symbol: The cognitive basis of grammar*. Berlin: Mouton de Gruyter.

Langacker, Ronald W. 1999. Losing control: Grammaticization, subjectification, and transparency. In Andreas Blank and Peter Koch (Eds.), *Historical semantics and cognition*, 147–175. Berlin: Mouton de Gruyter.

Langacker, Ronald W. 2005. Construction grammars: Cognitive, radical and less so. In Francisco J. Ruiz de Mendoza Ibáñez and María Sandra Peña Cervel (Eds.), *Cognitive Linguistics: Internal dynamics and interdisciplinary interaction*, 101–159. Berlin: Mouton de Gruyter.

Langacker, Ronald W. 2008. *Cognitive Grammar: A basic introduction*. Oxford: Oxford University Press.

Langacker, Ronald W. 2009. Cognitive (Construction) Grammar. *Cognitive Linguistics* 20: 167–176.

Langacker, Ronald W. 2011. Grammaticalization and Cognitive Grammar. In Heiko Narrog and Bernd Heine (Eds.), *The Oxford handbook of grammaticalization*, 79–91. Oxford: Oxford University Press.

Langacker, Ronald W. 2019. Construal. In Ewa Dąbrowska and Dagmar Divjak (Eds.), *Cognitive linguistics: Foundations of language*, 140–166. Berlin: De Gruyter.

Langer, Jonas. 1996. Heterochrony and the evolution of primate cognitive development. In Anne E. Russon, Kim A. Bard and Sue Taylor Parker (Eds.), *Reaching into thought : The minds of the great apes*, 257–277. Cambridge: Cambridge University Press.

Laurence, Stephen and Eric Margolis. 1999. Concepts and cognitive science. In Eric Margolis and Stephen Laurence (Eds.), *Concepts: Core readings*, 3–81. Cambridge, MA: MIT Press.

Laurence, Stephen and Eric Margolis. 2002. Radical concept nativism. *Cognition* 86: 25–55.

Lauwers, Peter and Dominique Willems. 2011. Coercion: Definition and challenges, current approaches and new trends. *Linguistics* 49 (6): 1219–1235.

Leclercq, Benoît. 2019. Coercion: A case of saturation. *Constructions and Frames* 11 (2): 270–289.

Leclercq, Benoît. 2020. Semantics and pragmatics in Construction Grammar. *Belgian Journal of Linguistics* 34: 225–234.

Leclercq, Benoît. 2022. Ad hoc concepts and the relevance heuristics: A false paradox? *Pragmatics* [online first].

Leclercq, Benoît. 2023. Modality revisited: Combining insights from Construction Grammar and Relevance Theory. In Ilse Depraetere, Bert Cappelle and Martin Hilpert et al., *Models of modals: From pragmatics and corpus linguistics to machine learning*, 60–92. Mouton de Gruyter.

Leclercq, Benoît and Cameron Morin. 2023. No equivalence: A new principle of no synonymy. *Constructions* 15: 1–16.

Lee, Poong S. 2017. Mental files concepts and bodies of information. *Synthese*: 1–20.

Lee-Goldman, Russell R. 2011. *Context in constructions*. Ph.D. dissertation, University of California at Berkeley.

Lemmens, Maarten. 2016. Cognitive semantics. In Nick Riemer (Ed.), *Routledge handbook of semantics*, 90–105. London: Routledge.

Lemmens, Maarten. 2017. A cognitive, usage-based view on lexical pragmatics: Response to Hall. In Ilse Depraetere and Raphael Salkie (Eds.), *Semantics and pragmatics: Drawing a line*, 101–114. Berlin: Springer International Publishing.

Leonetti, Manuel and Victoria Escandell-Vidal. 2004. Semántica conceptual /Semántica procedimental. In Milka Villayandre Llamazares (Ed.), *Actas del V Congreso de Lingüística General*, vol. II, 1727–1738. Madrid, Arco/Libros.

Leslie, Alan M. 1992. Pretense, autism, and the theory-of-mind module. *Current Directions in Psychological Science* 1: 18–21.

Leslie, Alan M. 1994. ToMM, ToBy, and agency: Core architecture and domain specificity. In Lawrence A. Hirschfeld and Susan A. Gelman (Eds.), *Mapping the mind: Domain specificity in cognition and culture*, 119–148. Cambridge: Cambridge University Press.

Levine, Alex and Mark H. Bickhard. 1999. Concepts: Where Fodor went wrong. *Philosophical Psychology* 12: 5–23.

Lewandowska-Tomaszczyk, Barbara. 1985. On semantic change in a dynamic model of language. In Jacek Fisiak (Ed.), *Historical semantics: Historical word-formation*, 297–323. Berlin: Mouton de Gruyter.

Lewandowska-Tomaszczyk, Barbara. 2007. Polysemy, prototypes and radial categories. In Dirk Geeraerts and Hubert Cuyckens (Eds.), *The Oxford handbook of cognitive linguistics*, 139–169. Oxford: Oxford University Press.

Li, Bai, Zining Zhu, Guillaume Thomas, Frank Rudzicz and Yang Xu. 2022. Neural reality of argument structure constructions. *Proceedings of the 60th Annual Meeting of the Association for Computational Linguistics* 1: 7410–7423.

Locke, John. [1690]1975. *An essay concerning human understanding*. New York: Oxford University Press.

Ludlow, Peter. 2003. Referential semantics for I-Languages? In Louise M. Antony and Norbert Hornstein (Eds.), *Chomsky and his critics*, 140–161. Oxford: Blackwell.

Macnamara, John. 1987. Logical competence. *Behavioral and Brain Sciences (Précis of Relevance)* 10: 724–725.

Margolis, Eric. 1998. How to acquire a concept. *Mind & Language* 13 (3): 347–369.

Mazzarella, Diana. 2013. Associative and inferential approaches to pragmatics: The state of the art of experimental investigation. *Methode: Analytic Perspectives* 2 (2): 172–194.

Mazzarella, Diana. 2014. Is inference necessary to pragmatics? *Belgian Journal of Linguistics* 28: 71–95.

Michaelis, Laura A. 2003a. Word meaning, sentence meaning, and syntactic meaning. In Hubert Cuyckens, René Dirven and John R. Taylor (Eds.), *Cognitive approaches to lexical semantics*, 163–209. Berlin: Mouton de Gruyter.

Michaelis, Laura A. 2003b. Headless constructions and coercion by construction. In Elaine J. Francis and Laura A. Michaelis (Eds.), *Mismatch: Form–function incongruity and the architecture of grammar*, 259–310. Stanford, CA: CSLI Publications.

Michaelis, Laura A. 2004. Type shifting in Construction Grammar: An integrated approach to aspectual coercion. *Cognitive Linguistics* 15: 1–67.

Michaelis, Laura A. 2005. Entity and event coercion in a symbolic theory of syntax. In Jan-Ola Östman and Myriam Fried (Eds.), *Construction grammars: Cognitive grounding and theoretical extensions*, 45–88. Amsterdam: John Benjamins.

Michaelis, Laura A. 2011. Stative by construction. *Linguistics* 49 (6): 1359–1399.

Michaelis, Laura A. 2017. Meaning of constructions. In Mark Aronoff (Ed.), *Oxford research encyclopedia of linguistics*. Available at: doi.org/10.1093/acrefore/978019 9384655.013.309.

Michaelis, Laura A. 2019. Constructions are patterns and so are fixed expressions. In Ruth Moehlig-Falke and Beatrix Busse (Eds.), *Patterns in language and linguistics*, 193–220. Berlin: Mouton de Gruyter.

Mioduszewska, Ewa. 2015. Ad hoc concepts, linguistically encoded meaning and explicit content: Some remarks on Relevance Theoretic perspective. In Wojciech Malec and Marietta Rusinek (Eds.), *Within language, beyond theories: Discourse analysis, pragmatics and corpus-based studies*, 81–96. Newcastle upon Tyne: Cambridge Scholars Publishing.

Moens, Marc and Mark Steedman. 1988. Temporal ontology and temporal reference. *Computational Linguistics* 14 (2): 15–29.

Moeschler, Jacques. 2016. Where is procedural meaning located? Evidence from discourse connectives and tenses. *Lingua* 175–176: 122–138.

Moeschler, Jacques. 2018. Truth-conditional pragmatics. In Jan-Ola Östman and Jef Verschueren (Eds.), *Handbook of pragmatics*, 49–79. Amsterdam: John Benjamins.

Murphy, Gregory L. 1991. Meaning and concepts. In Paula J. Schwanenflugel (Ed.), *The psychology of word meaning*, 11–35. Hillsdale, NJ: Erlbaum.

Murphy, M. Lynne. 2000. Knowledge of words versus knowledge about words: The conceptual basis of lexical relations. In Bert Peeters (Ed.), *The lexicon-encyclopedia interface*, 317–348. Amsterdam: Elsevier.

Murray, John D. 1995. Logical connectives and local coherence. In Robert F. Lorch and Edward J. O'Brien (Eds.), *Sources of cohesion in text comprehension*, 107–125. Hillsdale, NJ: Erlbaum.

Murray, John D. 1997. Connectives and narrative text: The role of continuity. *Memory and Cognition* 25: 227–236.

Narrog, Heiko and Bernd Heine. 2011. *The Oxford handbook of grammaticalization*. Oxford: Oxford University Press.

Nicolle, Steve. 1996. *Conceptual and procedural encoding in Relevance Theory: A study with reference to English and Kiswahili*. Ph.D. thesis, University of York, UK.

Nicolle, Steve. 1997a. A relevance-theoretic account of *be going to. Journal of Linguistics* 33: 355–377.

Nicolle, Steve. 1997b. Conceptual and procedural encoding: Criteria for the identification of linguistically encoded procedural information. In Marjolein Groefsema (Ed.), *Proceedings of the University of Hertfordshire Relevance Theory Workshop*, 47–56. Chelmsford: Peter Thomas and Associates.

Nicolle, Steve. 1998a. *Be going to* and *will*: A monosemous account. *English Language and Linguistics* 2: 223–243.

Nicolle, Steve. 1998b. A relevance theory perspective on grammaticalization. *Cognitive Linguistics* 9: 1–35.

Nicolle, Steve. 2011. Pragmatic aspects of grammaticalization. In Heiko Narrog and Bernd Heine (Eds.), *The Oxford handbook of grammaticalization*, 401–412. Oxford: Oxford University Press.

Nicolle, Steve. 2015. Diachronic change in procedural semantic content. *Cahiers de Linguistique Française* 32: 133–148.

Nikiforidou, Kiki. 2009. Constructional analysis. In Frank Brisard, Jan-Ola Östman and Jef Verschueren (Eds.), *Grammar, meaning and pragmatics*, 16–32. Amsterdam: John Benjamins.

Noël, Dirk. 2007. Diachronic construction grammar and grammaticalization theory. *Functions of Language* 14 (2): 177–202.

Norén, Kerstin and Per Linell. 2007. Meaning potentials and the interaction between lexis and contexts: An empirical substantiation. *Pragmatics* 17: 387–416.

Padilla Cruz, Manuel. 2022. Is free enrichment always free? Revisiting ad hoc concept construction. *Journal of Pragmatics* 187: 130–143.

Panther, Klaus-Uwe and Linda L. Thornburg. 2003. *Metonymy and pragmatic inferencing*. Amsterdam: John Benjamins.

Panther, Klaus-Uwe and Linda L. Thornburg. 2007. Metonymy. In Dirk Geeraerts and Hubert Cuyckens (Eds.), *The Oxford handbook of cognitive linguistics*, 236–263. New York: Oxford University Press.

Papafragou, Anna. 2000. *Modality: Issues in the semantics–pragmatics interface*. Amsterdam: Elsevier.

Paradis, Carita. 2003. Is the notion of linguistic competence relevant in cognitive linguistics? *Annual Review of Cognitive Linguistics* 1: 247–271.

Paradis, Michel. 2009. *Declarative and procedural determinants of second languages*. Amsterdam: John Benjamins.

Park, Kyu Hyun and Billy Clark. 2022. A relevance-focused production heuristic. *Journal of Pragmatics* 187: 176–185.

Peña Cervel, Mária Sandra. 2017. Revisiting the English resultative family of constructions: A unifying account. In Francisco José Ruiz de Mendoza Ibáñez, Alba Luzondo Oyón and Paula Pérez Sobrino (Eds.), *Constructing families of constructions: Analytical perspectives and theoretical challenges*, 175–204. Amsterdam: John Benjamins.

Perek, Florent. 2015. *Argument structure in usage-based Construction Grammar: Experimental and corpus-based perspectives*. Amsterdam: John Benjamins.

Perry, John. 1993. *The problem of the essential indexical and other essays*. New York: Oxford University Press.

Pickering, Martin J. and Steven Frisson. 2001. Processing ambiguous verbs: Evidence from eye movements. *Journal of Experimental Psychology: Learning, Memory and Cognition* 27: 556–573.

Pinker, Steven. 1989. *Learnability and cognition: The acquisition of argument structure*. Cambridge, MA: MIT Press.

Prinz, Jesse J. 2002. *Furnishing the mind: Concepts and their perceptual basis*. Cambridge, MA: MIT Press.

Pritchard, Timothy. 2019. Analogical cognition: An insight into word meaning. *Review of Philosophy and Psychology* 10: 587–607.

Pulvermüller, Friedemann, Bert Cappelle and Yury Shtyrov. 2013. Brain basis of meaning, words, constructions, and grammar. In Graeme Trousdale and Thomas Hoffmann (Eds.), *Oxford Handbook of Construction Grammar*, 397–416. Oxford: Oxford University Press.

Pustejovsky, James. 1991. The generative lexicon. *Computational Linguistics* 17 (4): 409–441.

Pustejovsky, James. 1995. *The generative lexicon*. Cambridge, MA: MIT Press.

Pustejovsky, James. 2011. Coercion in a general theory of argument selection. *Linguistics* 49 (6): 1401–1431.

Putnam, Hilary. 1988. *Representation and reality*. Cambridge, MA: MIT Press.

Quine, Willard Van Orman. 1953. Two dogmas of empiricism. In Willard Van Orman Quine (Ed.), *From a logical point of view*, 20–46. Cambridge, MA: Harvard University Press.

Quine, Willard Van Orman. 1960. *Word and object*. Cambridge, MA: MIT Press.

Radden, Günter, Klaus-Michael Köpcke, Thomas Berg and Peter Siemund. 2007. The construction of meaning in language. In Günter Radden, Klaus-Michael Köpcke, Thomas Berg and Peter Siemund (Eds.), *Aspects of meaning construction*, 1–15. Amsterdam: John Benjamins.

Rappaport Hovav, Malka and Beth Levin. 2008. The English dative alternation: The case for verb sensitivity. *Journal of Linguistics* 44: 129–167.

Reboul, Anne. 2000. Words, concepts, mental representations, and other biological categories. In Bert Peeters (Ed.), *The lexicon-encyclopedia interface*, 55–95. Amsterdam: Elsevier.

Reboul, Anne. 2001. Semantic transparency, semantic opacity, states of affairs, mental states and speech acts. In Luigi M. Anolli, Maria R. Ciceri and Giuseppe Riva (Eds.), *Say not to say: New perspectives on miscommunication*, 46–71. Amsterdam: IOS Press.

Reboul, Anne. 2008. Pragmatics. *Journal of Linguistics* 44 (2): 519–524.

Reboul, Anne. 2014. *Mind, values and metaphysics: Philosophical papers dedicated to Kevin Mulligan*, vol. 2. Heidelberg: Springer International Publishing.

Recanati, François. 1989. The pragmatics of what is said. *Mind & Language* 4: 294–328.

Recanati, François. 1993. *Direct reference: From language to thought*. Oxford: Blackwell.

Recanati, François. 2004. *Literal meaning*. Cambridge: Cambridge University Press.

Reddy, Michael. 1979. The conduit metaphor: A case of conflict in our language about language. In Andrew Ortony (Ed.), *Metaphor and thought*, 284–324. Cambridge: Cambridge University Press.

Ribeiro, Anna C. 2013. Relevance theory and poetic effects. *Philosophy and Literature* 37: 102–117.

Riemer, Nick. 2016. *Routledge handbook of semantics*. London: Routledge.

Romain, Laurence. 2017. Measuring the alternation strength of causative verbs: A quantitative and qualitative analysis of the interaction between verb, theme and construction. *Belgian Journal of Linguistics* 31: 213–236.

Romain, Laurence. 2022. Putting the argument back into argument structure constructions. *Cognitive Linguistics* 33 (1): 35–64.

Romero, Esther and Belén Soria. 2010. Introduction: Explicit communication and Relevance Theory pragmatics. In Belén Soria and Esther Romero (Eds.), *Explicit communication: Robyn Carston's pragmatics*, 1–24. Basingstoke: Palgrave Macmillan.

Rosch, Eleanor. 1973. Natural categories. *Cognitive Psychology* 4: 328–350.

Rosch, Eleanor. 1975. Cognitive representations of semantic categories. *Journal of Experimental Psychology* 104: 192–233.

Rosch, Eleanor. 1978. Principles of categorization. In Eleanor Rosch and Barbara B. Lloyd (Eds.), *Cognition and categorization*, 27–48. Hillsdale, NJ: Lawrence Erlbaum.

Rosch, Eleanor. 1983. Prototype classification and logical classification: The two systems. In Ellin K. Scholnick (Ed.), *New trends in conceptual representation: Challenges to Piaget's theory?*, 73–86. Hillsdale, NJ: Lawrence Erlbaum.

Rosch, Eleanor and Carolyn B. Mervis. 1975. Family resemblances: Studies in the internal structure of categories. *Cognitive Psychology* 7: 573–605.

Rubio-Fernández, Paula. 2008. Concept narrowing: The role of context-independent information. *Journal of semantics* 25: 381–409.

Ruiz de Mendoza, Francisco J. and María A. Gómez-González. 2014. Constructing discourse and discourse constructions. In María A. Gómez-González, Francisco J. Ruiz de Mendoza and Francisco Gonzálvez-García (Eds.), *Theory and practice in functional cognitive space*, 295–314. Amsterdam: John Benjamins.

Ryle, Gilbert. 1946. Knowing how and knowing that. *Proceedings of the Aristotelian Society* XLVI: 1–16.

Sampson, Geoffrey. 2005. *The 'language instinct' debate*. London: Continuum.

Sanders, Ted J. M. 2005. Coherence, causality and cognitive complexity in discourse. In Michel Aurnague, Myriam Bras, Anne Le Draoulec and Laure Vieu (Eds.), *Proceedings of the first international symposium on the exploration and modelling of meaning (SEM-05)*, 31–44. Biarritz, France.

Sandra, Dominiek. 1998. What linguists can and can't tell you about the human mind: A reply to Croft. *Cognitive Linguistics* 9: 361–378.

Sandra, Dominiek and Sally Rice. 1995. Network analyses of prepositional meaning: Mirroring whose mind – the linguist's or the language user's? *Cognitive Linguistics* 6 (1): 89–130.

Schmid, Hans-Jörg. 2007. Entrenchment, salience, and basic levels. In Dirk Geeraerts and Hubert Cuyckens (Eds.), *The Oxford handbook of cognitive linguistics*, 117–138. New York: Oxford University Press.

Schmid, Hans-Jörg. 2012. Linguistic theories, approaches and methods. In Martin Middeke, Timo Müller, Christina Wald and Hubert Zapf (Eds.), *English and American studies: Theory and practice*, 371–394. Stuttgart: Metzler.

Schmid, Hans-Jörg. 2014. Lexico-grammatical patterns, pragmatic associations and discourse frequency. In Thomas Herbst, Hans-Jörg Schmid and Susen Faulhaber (Eds.), *Constructions – Collocations – Patterns*, 239–293. Berlin: Mouton de Gruyter.

Schmid, Hans-Jörg. 2017. *Entrenchment and the psychology of language learning: How we reorganize and adapt linguistic knowledge*. Boston, MA: APA and Walter de Gruyter.

Schmid, Hans-Jörg. 2020. *The dynamics of the linguistic system: Usage, conventionalization, and entrenchment*. Oxford: Oxford University Press.

Scholl, Brian J. and Alan M. Leslie. 1999. Modularity, development, and "theory of mind." *Mind & Language* 14: 131–153.

Scott, Kate. 2011. Beyond reference: Concepts, procedures and referring expressions. In Victoria Escandell-Vidal, Manuel Leonetti and Aoife Ahern (Eds.), *Procedural meaning: Problems and perspectives*, 183–203. Bingley: Emerald Group Publishing.

Scott, Kate. 2013. *This* and *that*: A procedural analysis. *Lingua* 131: 49–65.

Scott, Kate. 2016. Pronouns and procedures: Reference and beyond. *Lingua* 175–176: 69–82.

Scott, Kate. 2017. Prosody, procedures and pragmatics. In Ilse Depraetere and Raphael Salkie (Eds.), *Semantics and pragmatics: Drawing a line*, 323–341. Berlin: Springer International Publishing.

Scott, Kate. 2021. Contrastive stress in English: Meaning, expectations and ostension. In Elly Ifantidou, Louis de Saussure and Tim Wharton (Eds.), *Beyond meaning*, 29–41. Amsterdam: John Benjamins.

Shin, Gyu-Ho and Hyunwoo Kim. 2021. Roles of verb and construction cues: Cross-language comparisons between English and Korean sentence comprehension. *Review of Cognitive Linguistics* 19 (2): 332–362.

Sinclair, John. 1991. *Corpus, concordance, collocation*. Oxford: Oxford University Press.

Sinclair, Mellinda and Walter K. Winckler. 1991. Relevance theory: Explaining verbal communication. *Stellenbosch Papers in Linguistics Plus* 18: 1–97.

Slattery, Timothy J., Patrick Sturt, Kiel Christianson, Masaya Yoshida and Fernanda Ferreira. 2013. Lingering misinterpretations of garden path sentences arise from competing syntactic representations. *Journal of Memory and Language* 69: 104–120.

Sperber, Dan. 1994. The modularity of thought and the epidemiology of representations. In Lawrence A. Hirschfeld and Susan A. Gelman (Eds.), *Mapping the mind: Domain specificity in cognition and culture*, 39–67. Cambridge: Cambridge University Press.

Sperber, Dan. 1996. *Explaining culture: A naturalistic approach*. Oxford: Blackwell.

Sperber, Dan. 2000a. Metarepresentations in an evolutionary perspective. In Dan Sperber (Ed.), *Metarepresentations: A multidisciplinary perspective*, 117–138. Oxford: Oxford University Press.

Sperber, Dan. 2000b. Introduction. In Dan Sperber (Ed.), *Metarepresentations: A multidisciplinary perspective*, 3–13. Oxford: Oxford University Press.

Sperber, Dan. 2000c. *Metarepresentations: A multidisciplinary perspective*. Oxford: Oxford University Press.

Sperber, Dan. 2001. In defense of massive modularity. In Emmanuel Dupoux (Ed.), *Language, brain and cognitive development: Essays in honor of Jacques Mehler*, 47–57. Cambridge, MA: MIT Press.

Sperber, Dan. 2005. Modularity and relevance: How can a massively modular mind be flexible and context-sensitive? In Peter Carruthers, Stephen Laurence and Stephen Stich (Eds.), *The innate mind: Structure and content*, 53–68. Oxford: Oxford University Press.

Sperber, Dan and Deirdre Wilson. 1987. Precis of relevance: Communication and cognition. *Behavioral and Brain Sciences* 10: 697–754.

Sperber, Dan and Deirdre Wilson. 1995. *Relevance: Communication and cognition* (2nd ed.). Oxford: Blackwell.

Sperber, Dan and Deirdre Wilson. 1998. The mapping between the mental and the public lexicon. In Peter Carruthers and Jill Boucher (Eds.), *Language and thought: Interdisciplinary themes*, 184–200. Cambridge: Cambridge University Press.

Sperber, Dan and Deirdre Wilson. 2002. Pragmatics, modularity and mind-reading. *Mind & Language* 17: 3–23.

Sperber, Dan and Deirdre Wilson. 2005. Pragmatics. *UCL Working Papers in Linguistics* 17: 353–388.

Sperber, Dan and Deirdre Wilson. 2008. A deflationary account of metaphor. In Ray W. Gibbs (Ed.), *The Cambridge handbook of metaphor and thought*, 84–105. New York: Cambridge University Press.

Sperber, Dan, Francesco Cara and Vittorio Girotto. 1995. Relevance theory explains the selection task. *Cognition* 57: 31–95.

Squire, Larry R. 2004. Memory systems of the brain: A brief history and current perspective. *Neurobiology of Learning and Memory* 82: 171–177.

Stefanowitsch, Anatol. 2003. A construction-based approach to indirect speech acts. In Klaus-Uwe Panther and Linda L. Thornburg (Eds.), *Metonymy and pragmatic inferencing*, 105–126. Amsterdam: John Benjamins.

Stemberger, Joseph P. and Brian MacWhinney. 1988. Are inflected forms stored in the lexicon? In Michael Hammond and Michael Noonan (Eds.), *Theoretical morphology*, 101–116. New York: Academic Press.

Stöver, Hanna. 2010. *Metaphor and Relevance Theory: A new hybrid model*. Ph.D. dissertation, University of Bedfordshire.

Suttle, Laura and Adele E. Goldberg. 2011. The partial productivity of constructions as induction. *Linguistics* 6: 1237–1270.

Sztencel, Magdalena. 2011. From words to concepts. *Kwartalnik Neofilologiczny* 3: 375–394.

Sztencel, Magdalena. 2012a. Against referential semantics. In Pierre Frath, Valérie Bourdier, Emilia Hilgert, Karine Bréhaux and Jocelyn Dunphy-Blomfield (Eds.), *Res-per-nomen III: La référence, la conscience et le sujet énonciateur*, 485–498. Reims: ÉPURE – Éditions et Presses Universitaires de Reims.

Sztencel, Magdalena. 2012b. Do we need specifically linguistic semantics? *Newcastle Working Papers in Linguistics* 18: 73–92.

Sztencel, Magdalena. 2018. *Semantics, pragmatics and meaning revisited: The case of conditionals*. Dordrecht: Springer International Publishing.

Tabossi, Patrizia, Rachele Fanari and Kinou Wolf. 2009. Why are idioms recognized fast? *Memory and Cognition* 37: 529–540.

Talmy, Leonard. 1988. The relation of grammar to cognition. In Brygida Rudzka-Ostyn (Ed.), *Topics in cognitive linguistics*, 165–205. Amsterdam: John Benjamins.

Talmy, Leonard. 2000a. *Toward a cognitive semantics*. Vol. 1, *Concept structuring systems*. Cambridge, MA: MIT Press.

Talmy, Leonard. 2000b. *Toward a cognitive semantics*. Vol. 2, *Typology and process in concept structuring*. Cambridge, MA: MIT Press.

Talmy, Leonard. 2018. *Ten lectures on cognitive semantics*. Leiden: Brill.

Taylor, John R. 1995. *Linguistic categorization: Prototypes in linguistic theory*. Oxford: Oxford University Press.

Taylor, John R. 2017. Lexical semantics. In Barbara Dancygier (Ed.), *Cambridge handbook of cognitive linguistics*, 246–261. Cambridge: Cambridge University Press.

Taylor, John R., Hubert Cuyckens and René Dirven. 2003. New directions in cognitive lexical semantic research. In Hubert Cuyckens, René Dirven and John Taylor (Eds.), *Cognitive approaches to lexical semantics*, 1–28. Berlin: Mouton de Gruyter.

Taylor, Kenneth A. 2001. Sex, breakfast, and descriptus interruptus. *Synthese* 128: 45–61.

Tendahl, Markus. 2009. *A hybrid theory of metaphor*. Basingstoke: Palgrave Macmillan.

Tendahl, Markus and Ray Gibbs. 2008. Complementary perspectives on metaphor: Cognitive Linguistics and Relevance Theory. *Journal of Pragmatics* 40 (11): 1823–1864.

Thompson, Sandra A. and Yuka Koide. 1987. Iconicity and "indirect objects" in English. *Journal of Pragmatics* 11 (3): 399–406.

Tolkien, John R. R. 1937. *The Hobbit*. Boston, MA: Houghton Mifflin.

Tomasello, Michael. 1992. *First verbs: A case study of early grammatical development*. Cambridge: Cambridge University Press.

Tomasello, Michael. 2003. *Constructing a language: A usage-based approach*. Cambridge, MA: Harvard University Press.

Tomasello, Michael. 2006. Acquiring linguistic constructions. In Deanna Kuhn and Robert S. Siegler (Eds.), *Handbook of child psychology:* vol. 2. *Cognition, perception, and language* (6th ed.), 255–298. New York: Wiley.

Tomasello, Michael and Dan I. Slobin. 2005. *Beyond nature nurture: Essays in honor of Elizabeth Bates*. Mahwah, NJ: Lawrence Erlbaum.

Traugott, Elizabeth C. 1989. On the rise of epistemic meanings in English: An example of subjectification in semantic change. *Language* 65: 31–55.

Traugott, Elizabeth C. 1995. Subjectification in grammaticalisation. In Susan Wright and Dieter Stein (Eds.), *Subjectivity and subjectivisation*, 31–54. Cambridge: Cambridge University Press.

Traugott, Elizabeth C. 1999. The rhetoric of counter-expectation in semantic change: A study of subjectification. In Andreas Blank and Peter Koch (Eds.), *Historical semantics and cognition*, 177–196. Berlin: Mouton de Gruyter.

Traugott, Elizabeth C. 2003. From subjectification to intersubjectification. In Raymond Hickey (Ed.), *Motives for language change*, 124–139. Cambridge: Cambridge University Press.

Traugott, Elizabeth C. 2008. The grammaticalization of *NP of NP* patterns. In Alexander Bergs and Gabriele Diewald (Eds.), *Constructions and language change*, 21–43. Berlin: Mouton de Gruyter.

Traugott, Elizabeth C. 2010. Revisiting subjectification and intersubjectification. In Kristin Davidse, Lieven Vandelanotte and Hubert Cuyckens (Eds.), *Subjectification, intersubjectification and grammaticalization*, 29–70. Berlin: Mouton de Gruyter.

Traugott, Elizabeth C. 2014. Grammaticalization: An interview with Elizabeth Closs Traugott. *ReVEL* 12 (22).

Traugott, Elizabeth C. 2015. Toward a coherent account of grammatical constructionalization. In Jóhanna Barðdal, Elena Smirnova, Lotte Sommerer and Spike Gildea (Eds.), *Diachronic Construction Grammar*, 51–79. Amsterdam: John Benjamins.

Traugott, Elizabeth C. and Richard B. Dasher. 2002. *Regularity in semantic change*. Cambridge: Cambridge University Press.

Traugott, Elizabeth C. and Ekkehard König. 1991. The semantics–pragmatics of grammaticalization revisited. In Elizabeth C. Traugott and Bernd Heine (Eds.), *Approaches to grammaticalization*, vol. 1, 189–219. Amsterdam: John Benjamins.

Traugott, Elizabeth C. and Graeme Trousdale. 2013. *Constructionalization and constructional changes*. Oxford: Oxford University Press.

Trousdale, Graeme. 2008a. Constructions in grammaticalization and lexicalization: Evidence from a composite predicate in the history of English. In Graeme Trousdale and Nikolas Gisborne (Eds.), *Constructional approaches to English grammar*, 33–67. Berlin: Mouton de Gruyter.

Trousdale, Graeme. 2008b. Words and constructions in grammaticalization: The end of the English impersonal construction. In Susan M. Fitzmaurice and Donka Minkova (Eds.), *Studies in the history of the English language IV: Empirical and analytical advances in the study of English language change*, 301–326. Berlin: Mouton de Gruyter.

Trousdale, Graeme. 2010. Issues in constructional approaches to grammaticalization. In Katerina Stathi, Elke Gehweiler and Ekkehard König (Eds.), *Grammaticalization: Current views and issues*, 51–71. Amsterdam: John Benjamins.

Trousdale, Graeme. 2012. Grammaticalization, constructions, and the grammaticalization of constructions. In Kristin Davidse, Tine Breban, Lieselotte Brems and Tanja Mortelmans (Eds.), *Grammaticalization and language change: New reflections*, 167–198. Amsterdam: Benjamins.

Ungerer, Tobias and Stefan Hartmann. 2023. *Constructionist approaches: Past, present, future*. Cambridge: Cambridge University Press.

van der Henst, Jean-Baptiste. 2006. Relevance effects in reasoning. *Mind & Society* 5 (2): 229–245.

van der Henst, Jean-Baptiste and Dan Sperber. 2004. Testing the cognitive and communicative principles of relevance. In Ira Noveck and Dan Sperber (Eds.), *Experimental pragmatics*, 141–171. New York: Palgrave Macmillan.

van der Henst, Jean-Baptiste, Laure Carles and Dan Sperber. 2002. Truthfulness and relevance in telling the time. *Mind & Language* 17: 457–466.

van der Henst, Jean-Baptiste, Dan Sperber and Guy Politzer. 2002. When is a conclusion worth deriving? A relevance-based analysis of indeterminate relational problems. *Thinking & Reasoning* 8: 1–20.

Vega Moreno, Rosa E. 2001. Representing and processing idioms. *UCL Working Papers in Linguistics* 13: 73–107.

Vega Moreno, Rosa E. 2003. Relevance Theory and the construction of idiom meaning. *UCL Working Papers in Linguistics* 15: 83–104.

Vega Moreno, Rosa E. 2005. Idioms, transparency and pragmatic inference. *UCL Working Papers in Linguistics* 17: 389–426.

Verschueren, Jef. 2018. Adaptability and meaning potential. In Rajend Mesthrie and David Bradley (Eds.), *The dynamics of language: Plenary and focus papers from the 20th international congress of linguists, Cape Town, July 2018*, 93–109. Cape Town: UCT Press.

Vicente, Agustín and Fernando Martínez-Manrique. 2010. On relevance theory's atomistic commitments. In Belén Soria and Esther Romero (Eds.), *Explicit communication: Robyn Carston's pragmatics*, 42–57. Basingstoke: Palgrave Macmillan.

Vicente, Begoña. 2005. Meaning in relevance theory and the semantics/pragmatics distinction. In Seana Coulson and Barbara Lewandowska-Tomaszczyk (Eds.), *The literal and non-literal in language and thought*, 179–200. Frankfurt: Peter Lang.

Wałaszewska, Ewa. 2011. Broadening and narrowing in lexical development: How relevance theory can account for children's overextensions and underextensions. *Journal of Pragmatics* 43: 314–326.

Walton, Alan L. 1988. *The pragmatics of English modal verbs*. Ph.D. thesis, University of London.

Wharton, Tim. 2004. Lexical acquisition and pragmatics. *UCL Working Papers in Linguistics* 16: 323–341.

Wharton, Tim. 2009. *Pragmatics and non-verbal communication*. Cambridge: Cambridge University Press.

Wharton, Tim. 2014. What words mean is a matter of what people mean by them. *Linguagem em (Dis)curso* 14 (3): 473–488.

Wiemer-Hastings, Katja and Xu Xu. 2005. Content differences for abstract and concrete concepts. *Cognitive Science* 29: 719–736.

Wierzbicka, Anna. 1988. *The semantics of grammar*. Amsterdam: John Benjamins.

Wilson, Deirdre. 2000. Metarepresentation in linguistic communication. In Dan Sperber (Ed.), *Metarepresentations: An interdisciplinary perspective*, 411–448. Oxford: Oxford University Press.

Wilson, Deirdre. 2003. Relevance Theory and lexical pragmatics. *Italian Journal of Linguistics / Rivista di Linguistica* 15: 273–291.

Wilson, Deirdre. 2005. New directions for research on pragmatics and modularity. *Lingua* 115: 1129–1246.

Wilson, Deirdre. 2009. Parallels and differences in the treatment of metaphor in Relevance Theory and Cognitive Linguistics. *Studies in Pragmatics* 11: 42–60.

Wilson, Deirdre. 2011. The conceptual-procedural distinction: Past, present and future. In Victoria Escandell-Vidal, Manuel Leonetti and Aoife Ahern (Eds.), *Procedural meaning: Problems and perspectives*, 3–31. Bingley: Emerald Group Publishing.

Wilson, Deirdre. 2012. Modality and the conceptual-procedural distinction. In Ewa Wałaszewska and Agnieszka Piskorska (Eds.), *Relevance Theory: More than understanding*, 24–43. Newcastle upon Tyne: Cambridge Scholars Publishing.

Wilson, Deirdre. 2016. Reassessing the conceptual-procedural distinction. *Lingua* 175: 5–19.

Wilson, Deirdre. 2017. Relevance Theory. In Yan Huang (Ed.), *The Oxford handbook of pragmatics*, 79–100. Oxford: Oxford University Press.

Wilson, Deirdre. 2022. Communication, comprehension and interpretation. In Herbert L. Colson, Teenie Matlock and Gerard J. Steen (Eds.), *Dynamism in metaphor and beyond*, 143–156. Amsterdam: John Benjamins.

Wilson, Deirdre and Robyn Carston. 2006. Metaphor, relevance and the 'emergent property' issue. *Mind & Language* 21 (3): 404–433.

Wilson, Deirdre and Robyn Carston. 2007. A unitary approach to lexical pragmatics: Relevance, inference and ad hoc concepts. In Noël Burton-Roberts (Ed.), *Pragmatics*, 230–259. Basingstoke: Palgrave Macmillan.

Wilson, Deirdre and Robyn Carston. 2019. Pragmatics and the challenge of 'non-propositional' effects. *Journal of Pragmatics* 145: 31–38.

Wilson, Deirdre and Dan Sperber. 1991. Pragmatics and modularity. In Steven Davis (Ed.), *Pragmatics: A reader*, 583–595. Oxford: Oxford University Press.

Wilson, Deirdre and Dan Sperber. 1993. Linguistic form and relevance. *Lingua* 90: 1–25.

Wilson, Deirdre and Dan Sperber. 2004. Relevance theory. In Laurence R. Horn and Gregory Ward (Eds.), *The handbook of pragmatics*, 607–632. Oxford: Blackwell.

Wilson, Deirdre and Dan Sperber. 2012. *Meaning and relevance*. Cambridge: Cambridge University Press.

Wittgenstein, Ludwig. 1958. *Philosophical investigations* (trans. G. E. M. Anscombe). Oxford: Basil Blackwell.

Wittke, Kacie, Ann M. Mastergeorge, Sally Ozonoff, Sally J. Rogers and Letitia R. Naigles. 2017. Grammatical language impairment in autism spectrum disorder: Exploring language phenotypes beyond standardized testing. *Frontiers in Psychology* 8: 532.

Wulff, Stefanie. 2008. *Rethinking idiomaticity: A usage-based approach*. London: Continuum.

Wulff, Stefanie. 2013. Words and idioms. In Thomas Hoffmann and Graeme Trousdale (Eds.), *The Oxford handbook of construction grammar*, 274–289. Oxford: Oxford University Press.

Xue, Bing and Lu Lin. 2022. 语用学与认知语言学融合的新路径 – 推论- 构式语用观 (Integrating pragmatics and cognitive linguistics: A call for inferential-constructional pragmatics). 外语与外语教学 *(Foreign languages and their teaching)* 2: 12–20.

Ye, Zheng, Weidong Zhan and Xiaolin Zhou. 2007. The semantic processing of syntactic structure in sentence comprehension: An ERP study. *Brain Research* 1142: 135–145.

Yeh, Wenchi and Lawrence W. Barsalou. 2006. The situated nature of concepts. *American Journal of Psychology* 119: 349–384.

Yoon, Soyeon. 2012. *Constructions, semantic compatibility, and coercion: An empirical usage-based approach*. Ph.D. thesis, Rice University, Texas.

Ziegeler, Debra. 2007a. Arguing the case against coercion. In Günter Radden, Klaus-Michael Köpcke, Thomas Berg and Peter Siemund (Eds.), *Aspects of meaning construction*, 99–123. Amsterdam: John Benjamins.

Ziegeler, Debra. 2007b. A word of caution on coercion. *Journal of Pragmatics* 39: 990–1028.

Zufferey, Sandrine. 2010. *Lexical pragmatics and theory of mind: The acquisition of connectives*. Amsterdam: John Benjamins.

Zufferey, Sandrine. 2015. *Acquiring pragmatics: Social and cognitive perspectives*. London: Routledge.

Zufferey, Sandrine, Jacques Moeschler and Anne Reboul. 2019. *Implicatures*. Cambridge: Cambridge University Press.

Index

Printed in the USA
CPSIA information can be obtained
at www.ICGtesting.com
LVHW050917161123
PP17968500003B/12